"Don Carson's *The God Who Is There* is a unique and important volume in many ways. It is neither a traditional systematic theology nor a Bible survey. It unpacks the whole biblical storyline through the lens of God's character and actions. As a ministry tool, it can be used for evangelism, since it so thoroughly lays out the doctrine of God, as Paul does on Mars Hill in Acts 17. And yet it also does what the catechisms of the Reformation churches did: give Christians a grounding in basic biblical beliefs and behavior. By all means, get this book!"

—**Tim Keller**, pastor, Redeemer Presbyterian Church, New York City

"This is a much-needed book. D. A. Carson is one of the few biblical scholars who are gifted to write simply and in a way that captivates. We live in a time when people quickly reject or accept the Bible without even knowing its contents. Carson does a masterful job of explaining the Scriptures so that a person who has never even opened the Bible can understand it. At the same time, those who grew up under its teaching will find valuable and obvious truths that will lead them to greater worship and appreciation of the God we serve."

—**Francis Chan**, author of *Crazy Love*

"What a wonderful resource! I love how Carson pulls together, in such an inviting way, God's story from his Word! This book is a treasure for those who want to know what the Bible says as well as those of us who have read it, taught it, and lived it for years."

—**Dr. Crawford W. Loritts Jr.**, speaker, author, radio host, and senior pastor of Fellowship Bible Church, Roswell, GA

"I am constantly on the lookout for good books for thoughtful students about issues of faith. The pickings are usually slim. D. A. Carson's *The God Who Is There* offers a helpful resource I can heartily recommend. It is challenging yet respectful, thought-provoking yet accessible, faithful to the historic Christian faith yet relevant to our ever-changing world. I hope many students and faculty will give it serious consideration."

—**Randy Newman**, staff member, Campus Crusade for Christ; author of *Questioning Evangelism* and *Corner Conversations*

"If you've ever wanted to hear God's story, then this book is for you. If you've ever wanted to come face-to-face with the God who made, loves, and rescues you, then this book is for you. And if you've never picked up the Bible or wandered into a Christian church, then this book is *especially* for you."

—**Sam Chan**, lecturer in theology, preaching, ethics, and evangelism,
Sydney Missionary and Bible College, Australia

"This may well prove to be one of the finest and most influential books D. A. Carson has written. A comprehensive apologia for the Christian faith, it is rooted in engaging exposition of major biblical texts, tracing the chronological story of God's gospel grace with rich theological insight. Skillfully related to the objections and issues raised by twenty-first-century culture, it will inspire and equip any Christian who desires to communicate Christ more effectively and can confidently be given to any inquirer seeking to discover the heart of biblical faith. It is the best book of its kind I have read in many years."

—**David J. Jackman**, former president, Proclamation Trust, London, England

THE
GOD
WHO IS
THERE

Finding Your Place in God's Story

D. A. CARSON

BakerBooks

a division of Baker Publishing Group
Grand Rapids, Michigan

© 2010 by D. A. Carson

Published by Baker Books
a division of Baker Publishing Group
P.O. Box 6287, Grand Rapids, MI 49516-6287
www.bakerbooks.com

Printed in the United States of America

Library of Congress Cataloging-in-Publication Data
Carson, D. A.
    The God who is there : finding your place in God's story / D. A. Carson.
        p.   cm.
    Includes bibliographical references and index.
    ISBN 978-0-8010-1372-0 (pbk.)
    1. Bible—Criticism, interpretation, etc. 2. God (Christianity) I. Title.
BS511.3.C376 2010
220.6′1—dc22   2010013664

11   12   13   14   15   16   7   6   5   4   3

For Ben and Lynae Peays

Contents

Preface

If you know nothing at all about what the Bible says, the book you are now holding in your hands is for you.

If you have recently become interested in God or the Bible or Jesus but quite frankly you find the mass of material rather daunting and do not know where to begin, this book is for you.

If you have been attending a Christian church for many years in an indifferent fashion—it's a nice extracurricular activity now and then—but have recently come to the conclusion you really ought to understand more than you do, this book is for you.

If you have quite a few of the pieces of the Bible stored in your mind but have no idea how the exodus relates to the exile or why the New Testament is called the New Testament, this book is for you.

If in your experience the Bible has lots of data but you do not see how it conveys God to you or introduces Jesus in a fashion that is utterly humbling and transforming, this book is for you.

This book is not for everyone. The person who does not want more than a bumper sticker introduction to Christianity may find this book a bit much. What I have tried to do here is run through the Bible in fourteen chapters. Each chapter focuses on one or more passages from the Bible, unpacks it a little, and tries to build connections with the context, drawing the lines together to show how they converge in Jesus. By and large I have assumed very little prior acquaintance with the Bible. What I do assume, however, is that a reader will get hold of a Bible and have it near at hand. In the first chapter I will tell you how to find your way around in a Bible.

I have presented the material in these chapters as talks in various places. Most recently, however, I gave them as a series spread over two weekends in the Twin Cities. The series was videorecorded and is available on DVD. Each individual talk can also be downloaded as a free video file from thegospelcoalition.org. The video series fairly closely parallels the chapters of this book. In addition, *The God Who Is There Leader's Guide* (also published by Baker) corresponds to this book and to the video series for those who want to organize a small group discussion of the material and find additional resources.

My warm thanks to those who have helped bring this series together. The list of names could be surprisingly long, but I'll especially mention Lucas Naugle and his video crew for their competence and professionalism, the various staff members at Desiring God Ministries for organizing the talks in the Twin Cities, Andy Naselli for the initial transcription, and Ben Peays, the executive director of The Gospel Coalition, for tirelessly working out details. I am especially thankful for those who have listened to parts of this material on earlier occasions and asked probing and intelligent questions that forced me to be a little clearer than I would otherwise have been.

I must tell you right away that I do not pretend to be a neutral bystander, coolly weighing what some will think of as the pros and cons of the Christian faith. I will try to be as careful as I can in handling the Bible, but I must tell you I am a Christian. What I have found of God in Jesus Christ is so wonderful, I am eager for others to know it too—and to know him.

Since in this book I try to explain things instead of taking them for granted, I'll begin with a small explanation right now. For years I have usually placed after my name, in the prefaces of the books I have written, the Latin phrase *Soli Deo gloria*, and I am about to use it again. The phrase means "Glory to God alone" or "To God alone be glory." It was one of five phrases developed about five hundred years ago to summarize a great deal of Christian truth— in this case the truth that everything that is done should be done for God's praise, to the exclusion of human self-glorification and pomposity. The great composer Johann Sebastian Bach appended the initials of the phrase, "SDG," to the musical manuscripts of each of his cantatas; it was similarly used by his contemporary George Frideric Handel (best known for what we commonly call "Handel's Messiah"). It is a small acknowledgment of something found in the very Bible that we are about to read, in 1 Corinthians 10:31: "So whether you eat or drink or whatever you do, do it all for the glory of God." And if you do not know what "1 Corinthians" means, read on!

Don Carson
Soli Deo gloria

1

The God Who Made
Everything

Before plunging into the first passage of the Bible, it might be helpful if I tell you where we are going in this series.

There was a time in the Western world when many people had read the Bible reasonably thoroughly and therefore knew how it was put together. Even those who were atheists were, shall I say, *Christian* atheists. That is to say, the God they disbelieved in was the God of the Bible. Their understanding of the God whom they found unbelievable was in some measure shaped by their reading of the Bible. But today, of course, a rising number of people really do not know how the Bible works at all. They have never read it, or at least have never read it closely. So the first place to begin in trying to understand what Christianity is, and who Jesus is, is to start again to read the Bible.

There are many ways by which we could introduce Christianity. We could, for example, do a brief survey of the history of the Christian church. Or we might start analyzing what Christians in various parts of the world believe. But the best way to get at it is to examine Christianity's foundation documents. There are sixty-six of them. They vary in length from one page to small books. They were written over a period of 1500 years in three languages. The biggest part was written in Hebrew; a very tiny part was written in a language like Hebrew called Aramaic; and the last part was written in Greek. So all of our Bibles today—the Bibles that we hold in our hands and pick up and read and treasure—are translations of what was originally given in these languages.

These sixty-six foundation documents are highly diverse in form and literary genre: some are letters; some are oracles from God; some are written in poetry; some are laments; some contain genealogies; some reflect intense mental and spiritual wrestling as believers try to understand what on earth God is doing; some are written in a genre that we just do not use anymore called "apocalyptic," which uses astonishing symbolism that is visually striking. Moreover, these sixty-six documents, often called the "books" of the Bible, are surprisingly varied in terms of accessibility: some parts you can read very easily, while other parts are full of archaic symbolism, symbolism that has to be explained because it belongs to a time and place very different from our own.

Now all of these foundation documents, these "books," have been put together to constitute "the Book." That's all "Bible" means. It's the Book. It's the book of Christianity's foundation documents, and we who are Christians insist that God has disclosed himself supremely in the pages of these documents. Because most people do not read the languages in which the Bible was first written (Hebrew, Aramaic, and Greek), they read them in an English (or some other language) translation. There are many translations of the Bible into English. For our purposes, it will not make much difference which translation you choose. Common ones today are the New International Version (NIV), the English Standard Version (ESV), and Today's New International Version (TNIV). You can remind yourself of these abbreviations on the copyright page at the beginning of this book. If at some point the translations differ in an important way, I'll take a moment to explain the difference.

In these chapters I shall sketch in what the Bible says so as to make sense of what Christianity means and looks like if it is constrained by its own foundation documents. Sometimes Christians themselves abandon these foundation documents and thus betray, sometimes unwittingly, the very heritage they have received. The Christian claim, however, is that this Bible discloses the God who is there.

In this first chapter we reflect on "the God who made everything." We begin with the first book in the Bible, called Genesis. The books of the Bible are organized by chapters and verses; that is, if you open the Bible anywhere, you will find a break with a big number (that's the heading of a chapter) and then some small numbers (those are verses). So a reference such as "Genesis 3:16" means the book of Genesis, the third chapter, the sixteenth verse. If you are not familiar with the Bible, the easiest way to orientate yourself to its organization is by opening up the first few pages where you will find the table of contents listing the names of the books of the Bible in order: Genesis, Exodus, Leviticus, Numbers, and so on, all the way through—all sixty-six of them. Then you will be able to find the page number so you can locate the book, and when you turn to the book you will be able to find the chapter number and verse number. Over the course of these fourteen chapters, I shall refer to a lot of books of the Bible and a lot of specific passages. If you want to look them up, you will be able to do so. But usually we shall focus on one passage at a time, and work away at it—and in that case it would be best if you find the passage in your Bible and follow along.

One more small detail. A casual glance at the table of contents of a Bible shows it is divided into two unequal parts. The first two-thirds of the Bible is often referred to as the "Old Testament," and it is made up of thirty-nine of the sixty-six books. It sweeps through from the creation to the period before Jesus. The last third of the Bible, give or take, is called the "New Testament" and is comprised of the remaining twenty-seven books. It starts with Jesus and steadfastly focuses on him. The books of the New Testament all spring from the first one hundred years of the common era, even though what is found there also points to the very end of history. As for the expressions "Old Testament" and "New Testament," they will be explained later in this book.

Genesis 1–2

So we begin with Genesis 1. You might want to read through these two short chapters, because in what follows I shall be picking up parts of them. This is what the opening line of the Bible says:

> [1]In the beginning God created the heavens and the earth. [2]Now the earth was formless and empty, darkness was over the surface of the deep, and the Spirit of God was hovering over the waters.
> [3]And God said, "Let there be light," and there was light. [4]God saw that the light was good, and he separated the light from the darkness. [5]God called the light "day," and the darkness he called "night." And there was evening, and there was morning—the first day.
>
> Genesis 1:1–5

Then in successive days, various things are created by this God who says, "Let there be this" or "Let there be that." And occasionally a refrain is added: "And God saw that it was good" (Gen. 1:10). So eventually you get to day five, and the water teems with living creatures and birds fly above the earth across the vault of the sky (1:20). "God created the great creatures of the sea and every living and moving thing with which the water teems, according to their kinds, and every winged bird according to its kind" (1:21).

And then the sixth day: "Let the land produce living creatures according to their kinds: livestock, creatures that move along the ground, and wild animals, each according to its kind" (1:24). Again, at the end of the description: "And God saw that it was good" (1:25).

> [26]Then God said, "Let us make human beings in our image, in our likeness, so that they may rule over the fish in the sea and the birds in the sky, over the

livestock and all the wild animals, and over all the creatures that move along the ground."

²⁷So God created human beings in his own image, in the image of God he created them; male and female he created them.

²⁸God blessed them and said to them, "Be fruitful and increase in number; fill the earth and subdue it. Rule over the fish in the sea and the birds in the sky and over every living creature that moves on the ground."

²⁹Then God said, "I give you every seed-bearing plant on the face of the whole earth and every tree that has fruit with seed in it. They will be yours for food. ³⁰And to all the beasts of the earth and all the birds in the sky and all the creatures that move on the ground—everything that has the breath of life in it—I give every green plant for food." And it was so.

³¹God saw all that he had made, and it was very good. And there was evening, and there was morning—the sixth day.

¹Thus the heavens and the earth were completed in all their vast array.

²By the seventh day God had finished the work he had been doing; so on the seventh day he rested from all his work. ³Then God blessed the seventh day and made it holy, because on it he rested from all the work of creating that he had done.

Genesis 1:26–2:3

Then the rest of chapter 2 offers a kind of expansion on the creation of human beings that we'll come to in due course.

Genesis 1–2 and Science

Because much of twenty-first-century culture is convinced that contemporary scientific thought is fundamentally incompatible with the opening chapters of Genesis, I had better say something about the approach I adopt here. Four things to note:

1. There is more ambiguity in the interpretation of these chapters than some Christians recognize. Some Christians are convinced, for example, that this pair of chapters, read responsibly, insists that the world is not more than four thousand years older than the coming of Jesus. Others insist that it is entirely compatible with vast ages. In particular, some think that each "day" represents an age. Others infer that there is an enormous gap between verse 1 and verse 2 of Genesis 1.

Still others see the seven-day week of Genesis 1 as a literary device: creation week is symbol laden and focusing on other points of interest rather than describing a literal week.

Others devote their energy to comparing these two chapters with other creation accounts in the ancient world in which the book of Genesis was written. In the Babylonian era, for example, there was a document called the *Enuma Elish*, which describes the creation of the world. It has been argued that the biblical account is basically shaped along the lines of those Babylonian myths.

In short, there are significant differences of opinion among Christians, let alone among those who want to write the entire account off. What shall we do with this?

I hold that the Genesis account is a mixed genre that feels like history and really does give us some historical particulars. At the same time, however, it is full of demonstrable symbolism. Sorting out what is symbolic and what is not is very difficult. How we shall negotiate this tension I will tell you in a moment.

2. There is more ambiguity in the claims of science than some scientists recognize. Recently, of course, the media have focused on the fresh literary adventures of people like Richard Dawkins (*The God Delusion*), Sam Harris (*The End of Faith: Religion, Terror, and the Future of Reason*), Christopher Hitchens (*God Is Not Great: How Religion Poisons Everything*), and others. Together their writings comprise what is now sometimes called "the new atheism." Correspondingly, robust responses of various sorts have been written. One thinks, for instance, of R. Albert Mohler (*Atheism Remix*); of David Bentley Hart (*Atheist Delusions: The Christian Revolution and Its Fashionable Enemies*); of Paul Copan and William Lane Craig (editors of *Contending with Christianity's Critics: Answering New Atheists and Other Objectors*); or of an essay by William Lane Craig that interacts, in particular, with Dawkins ("Five Arguments for the Existence of God").

All the books of the new atheism are based on the assumption of philosophical materialism: all that exists is matter, energy, space, and time—nothing else. So anything that claims to go beyond that or belong to some domain that cannot be reduced to these realities must necessarily be dismissed, even laughed at, as the trailing edge of a superstition that was declared foolish a long time ago and should immediately be abandoned.

And yet I personally know many front-rank scientists who are Christians. I have spoken at many universities, and one of the interesting things I discover is that if I attend nearby local churches and meet some of the faculty in the universities who belong to these local churches and who are committed believers, their numbers tend to be made up of more science and math professors and the like than arts, psychology, and English literature professors. It is simply not the case that anyone who is a scientist cannot be a Christian. So I am happy to recommend to you some books that talk about scientists who are Christians: for example, the little book by Mike Poole, *God and the Scientist*; or another one edited by William A. Dembski, *Uncommon Dissent: Intellectuals Who Find Darwinism Unconvincing*; or the volume by Li Cheng, a Chinese atheist and scientist who became a Christian, *Song of a Wanderer: Beckoned by Eternity*. More debate is going on than is sometimes perceived.

Even if your understanding of origins belongs to the dominant modern paradigm in which our entire known universe developed out of a big bang that took place something like fifteen billion years ago from an unimaginably condensed mass and became our universe, there is an obvious question to ask. Whether or not you subscribe to the view that this big bang took place under the guidance of God, sooner or later you are forced to ask the question, "Where did that highly condensed material come from?"

This is where some theorists display great cleverness. Alan Guth has written a book called *The Inflationary Universe*. He proposes that this very condensed material that ultimately exploded in the big bang emerged out of nothing. And if you say that the physics doesn't work, he says, "Yes, but at the big bang, there is what physicists call a 'singularity.'" A singularity is an occurrence in which the normal laws of physics no longer operate. That means that we no longer have any access to them. At that point it's the wildest speculation, which causes a critic named David Berlinski to write, "A lot of stuff that gets into print is simply nonsensical. Alan Guth's derivation of something from nothing is simply incandescent [horse manure]. [Now he uses another word for "manure," but I spare you.] Don't tell me you're deriving something from nothing when it's transparently obvious to any mathematician that this is incandescent nonsense."[1]

In other words, there are complications in the domain of science that suggest that science does not constitute a solid wall or barrier that makes it impossible for Christians who bow to the authority of Scripture and Christians who really want to learn from science to talk intelligently with each other.

3. Whatever one makes of current debates over intelligent design—one of the dominant debates of the day—there is a version of it that I find almost inescapable. Let me explain. During the last twenty-five years, various groups of people—mostly Christians but some non-Christians as well—have pointed to what they call "irreducible complexity," that is, structures in nature and in the human being that are so complex that it is statistically impossible that they could have come to be by chance. To appeal to a chance mutation, or to the mere selection of the fittest, or to any of the other appeals on offer in the various heritages that spring from Darwinism, simply makes no sense. Living systems have an irreducible complexity to them that makes it statistically impossible that all of the necessary but highly improbable steps were taken at the same time—and without such statistically impossible simultaneity, life could not be. What this suggests, it is argued, is the need for a designer.

Some argue back—many unbelievers and some believers—"Yes, yes, but such unlikely simultaneous advantageous developments might simply mean that we do not understand the mechanisms. If you start inserting God wherever we do not have an explanation, then you end up putting God into the gaps of our ignorance, and as we learn more, the gaps get filled in and God shrinks.

We do not need a God of the gaps. A God of the gaps is not only bad science, it is bad theology." And so the debate continues.

Whatever you make of that debate—and the literature is already voluminous—what I find interesting is that many writers who do not in any sense claim to be Christians sometimes speak of their marvel at the unimaginable complexity and splendor of the universe—a marvel that rises to the level of what might be called "worship." For example, I think of a fascinating book by Martin J. Rees, *Just Six Numbers: The Deep Forces That Shape the Universe*. If the physical realities that these numbers describe generated a little higher number or a little lower number, the universe as we know it could not exist. There must, for example, be just exactly the right distance between one particle and another particle at the subatomic level to balance the various forces at play. Just six numbers, so tightly constrained in their upper and lower limits, make the physical universe possible. How did *that* happen? Other writers describe the astonishing complexity of the eyeball, and although they may be unabashed philosophical materialists in their orientation, they are so impressed by the complexity and glory of it all that they almost begin to treat nature as a god.

From a Christian point of view their instincts are jolly good—except that there is a God who has disclosed himself in the glory of what we call nature. I am not sure that it is right to argue from the complexity and glory of the six numbers, or from the stiffness of the woodpecker's tail feathers, or from the irreducible complexity of a cell or of the eyeball, to the conclusion that God exists. At the end of the day God is not merely an inference, the end of an argument, the conclusion after we have cleverly aligned the evidence. But if you begin with this God, the testimony to his greatness in what we see all around us is heart stopping. It takes an enormous act of will on the part of even the most cynical of scientists instead to look at it all and say, "Ah, it's just physics. Stop admiring it. Don't do that. There's no design. It's just molecules bumping into molecules."

4. Finally, let me say where I am coming from as we work through these texts. About thirty years ago a Christian thinker named Francis Schaeffer wrote a little book called *Genesis in Space and Time: The Flow of Biblical History*. He argues that one of the ways to minimize some of the endless debates that cloud discussions of origins is by asking, "What is the least that Genesis 1 and the following chapters must be saying for the rest of the Bible to make any sense?" So I will refrain from telling you everything that I think that these chapters are saying. It would take too long in any case. What I want to suggest to you is that however complex the debates over the symbolism and literary genre of Genesis 1–2 and however debated their relationship to contemporary science, there is an irreducible minimum that these chapters must be saying for the Bible to have any coherence at all, and that is what I shall lay out for you in the next few pages.

So what do Genesis 1–2 tell us?

Some Things about God

1. God simply is. The Bible does not begin with a long set of arguments to prove the existence of God. It does not begin with a bottom-up approach, nor does it begin with some kind of adjacent analogy or the like. It just begins, "In the beginning God" (Gen. 1:1). Now, if human beings are the test of everything, this makes no sense at all because then we have the right to sit back and judge whether it is likely that God exists, to evaluate the evidence and come out with a certain probability that perhaps a god of some sort or another exists. Thus we become the judges of God. But the God of the Bible is not like that. The Bible begins simply but dramatically: "In the beginning God." He is. He is not the object whom we evaluate. He is the Creator who has made us, which changes all the dynamics.

This way of looking at God is bound up with some developments in Western thought that we should pause to appreciate. Right through the early part of the Renaissance (roughly fourteenth to seventeenth centuries) and down through the time of the Reformation (sixteenth century), most people in the Western world presupposed that God exists and that he knows everything. Human beings exist, and because God knows everything, what we know must necessarily be some small subset of what he knows. In other words, all of our knowledge—because he knows everything—must be a subset of what he knows exhaustively and perfectly. In this way of looking at reality, all of our knowledge must come to us in some sense by God disclosing what he knows—by God disclosing it in nature, by God disclosing it by his Spirit, or by God disclosing it in the Bible. That was simply presupposed.

But the first half of the 1600s witnessed the rise of what is now called Cartesian thought (under the influence of René Descartes and those who followed him). The traditional way of thinking about knowledge changed. More and more people based their knowledge on an axiom that Descartes made popular: "I think, therefore, I am." Every first-year philosophy student today is still introduced to Descartes's axiom. Descartes himself thought that this axiom was a foundation for all human knowing. After all, if you are thinking, you cannot deny your own existence; the very fact that you are thinking shows that you exist. Descartes was looking for a foundation that Christians and atheists and Muslims and secularists and spiritual types could all agree was indisputable. From this foundation and other approaches, he then gradually built up an entire system of thought to try to convince people to become Roman Catholics.

But notice how his axiom runs: "*I* think, therefore, *I* am." Two hundred years earlier, no Christian would have said that very easily because *God's* existence and *God's* absolute knowledge were already givens. *Our* existence was seen as dependent on him, and *our* knowledge a mere tiny subset of his. It was very widely thought proper to begin with God, not with the "I" in "I think, therefore, I am." If we exist, it is because of *God's* power. Our knowledge, even our existence, is finally dependent on him. But this side of Cartesian thought, we begin with "I." I begin with me. And that puts me in a place where I start evaluating not only the world around me but also morals and history and God in such a way that God now becomes, at most, the inference of my study. That changes everything.

But the Bible does not run along those lines. God simply is.

2. *God made everything that is non-God.* God made everything else. This introduces an irreducible distinction between Creator and creature. God is not a creature; correspondingly, in this absolute sense, we are not creators. If someone were to ask, "Yes, but where did God come from?" the answer the Bible gives is that his existence is not dependent on anything or anyone else. *My* existence is dependent, finally, on him; *his* existence is self-existence. God has no cause; he just is. He always has been. By contrast, everything else in the universe began somewhere, whether in a big bang or in human conception—somewhere. God made it all. That means that everything in the universe apart from God is finally dependent upon God.

3. *There is only one of him.* This emerges strongly in the Bible. God openly says, "Let there be this," "Let there be that," "God made everything," "He saw that it was very good." Later on in the Bible this point is stressed again and again. For example, in verses that Jews reverently recite to this day called the Shema (found in the fifth book of the Bible: Deuteronomy 6), we read the words, "Hear, O Israel: The LORD our God, the LORD is one" (Deut. 6:4).[2] There is only one of him.

Yet even in this first chapter of the Bible there is a hint of complexity to his oneness. It is just a hint, and it is hard to know exactly what it means, but it is quite striking. We read through the account of creation "God said this," "God said that," "God said the other." Then when it comes to human beings, we read, "Then God said, 'Let *us* make human beings in *our* image, in *our* likeness'" (Gen. 1:26, emphasis added). That could be a "royal we." If you listen to BBC broadcasts, you might have listened to Her Majesty Queen Elizabeth II saying "we" and "us" where she is clearly referring to herself. Even the comics pick it up and picture her saying, "We are not amused." The Bible could conceivably be using a kind of editorial "we" here. But it is striking that it is introduced here when human beings are made and that the text goes on to speak of the first person plural not only when God says, "Let us," but also in the expressions "in *our* image, in *our* likeness." We dare not build too much on these details just yet. It is strange language just the same, however, especially in a Bible that insists again and again that there is but one God and that God is one. Could it be that already there is a hint that this one God is a complex being, a complex unity? This is something that will draw our attention repeatedly as we press on in the Bible.

However we understand the plural, the Bible here says that God makes creatures who bear his image. Here again is Genesis 1:26–27:

²⁶Then God said, "Let us make human beings in our image, in our likeness, so that they may rule over the fish in the sea and the birds in the sky, over the livestock and all the wild animals, and over all the creatures that move along the ground."

²⁷So God created human beings in his [singular] own image, in the image of God he created them [plural]; male and female he created them [plural].

We shall come back in a moment to what being made in God's image might mean.

4. *God is a talking God.* The first action that is described under this general rubric "God created the heavens and the earth" is "God said, 'Let there be light'" (1:3). I suppose one could understand this to be a kind of metaphorical way of saying that God brought the heavens and earth into being by his power and that he did not actually utter any words; the expression is metaphorical. Fine. Could be. Except that once Adam and Eve are made, then he actually addresses them and gives them some responsibilities: "This is what you are to do. This is what marriage will look like." He *speaks* to them. So the God of the Bible in the very first chapter is not some abstract "unmoved mover," some spirit impossible to define, some ground of all beings, some mystical experience. He has personality and dares to disclose himself in words that human beings understand. Right through the whole Bible, that picture of God constantly recurs. However great or transcendent he is, he is a talking God.

5. *Everything God makes is good—very good.* As the account progresses, you discover that there is no hint in Genesis 1–2 of death or decay, of butchery, malice, hate, one-upmanship, arrogance, pride, or destruction. There is no hint of any of this. Everything is very good. Regardless of all the difficulty we have understanding God's sovereignty in a world where there is suffering and evil—we shall come back to such themes as we make our way through the Bible—the Bible insists that God is good, and the foundations of this claim are already here in the first chapter.

6. *God comes to an end of his creative work, and he rests.* That is, he stops doing his work of creation. When we are told that God rested from his work, the Bible does not mean that God says, in effect, "Phew, am I tired. I'm glad that's over. I've really got to sit down and put my feet up." That is rather misreading the text. He comes to the end of his week of creation—however we understand this "week"—and at the end of his creative work he stops. He rests and designates this seventh day in a special way, a way that will be picked up later.

7. *The creation proclaims his greatness and glory.* Another facet of God's self-disclosure in these first two chapters of the Bible is only implied in the account, but it is teased out in later chapters of the Bible. When you hold a Stradivarius violin in your hands, the more you know about the history of violin making, the more you are impressed by the craftsman who built the

instrument you are holding. Similarly, the more we know about the created order—its vastness, its complexity, its physics, the ability of a tiny hummingbird to travel 1500 miles in migration and return to the same tree, the sweep from the unimaginable dimensions of an expanding universe to the minuteness of subatomic particles with incredibly short half-lives—the more our response ought to be adoration and genuine awe before the Creator. This response surfaces many times in the Bible. For instance:

> [1]The heavens declare the glory of God;
> the skies proclaim the work of his hands.
> [2]Day after day they pour forth speech;
> night after night they display knowledge.
> [3]They have no speech, they use no words;
> no sound is heard from them.
> [4]Yet their voice goes out into all the earth,
> their words to the ends of the world.
>
> Psalm 19:1–4

These are some of the things about God that these opening two chapters say right on the surface of the text. They also tell us some things about ourselves.

Some Things about Human Beings

1. *We are made in the image of God*. Because human beings are creatures, it is not surprising that we have many attributes in common with other creatures. We know this today from genetics. What percentage of my genes are shared with a chimp or a piglet? When the piglet dies and returns to the dust, it does exactly what I do: I return to the dust too. You and I are part of this created order.

If you keep stressing only the continuity human beings share with animals, then eventually you might come out with the kind of position that Peter Singer at Princeton University adopts. He argues, in effect, that all animal life ought to have, more or less, exactly the same kind of rights that human beings have; conversely, human beings are not intrinsically more important than, say, dolphins or chimpanzees. After all, genetically speaking we are mostly the same stuff. We are physical beings; they are physical beings. They are born, they live, they die; we too are born, we live, we die. But Genesis does not see things quite that way. It insists that human beings and human beings alone are made in the image of God.

As you can imagine, that expression "image of God" has over the millennia generated endless discussion. What does it mean to be "made in the image of God"? Philosophers and theologians have written long tomes saying, "Well, it has something to do with the facility of language, or with our self-identity, our reasoning processes, love that might be altruistic, our capacity to know God," and so on. But if you were reading the Bible for the first time and did not know anything about these debates, I suspect that your approach to this "image of God" language would be a little simpler. It becomes a kind of master concept that is filled in as you read on in the Bible. The point at this early juncture is that as God's image-bearers, we reflect God. The ways in which we reflect God will get filled in as the Bible unfolds.

In what ways do human beings start reflecting God, even in this first chapter? God is a talking God. He speaks to human beings, *and they speak back to him*. There is a commonality of speech, propositions, and knowledge that is not merely felt but can be articulated.

There is also something of creativity. Of course, our creativity is not like God's. In this chapter, God makes things; *he* makes things out of nothing. We cannot do that. But implanted in human beings, as a reflection of God, is a certain creativity. We work with our hands. My wife does spectacular needlepoint, silk and metal thread work; she makes quilts and dresses for little girls. My daughter is an inventive and creative cook. I like working with my hands in wood. Some write. Some are remarkably creative in their physicality. I have a son who studies every new physical challenge that comes along and plunges in, and he is almost an artist as he learns scuba diving or spelunking or whatever the new challenge is. Where does this creative urge come from? By and large creativity is not characteristic of elephants, black widow spiders, or rocks.

Human beings enjoy a capacity to work. God is depicted as engaged in the work of creation week, which ends in "rest" as he comes to the end of it. What he gives to the man and the woman is certain responsibilities to work in this world, to tend the garden. Work is teased out throughout all of Scripture as something intrinsically honorable. Christians should never descend to the place where working on the manufacturing floor or working as a secretary or working driving a bus or doing research chemistry is "secular," somehow divorced from God. We are not to say, "I work as I must to pay the bills, and then Sunday is when I am supposed to be spiritual. Monday I go back to trying to develop a new chemical that will fight cancer. That is work, and it has nothing to do with God." Rather, if this is God's universe and we are made in his image, then as we work, our work too reflects him and is offered back up to him with integrity and gratitude. Work is significant because we are made in the image of God. Work carried out in this way changes our perspective about who we are.

We must recognize, of course, that there are unbridgeable differences between God and us. We have already seen that he alone is self-existent; we are not, for like everything else in the creation we are dependent creatures. God never tells us to be something we are intrinsically incapable of being.

He never says to us, "Be self-existent, for I am self-existent." Later on, when the Bible unpacks God's omnipotence—that is, his unlimited power—he does not say, "Be omnipotent, for I am omnipotent." Nevertheless, in many domains, precisely because we *have* been created in the image of God, we are *supposed* to mirror him. That is why, later on in the Bible, God will say, "Be holy, for I am holy." (We'll glimpse a little later what holiness is.) We are to reflect God in certain ways. In these chapters, God is presented not only as the Creator but as the sovereign ruler over all. And in some small measure, God's function as the sovereign ruler is to find his image in these created human beings, this man and this woman, for they have been put in charge of the rest of the created order—not to rape it or exploit it or to become economically selfish with it, but to be God's own stewards over the good world that God has made. We have been made in his image and charged with the responsibility of looking after his creation. In so doing, we are reflecting something of God.

Even the capacity to know God, to delight in him, is wonderful. Peter Williams wrote a book called *I Wish I Could Believe in Meaning: A Response to Nihilism*. Nihilism is the view that life has no intrinsic or objective meaning. Many paths wind their way toward nihilism, but none is more seductive than that which says human beings are nothing more than a usefully arranged collection of molecules, beings who have arisen by sheer chance from the primordial muck. Where is the meaning in beings of this sort? From the Bible's point of view, however, meaning in life is bound up with the fact that we were made by God, in his image, and for God, with an eternal destiny. This radically changes our perception of what human beings are. Otherwise we slouch toward what one philosopher has called "self-referential incoherence." What he means by this is that we compare ourselves with ourselves. We have no external standard by which anything should be judged; we cannot find an anchor for our being anywhere. So we drown ourselves in temporary pleasures or pursuit of money or self-promotion, but we have no anchoring that locates us and gives us a meaning beyond ourselves. There is no scale.

Human beings were made in the image of God, and as his image-bearers we were made to work, to rule, to serve as God's stewards, to be surpassingly God-centered.

2. *We human beings were made male and female.* In Genesis 1, where the creation account is first given, we are told, "So God created human beings in his own image, in the image of God he created them; male and female he created them" (1:27). But in Genesis 2, where the creation of humans beings is expanded upon, not only what they hold in common but how they are different is exposed: "The LORD God said, 'It is not good for the man to be alone. I will make a helper suitable for him'" (2:18). Older English versions have "I will make a *help meet* for him," and from these italicized words we have derived our word *helpmeet* and hence *helpmate*: "a helper suitable for him."

[19]Now the LORD God had formed out of the ground all the wild animals and all the birds in the sky. He brought them to the man to see what he would name them; and whatever the man called each living creature, that was its name. [20]So the man gave names to all the livestock, the birds in the sky and all the wild animals.

But for Adam no suitable helper was found. [21]So the LORD God caused the man to fall into a deep sleep; and while he was sleeping, he took one of the man's ribs and then closed up the place with flesh. [22]Then the LORD God made a woman from the rib he had taken out of the man, and he brought her to the man. [23]The man said,

> "This is now bone of my bones
>   and flesh of my flesh;
> she shall be called 'woman,'
>   for she was taken out of man."

[24]For this reason a man will leave his father and mother and be united to his wife, and they will become one flesh.

Genesis 2:19–24

So while the opening chapters insist that human beings, male and female, were equally made in the image of God, they also insist that the woman was made as a helper. But the man and the woman come together in one union, a sexual union, a marriage union. A pattern is set, Genesis 2 tells us, in which, generation after generation, the man will leave his family, the woman will leave her family, and the two will settle into a new relationship, a new marriage, the two becoming one.

This is a rather different picture of marriage than some others offer. The man and the woman are not simply animals having it on; nor is this a picture of, say, an ancient Near Eastern harem with the most powerful monarch possessing the most women, while each woman is nothing more than property, a decidedly and intrinsically inferior being. In the biblical picture she comes from the man. She is one with him. She is different, transparently—for a start, she is not identical but his sexual and emotional counterpart, so that in marriage the two become "one flesh"—but here there is a vision of marriage that ultimately becomes a model of other relationships unpacked in later chapters in the Bible.

3. *The man and his wife were innocent.* We read in the last verse of Genesis 2, "The man and his wife were both naked, and they felt no shame" (v. 25). I'm sure you've seen some line-drawing cartoons of Adam and Even in the garden, with a little snake coming down a branch and an apple hanging down from somewhere. In these line diagrams, you don't want to make them indecent, so the woman's hair covers her breasts appropriately, and fig leaves and other branches cover the man in the appropriate spots. Some one-liner is attached to the cartoon, and we all giggle. But what does nakedness signify here at the end of Genesis 2?

Do you know that there is a theory to nudist colonies? Oh, I know that some nudist colonies are merely an excuse for sexual orgy. But the best nudist colonies—if I may speak of nudist colonies on a moral scale—have a certain philosophy to them. The idea is that if you could be completely open and transparent in one part of your life, then sooner or later you could foster openness and transparency in every part of your life. So we begin with physical transparency—complete openness, nakedness—and maybe down the road we'll all become wonderfully open, candid, honest, caring, loving people. It never works. But that's the theory. The reason it never works is that we have so much to be ashamed of; there is so much we need to hide.

In this account, however, Adam and Eve have nothing to hide and therefore nothing to be ashamed of. Tell me, you men, would you like your mother, wife, or daughter to know absolutely everything you think and feel? You women, would you like your father, husband, or son to know absolutely everything you think and feel? We hide all kinds of things, don't we? Why? Because we have so much of which we ought to be ashamed. What would it be like never ever to have told a lie? Never ever to have nurtured bitterness? Never ever to have succumbed to controlling lust? Never ever to have burned up with hate? Never ever to be puffed up in arrogance—but to always love God with heart and soul and mind and strength and always love the other as yourself? Then you would have absolutely nothing to be ashamed of. You could afford to be naked. No wonder the very word "Eden" means "delight."

Some Things about How Genesis 1–2 Fit into the Whole Bible and into Our Lives

Here I am merely going to prime the pump. These few paragraphs will prepare the way for some of the things teased out in the rest of the book.

1. *These two chapters constitute the necessary background to Genesis 3.* Without understanding how good everything is, we cannot fully grasp what happens in the next chapter, which depicts what is sometimes called "the fall," the onset of massive rebellion.

2. *This doctrine of creation actually surfaces again in the Bible, in passages written* after *the coming of Jesus.* However, this notion of creation is transformed: what is promised is a new creation and ultimately a new heaven and a new earth. The biblical vision of the future looks back to the old creation, which tragically succumbed to rebellion, hatred, idolatry, and sin. What is finally needed is for God to do a new creative act, to begin again, to create people over again, to create a new existence. In some of the New Testament writings, that prospect is called "new creation." We press toward a new heaven and a new earth, the home of righteousness. We shall examine that prospect more closely in the last chapter of this book. The terminology for it, however, is drawn from Genesis 1–2.

Likewise, Adam is depicted as the ancestor of the human race, our race, which falls away in ugliness, decay, and idolatry. Much later, Jesus is called the second Adam—that is, Jesus begins another humanity, a new race, that works on quite different principles. Christians must belong to this second Adam or all that the Bible speaks about as "the gospel," the good news, makes no sense at all. Similarly, the theme of rest and the theme of the garden will also continue, as we'll see.

3. *Above all, this vision shapes our worldview.* For example, in pagan polytheism (that is, in views of the world in which there are many gods), the gods have different domains of operation: there is a god or goddess of war, another of the sea, another of love, and so forth. Here is one God who has made it all. This differs, for example, from hedonism, where the point of human existence is, quite simply, to find as much pleasure as you possibly can, by whatever means possible, before you die. But here the pursuit of pleasure is bound up with God himself. We were made initially *by* God and *for* God, and the best and highest pleasure is a God-centeredness that secular hedonists cannot possibly imagine. Their pleasures are too fleeting, too small, too narrow.

Alternatively, pantheism teaches us that the entire material world and godness are all part of the same thing. There is no differentiation. Thus I am god and you are god and we are all in this god-existence together. "I am really quite a spiritual person, you know, and for me it is the vibration of crystals that enables me to be in sync with the universe and makes me feel transcendently other." This is a frame of reference that many adopt. It simply is not the worldview of the Bible. God made everything, and we human beings who have been made in his image find our greatest fulfillment, purpose, happiness, and integrity in being rightly related to him.

4. *What the Bible says about creation is what grounds the notion of human accountability and responsibility.* Why should I obey God? If he wants to take me in directions that I do not like, who is he to tell me what to do? Surely I am free to choose other gods or invent my own. I can belt out the popular song, "I did it my way." Who is he to boss me around? I defy him.

Unless he made me; unless he designed me. In that case I owe him everything—life and breath and everything else, such that if I do not see it that way then I am out of line with my Maker. I am out of line with the one who designed me and with what I am designed by God himself to be. I am fighting against myself as well as against the God who made me. All of human accountability and responsibility before God is grounded in the first instance in creation. He made us, and we owe him. If we do not recognize this simple truth, then, according to the Bible, that blindness is itself a mark of how alienated from him we are. It is for our good that we recognize it, not because he is the supreme bully but because without him we would not even be here, and we will certainly have to give an account to him.

Now we are set up for the Bible's analysis of what is wrong with us.

2

The God Who Does Not Wipe Out Rebels

The passage in the Bible that we will focus on is Genesis 3. I said at the end of the last chapter that Genesis 1–2 set the stage for what goes wrong. In general terms, that is correct. What I neglected to say, however, is that there is a particular element in Genesis 2 that sets the stage for Genesis 3—namely, Genesis 2:17 records one prohibition that God gives to Adam and Eve: "But you must not eat from the tree of the knowledge of good and evil, for when you eat of it you will certainly die." They are to work the garden and enjoy it in all its fruitfulness. It is a perfect delight. *But* there is a prohibition: they are not to eat of the tree of the knowledge of good and evil. And if they do eat of it, they will die.

We shall consider in due course why God issued the prohibition. Wasn't this sort of setting them up for failure? In any case, without noting that prohibition, we cannot possibly understand Genesis 3.

In this chapter we shall follow the biblical text so closely that it is worth laying it out here. I shall then offer a couple of introductory comments, then unpack Genesis 3 in four steps before showing how this material from the first book of the Bible is absolutely essential to any fair understanding of the whole Bible—and why that is important to you and me.

> [1]Now the serpent was more crafty than any of the wild animals the LORD God had made. He said to the woman, "Did God really say, 'You must not eat from any tree in the garden'?"
> [2]The woman said to the serpent, "We may eat fruit from the trees in the garden, [3]but God did say, 'You must not eat fruit from the tree that is in the middle of the garden, and you must not touch it, or you will die.'"

⁴"You will not certainly die," the serpent said to the woman. ⁵"For God knows that when you eat of it your eyes will be opened, and you will be like God, knowing good and evil."

⁶When the woman saw that the fruit of the tree was good for food and pleasing to the eye, and also desirable for gaining wisdom, she took some and ate it. She also gave some to her husband, who was with her, and he ate it. ⁷Then the eyes of both of them were opened, and they realized they were naked; so they sewed fig leaves together and made coverings for themselves.

⁸Then the man and his wife heard the sound of the LORD God as he was walking in the garden in the cool of the day, and they hid from the LORD God among the trees of the garden. ⁹But the LORD God called to the man, "Where are you?"

¹⁰He answered, "I heard you in the garden, and I was afraid because I was naked; so I hid."

¹¹And he said, "Who told you that you were naked? Have you eaten from the tree that I commanded you not to eat from?"

¹²The man said, "The woman you put here with me—she gave me some fruit from the tree, and I ate it."

¹³Then the LORD God said to the woman, "What is this you have done?"

The woman said, "The serpent deceived me, and I ate."

¹⁴So the LORD God said to the serpent, "Because you have done this,

> "Cursed are you above all livestock
>   and all wild animals!
> You will crawl on your belly
>   and you will eat dust
>   all the days of your life.
> ¹⁵And I will put enmity
>   between you and the woman,
>   and between your offspring and hers;
> he will crush your head,
>   and you will strike his heel."

¹⁶To the woman he said,

> "I will make your pains in childbearing very severe;
>   with pain you will give birth to children.
> Your desire will be for your husband,
>   and he will rule over you."

¹⁷To Adam he said, "Because you listened to your wife and ate from the tree about which I commanded you, 'You must not eat of it,'

> "Cursed is the ground because of you;
>   through painful toil you will eat of it
>   all the days of your life.
> ¹⁸It will produce thorns and thistles for you,
>   and you will eat the plants of the field.

> [19]By the sweat of your brow
>   you will eat your food
> until you return to the ground,
>   since from it you were taken;
> for dust you are
>   and to dust you will return."

[20]Adam named his wife Eve, because she would become the mother of all the living.

[21]The LORD God made garments of skin for Adam and his wife and clothed them. [22]And the LORD God said, "The man has now become like one of us, knowing good and evil. He must not be allowed to reach out his hand and take also from the tree of life and eat, and live forever." [23]So the LORD God banished him from the Garden of Eden to work the ground from which he had been taken. [24]After he drove them out, he placed on the east side of the Garden of Eden cherubim and a flaming sword flashing back and forth to guard the way to the tree of life.

Genesis 3

Understanding Genesis 3

How shall we understand this chapter? In another part of the Bible—one that we're not going to have time to explore in detail—the account is told of King David seducing a woman next door, and when he is caught, he arranges to have her husband killed (see 2 Samuel 11). So you have a powerful man (David), a weak man (the woman's husband), and something that is desired (the woman).

Nathan the prophet is sent by God to confront King David about his cleverly concealed adultery and murder (see 2 Samuel 12). Because the king is an autocrat, the prophet approaches with a certain amount of care, and so he begins with a parable. "Your majesty," he says, "something rather sad has taken place out in the country. There is a very rich farmer with herds and cattle, with flocks you wouldn't believe. Next door is a dirt farmer with just one little lamb—and he doesn't even have that anymore. Some people came by to see the rich man, and to prepare a feast for the visitors the rich farmer went and swiped the one poor little lamb from the dirt farmer." So here we have a very powerful man (the rich farmer), a weak man (the dirt farmer), and something that's desired (the dirt farmer's only lamb): the parable is meant to mirror David's treachery. Initially David does not see the connection, but eventually he does. He is exposed and crushed by his own idolatrous corruption.

It is easy to see why Nathan tells the parable, to figure out what the parable is supposed to do: it is setting up an analogous situation by telling something similar to what took place, something with the same essential ingredients: a rich man, a weak man, and something that is desired. Yet if you compare the stories closely, you also see differences. What is desired in the first instance is a woman; what is desired in the second instance is a lamb. In the first instance, the weak man is killed so that David can hide his sin, but in the second instance, what is desired is killed (the lamb itself). The stories are not exactly parallel. If they were exactly the same, it would not be an analogy or a parable. In other words, sometimes stories get the gist of the thing right, but they are sufficiently symbol laden that you have to work your way through the details to understand the point.

So in Genesis 3. This serpent may be the embodiment of Satan, or he may be the symbol for Satan, and the Bible doesn't really care to explain which. What it does say about Satan can be drawn out pretty precisely, but we cannot understand exactly what the communication arrangements were in Eden, and they do not adversely affect the main points of the narrative.

With that introduction, let me suggest four things that emerge unmistakably from Genesis 3.

1. The Deceitful Repulsiveness of That First Rebellion (Gen. 3:1–6)

We are introduced to the serpent. According the last book of the Bible, Satan himself stands behind this serpent in some sense (see Rev. 12). Moreover, his smooth talk aligns him with another description of Satan where we are told that he masquerades as an angel of light (see 2 Cor. 11:14), deceiving, if it were possible, the very chosen ones of God (see Matt. 24:24): he is a smart-mouth.

Here we are also told that he was made by God: "the serpent was more crafty than any of the wild animals the LORD God had made" (Gen. 3:1). In other words, the Bible does not set Satan or the serpent up as a kind of anti-God who stands over against God as his equal but polar opposite, like matter and antimatter, with exactly the same power, such that if they were to collide they would explode in a fireball of released energy that leaves nothing else behind. In the Bible there is no picture of God matched by an equivalent anti-God, a bit like the light side and the dark side in the Force, where the individual human being leans one way or the other to determine which side of the Force wins. This is not the picture. The picture painted by the first sentence of this chapter is that even Satan himself is a dependent being, a created being. This passage does not tell us how or when he fell. Elsewhere he is portrayed as part of the angelic number who rebelled against God. But none of that is described here. He just shows up.

We are told, according to our English versions, that he was the most crafty of the wild animals that God had made. In many sectors of the English-speaking world, the word *crafty* suggests surreptitiousness, sneakiness. Does it have such negative overtones to you? It certainly does to me. But the word that is used here in Hebrew can be either positive or negative, depending on the context. In many places it is rendered something like "prudence." For example, "A prudent man keeps his knowledge to himself" (Prov. 12:23 NIV). This passage does not refer to a crafty man, a sneaky little blighter who keeps his knowledge to himself; it conjures up, rather, someone who is wise and prudent. Or again, "The prudent are crowned with knowledge" (Prov. 14:18). This does not mean the crafty are crowned with knowledge. Similarly in the first verse of Genesis 3: I suspect that what is being said is that the serpent, Satan, was crowned with more prudence than all the other creatures, but in his rebelling the prudence became craftiness; the very same virtue that was such a strength became twisted into a vice. One recalls the observation of Sherlock Holmes: "Ah, me! it's a wicked world, and when a clever man turns his brains to crime it is the worst of all."[1]

The serpent approaches the woman (what the modes of communication were, I have no idea) and avoids offering her a straight denial or a direct temptation. He begins instead with a question: "Did God really say *that*? Did God really say, 'You must not eat from any tree in the garden'?" Notice what he is doing. He expresses just the right amount of skepticism, a slightly incredulous "Can you really believe that God would say that?"—like an employee asking, "Can you believe what the boss has done this time?" The difference is that the person whose word is being questioned is the maker, the designer, God the sovereign. In some ways the question is both disturbing and flattering. It smuggles in the assumption that we have the ability, even the right, to stand in judgment of what God has said.

Then the devil offers exaggeration. God did forbid one fruit, but the way the serpent frames his question—"Did God really say, 'You must not eat from *any* tree in the garden'?"—casts God as the cosmic party pooper: "God basically exists to spoil my fun. I might want a snack, but God says, 'No.' I want to do something, but God says, 'No, no, no.' He is just the cosmic killjoy. Can you believe that God said that?!"

The woman replies with a certain amount of insight, wisdom, and grace— at least initially. She corrects him on his facts, on his exaggeration: "We may eat fruit from the trees in the garden," she insists (3:2). Then she adds, still correctly, "But God did say, 'You must not eat fruit from the tree that is in the middle of the garden'" (3:3, referring back to 2:17). His exaggeration is neatly set aside. But then she adds her own exaggeration. She adds, "and *you must not touch it*, or you will die" (3:3, emphasis added). God had not said anything about not touching it. It is almost as if the prohibition to eat has got under her skin, making her sufficiently riled up that she has to establish the *meanness* of the prohibition. The first sin is a sin against the goodness of God.

We gain a little insight into the terrible slippage going on in the woman's mind if we conjure up what she *should* have said. Perhaps something like this: "Are you out of your skull? Look around! This is Eden; this is paradise! God knows exactly what he is doing. He made everything; he even made me. My husband loves me and I love him—and we are both intoxicated with the joy and holiness of our beloved Maker. My very being resonates with the desire to reflect something of his spectacular glory back to him. How could I possibly question his wisdom and love? He knows, in a way I never can, exactly what is best—and I trust him absolutely. And you want me to *doubt* him or question the purity of his motives and character? How idiotic is that? Besides, what possible good can come of a creature defying his Creator and Sovereign? Are you out of your skull?"

Instead, the woman flirts with the possibility that God is nothing more than a cosmic party pooper, bent on limiting the pleasure of his creatures.

Then comes the first overt contradiction of God. The serpent declares, "You will not certainly die" (3:4). The first doctrine to be denied, according to the Bible, is the doctrine of judgment. In many disputes about God and religion, this pattern often repeats itself, because if you can get rid of that one teaching, then rebellion has no adverse consequences, and so you are free to do anything.

Far from recognizing the threat of judgment, the serpent holds out that rebellion offers special insight, even divine insight: "God knows that when you eat of it your eyes will be opened, and you will be like God, knowing good and evil" (3:5). Here is the big ploy, the total temptation. The heart of the vicious deceitfulness central to what the serpent promises is that what he says is partly true and totally false. It is true, after all: her eyes will be opened, and in some sense she will see the difference between good and evil. She will determine it for herself. God himself says so at the end of the chapter: "The man has now become like one of us, knowing good and evil" (3:22).

And yet this is an entirely subversive promise. God knows good and evil with the knowledge of omniscience: he knows all that has been, all that is, all that will be, all that might be under different circumstances—he knows it all, including what evil is. But the woman is going to learn about evil by personal experience; she is going to learn about it by becoming evil.

An illustration may help. My wife is a cancer survivor. She is a fairly high-risk survivor, and so the doctors still watch her very closely. The oncologists know a great deal about the disease—from the outside. She knows cancer from the inside. God knows all there is to know about sin, but not by becoming a sinner. The woman will find out about the knowledge of good and evil from the inside. In that sense, what the serpent promises is a total lie.

Indeed, the expression in Hebrew, "the knowledge of good and evil," is often used in places where to have the knowledge of good and evil is to have the ability to pronounce what is good and pronounce what is evil. That's what God had done, if you recall. He had made something and declared that "it was good" (1:10). He made something else, and "it was good" (1:12, 18, 21, 25). He finished his work of creation, and "it was very good" (1:31). For God has this sovereign, grounded-in-infinite-knowledge ability to pronounce what is good. Now this woman wants this God-like function. God says, in effect, "It is not good to eat that particular fruit. You will die." But if she does, instead of delighting in the wisdom of her Maker, she is pronouncing, independently, her own choices as to what is good and evil. She is becoming "like God," claiming the sort of independence that belongs only to God, the self-existence that belongs only to God, the moral absoluteness that belongs only to God.

To be like God, to achieve this by defying him, perhaps even outwitting him—this is an intoxicating program. This means that God himself must from now on be regarded, consciously or not, as at least a rival and maybe an enemy: "I pronounce my own good, thank you very much, and I do not need you to tell me what I may or may not do."

Doubtless here is where we need to think a little more about this tree. What was the fruit? There is no biblical text that says it was an apple, as if God really hates apples but is rather partial to pineapples and pears. It is not necessary to suppose that the fruit is magical, such that by ingesting it—whatever it is—a switch suddenly goes on in the brain, the chemistry changes, and now you suddenly start pronouncing good and evil. That is not quite the point. Regardless of what this fruit is, it is an inevitable test. If God makes image-bearers and pronounces what is good and what is evil, if he orders the whole system, then to come along at any point and say, "No, I will declare my own good. What you declare to be evil, I will declare to be good. What you say is good, I will declare to be evil"—this is why the tree bearing this fruit is said to be the tree of the knowledge of good and evil. What is crucial is not the tree but the rebellion. What is so wretchedly tragic is God's image-bearer standing over against God. This is the de-god-ing of God so that I can be my own god. This, in short, is idolatry.

Throughout the history of the Christian church, some Christians have argued that the tree is a symbol for sex. But that suggests there is something intrinsically evil about sex. That sort of inference flies in the face of what the Bible says. When God brings the man and woman together in this first marriage, he himself is establishing the union, he himself is declaring it very good. Much later in the Bible, one of the writers says, "Marriage should be honored by all, and the marriage bed kept pure" (Heb. 13:4). Nothing in the Bible says that sex is intrinsically evil, though like all of God's good gifts it can be abused, distorted, twisted, and perverted.

We should not think that the serpent's temptation is nothing more than an invitation to break a rule, arbitrary or otherwise. That is what a lot of people think that "sin" is: just breaking a rule. What is at stake here is something deeper, bigger, sadder, uglier, more heinous. It is a revolution. It makes me god and thus de-gods God.

"When the woman saw that the fruit of the tree was good for food and pleasing to the eye, and also desirable for gaining wisdom"—that is, physically appealing, aesthetically pleasing, transforming in the domain of wisdom—"she took some and ate it" (Gen. 3:6). For those of you who know the language "take and eat," which Christians recite at the Lord's Supper, it is impossible not to recall the later use of this pair of verbs. "She took . . . and ate." "So simple the act and so hard the undoing," someone has said. "God will taste poverty and death before 'take and eat' become verbs of salvation."[2]

"She also gave some to her husband, who was with her, and he ate it" (3:6). Apparently, he was with her in all of this, entirely complicit, no less guilty than she in the deceit and repulsiveness of the slide to self-destruction.

2. The Initial Consequences That Erupted from This First Rebellion (Gen. 3:7–13)

Above all, there is a massive inversion: God creates the man who loves his wife, who comes from him, and together they are to be vice-regents over the created order. Now instead one of the creation order, the serpent, seduces the woman, who hauls in the man, and together they defy God—the order of creation is turned on its head. And, of course, there is death. This should not be surprising. If God is the Creator and gives life, then if you detach yourself from this God, if you defy this God, what is there but death? He is the one who gave life in the first place. He did not bring the universe and his own image-bearers into existence so that they might be completely autonomous from him, somehow achieving the self-existence that belongs only to God. So if one walks away from him, what is there but death? If you pronounce your own good and evil and decide you want to be a god yourself, thus detaching yourself from the living God who made you and who alone gives life, there is nothing but death.

What kind of death? Christians have wrestled with this question. In the fourth century, a Christian thinker by the name of Augustine wrote, "If it be asked what death God threatened them with, whether bodily or spiritual or that second death [this language is used for hell itself], we answer, It was all. . . . [God] comprehends therein, not only the first part of the first death, wheresoever the soul loses God [that is, we die spiritually; we hide from God and become dead to God], nor the latter only, wherein the soul leaves the body, . . . but also . . . the second which is the last of deaths, eternal, and following after all."[3] You cannot cut yourself off from the God of the Bible without consequences. God himself has ordained that the attempt to displace God brings with it the punishment of death.

But note the results that are immediately emphasized by the text. The eyes of the man and the woman are opened; they know they are naked. In consequence they sew fig leaves together for a covering (see Gen. 3:7). At one level the serpent had kept his promise, but this new consciousness of good and evil is not a happy result. There is no pleasure here, but there is the loss of the knowledge of God and, finally, little but shame and guilt. Now they have something to hide, so they sew fig leaves, which is meant to be a bit silly. You cannot hide moral shame with fig leaves.

But this is also a way of saying that there is no way back to Eden. You cannot undo the loss of innocence. If you commit a theft, you can return what you have stolen. In that case you can undo the wrong. Even in that case, however, the stain in your own being cannot be undone. If you commit adultery, you cannot undo it at all. And if you or I defy God, we cannot undo the defiance. It cannot be undone. We cover ourselves in shame. There is no way back to innocence. In the Bible, there is only a way forward—to the cross.

One of the results of this guilt is broken fellowship with God (see Gen. 3:8–10). However spectacularly wonderful the pleasure of enjoying intimacy with God, captured in the picture of walking with God in the cool of the day (3:8), now it is gone. We can catch some small glimpse of this wretched slide through human analogies. If you have been married for ten years in a really good marriage characterized by genuine intimacy and not a little joy, and then for some abysmal reason you slip up and sleep with someone you should not be sleeping with, and you know it and your spouse knows it, the old easy intimacy is shattered. You cannot look each other in the eye anymore. Shame engulfs you. You hide. Even if good efforts are made to heal the breach, there are certain things you cannot talk about anymore. That is why throughout the Bible human sin before God is sometimes described as analogous to sexual betrayal. One Old Testament writer, the prophet Hosea, looks at the ways in which God's people have betrayed him, and actually pictures God—this is hard to believe—as the Almighty cuckold, the ultimate betrayed husband. After all, God's own people abandon him and chase other gods even though he has given them life and intimate fellowship.

This sin results not only in a broken relationship with God but in broken human relationships too. The account is almost funny in a sad, pathetic sort of way. God asks, "Have you eaten from the tree that I commanded you not to eat from?" (Gen. 3:11). "The woman you put here with me," Adam says—it's her fault (3:12). This is not the last time a man has blamed his wife. But she is no better: "It's not my fault, God. That serpent really fooled me." One of the things that commonly occurs in the wake of defying God is this: we deny that we have any responsibility for what happened. Everything we do that's wrong is someone else's fault.

To put this another way: one of the inevitable results of guilt and shame is *self*-justification. Adam justifies himself by blaming Eve; Eve justifies herself by blaming the serpent. Our only hope of being reconciled to God, however, is for *God* to justify us, for *God* to vindicate us. *Self*-justification cannot cut it, for we are guilty; in fact, self-justification is merely one more evidence of idolatry—the idolatry of thinking we have the resources to save ourselves, the idolatry that is still so impressed by self that it cannot readily admit guilt. At the beginning of the twentieth century, when the editors of the *Times* of

London asked several eminent writers to contribute pieces under the theme "What's wrong with the world," G. K. Chesterton replied,

> Dear Sirs,
>   I am.
> Sincerely yours,
> G. K. Chesterton

That reflects a profoundly Christian perspective—but the man and the woman in Genesis 3 are nowhere near recognizing it.

And these are but the initial results that erupt in the wake of this rebellion.

3. The Explicit Curses That God Pronounces (Gen. 3:14–19)

In the wake of this rebellion, God pronounces three curses.

THE FIRST CURSE: TO THE SERPENT

God says to the serpent,

> [14]Because you have done this,
>
>> Cursed are you above all livestock
>>   and all wild animals!
>> You will crawl on your belly
>>   and you will eat dust
>>   all the days of your life.
>> [15]And I will put enmity
>>   between you and the woman,
>>   and between your offspring and hers;
>> he will crush your head,
>>   and you will strike his heel.
>
> Genesis 3:14–15

Some people think that this is a kind of fairy tale, an origins myth, a just-so story about how the serpent lost its legs. "Once upon a time, snakes all had legs, and this is how they lost their legs." Is that what this is about?

I do know this: sometimes God picks up something that is already there and uses it in a new symbol-laden way. In the next chapter of this book, we shall be introduced to a man called Abraham, who is told, among other things, to establish the practice of circumcision for all the men in his family and household. What you must understand is that circumcision was not invented by God or by Abraham; circumcision was widely practiced throughout the ancient Near East of Abraham's day. It was not an unknown rite. But when God imposed it, as we shall see, he gave it a new, special symbol-ladenness in the context of his relationship with Abraham. Circumcision itself was not a brand-new phenomenon, but it gained a new symbol-relationship to reality. So also here: this snake may well have been squirreling and slithering along the ground, but now its mode of transport becomes a deeply symbol-laden thing. The devil himself is cast out and is rejected, a slimy thing running along the ground.

Later symbolism in the Bible runs along these same lines. The prophet Isaiah (late eighth century BC), for example, describes a day coming when "The wolf and the lamb will feed together, and the lion will eat straw like the ox, but dust will be the serpent's food" (Isa. 65:25). This is not because serpents are somehow less moral than lions, but in the symbolism of the day, the serpent was connected with the devil and all that was slimy, low down, and disgusting.

When God says, "I will put enmity between you [the serpent] and the woman, and between your offspring and hers" (3:15), this does not mean that all women will hate snakes. I know some who do, including my wife. My wife, whatever her many gifts and graces, was not called to be a herpetologist. But there are some women herpetologists. The curse reported here in Genesis 3 probes at a level much beyond mere women and snakes. In fact, the text immediately goes on to name not only the woman but the offspring: there will be enmity "between your offspring and hers." But if this expression means "all the offspring of the woman and all the offspring of snakes," then the enmity pronounced is between all human beings and all snakes, and we would not have any herpetologists at all! That is simply not the point.

From the woman, from the human race, will ultimately come the seed that will crush the serpent's head. Did you see Mel Gibson's film *The Passion of the Christ*? Whatever the film's strengths and weaknesses, the opening scene where Jesus is in agony as he prays in the Garden of Gethsemane is truly memorable. As Jesus is praying, a snake starts crawling over one of his limbs. Jesus stands up and suddenly slams his foot down on the snake's head. The symbolism is right out of Genesis 3. By going to the cross, Jesus will ultimately destroy this serpent, this devil, who holds people captive under sin, shame, and guilt. He will crush the serpent's head by taking their guilt and shame on himself.

Genesis 3:15 is sometimes called in Christian circles the "protevangelium," that is, the first announcement of the gospel, the first announcement of good news. This side of the fall, the picture is dark with threat of doom, but now there is promise that from the woman's seed—from the human race—will arise one who will crush the serpent's head. In fact, that promise is extended in the New Testament, the last third of the Bible, beyond Christ to Christians. In a letter written in about the middle of the first century to Christians in Rome, the apostle Paul writes, "The God of peace will soon crush Satan under your feet" (Rom. 16:20). There is a sense in which Christians, by living under the gospel and being reconciled to God because of the gospel, are destroying the devil and his work.

The Second Curse: To the Woman

To the woman he said,

> "I will make your pains in childbearing very severe;
>   with pain you will give birth to children.
> Your desire will be for your husband,
>   and he will rule over you."

Genesis 3:16

The first categorical command that God gave the man and woman was "Be fruitful and increase in number; fill the earth and subdue it" (Gen. 1:28). But now, this side of the fall, even this most fundamental of rights and privileges—part of their very being—now becomes a pain-filled thing. The whole created order is out of whack. Even introducing new life is bound up with loss.

"Your desire will be for your husband, and he will rule over you" (3:16). As you can imagine, this passage has been interpreted many different ways. It is worth reflecting on the fact that the two verbs that are used together here occur as a pair in only one other place within the first five books of the Bible (Genesis, Exodus, Leviticus, Numbers, and Deuteronomy), namely, in the next chapter. So if a first reader were reading along in Genesis 3 and thinking, "I really do not have a clue what this means," that reader would have to press on for only a few more verses before stumbling across the same pair of verbs again, this time in a passage that is clearer. That might prompt the reader to say, "Aha, that makes sense"—and then apply the same meaning in Genesis 3:16.

The second passage is found in Genesis 4. Here we learn that one of the sons of Adam and Eve, Cain, wants to kill the other son, Abel. The chapter portrays the first homicide. When God explains to Cain why he, God, is angry with Cain, he says, "If you do what is right, will you not be accepted? But if you do not do what is right, sin is crouching at your door; it [i.e., sin] *desires to have* you [i.e., to control you, to manipulate you, to boss you around], but *you must rule over* it" (Gen. 4:7, emphasis added). So also here in the wake of the fall: the woman *desires to have* her husband to control him, and he *rules over* her with a certain kind of brutal force. There is sin on both sides: she wants to control, and he, being physically stronger than she is, beats up on her. What we have here in Genesis 3:16 is the destruction of the marriage relationship. The tentacles of rebellion against God corrode all relationships.

When you read on through the following chapters you plow your way through the first homicide to double murders, polygamy, genocide, rape—on and on—all because at the beginning someone said, "I will be God."

The Third Curse: To Adam

[17]To Adam he said, "Because you listened to your wife and ate from the tree about which I commanded you, 'You must not eat of it,'

"Cursed is the ground because of you;
  through painful toil you will eat of it
  all the days of your life.
[18]It will produce thorns and thistles for you,
  and you will eat the plants of the field.
[19]By the sweat of your brow
  you will eat your food
until you return to the ground,
  since from it you were taken;
for dust you are
  and to dust you will return."

Genesis 3:17–19

"Because you listened to your wife and ate from the tree about which I commanded you" (3:17). Adam listened to the woman instead of to God. At the end of the day, prime allegiance must be to God himself, to God alone.

"Cursed is the ground because of you" (3:17). The whole created order of which we are a part is now not working properly. It is under a curse, subjected by God himself to death and decay.

We could press on to develop this theme, but we must take the last step in this chapter.

4. The Long-Term Effects That Flow from This Rebellion (Gen. 3:20–24)

"The LORD God made garments of skin for Adam and his wife and clothed them" (Gen. 3:21). They had used fig leaves. If God uses garments of skin, then blood has been shed—a sacrificial animal. At this stage in the Bible's storyline there is no system of sacrifice; that comes later—a priestly system with prescribed sacrifices and ritual. But God knows that they need to be covered. They have so much shame to hide. He does not say to them, "Take off those stupid fig leaves. If you just expose yourselves and be honest with one another, we can all get back together again and live happily ever after." There is no way back. He covers them with something more durable, but at the price of an animal that sheds its blood.

This is the first sacrifice in the long trajectory of bloody sacrifices that reaches all the way down to the coming of Jesus. When he appears, he is declared to be "the Lamb of God who takes away the sin of the world" (John 1:29). By his bloody sacrifice—by his death—we are covered over. Our shame and our guilt are addressed because he dies in our place. A lamb cannot do that. Here in Genesis 3 the death of an animal to cover the man and the woman is a picture of what is to come, the first step of an entire institution of sacrifices that points us finally to the supreme sacrifice and what Jesus did to take away our sin and cover up our shame.

Conclusion

I want to reflect on how this chapter fits into the Bible and into our lives.

The first important point is that Genesis 3 describes willful rebellion. Some of the hard questions that a strictly materialistic Darwinism must face are "Where do morals come from? Where does meaning come from? Where do notions of right and wrong come from?"

During the last two or three decades, a field of scientific philosophical endeavor has arisen that is now commonly labeled sociobiology. One writer has entitled his book *The Selfish Gene*, in which he argues that because of the way we have developed along evolutionary lines, we have genes that protect us. Those genes that move us toward certain behavior that keeps us alive and reproducing are going to strengthen those people whose behavior is most advantageous. Those who do not develop this advantageous behavior will drop away, and therefore, statistically you will get a higher and higher percentage of human beings who boast the kinds of genes that are nicely adapted to generating the advantageous behavior. Even a very selfish gene might learn somewhere along the line that cooperation with other people with similar genes is better than merely going it alone, so even this is a kind of expanded selfishness. Now you have a genetic predisposition towards working cooperatively and sharing, which might not fit some individualistic view of the survival of the fittest, but at the corporate level—a sociobiology level—this view of the function of the selfish gene makes a lot of sense. In other words, people can develop a bias toward certain behavior that is then called good or evil but which is nothing more than happy selections of genes that equip you, across the generations, with advantageous behavior. In short, sociobiology has become a systematic attempt to explain notions of right and wrong not at some moral level but purely at the naturalistic genetic level.

I would be the last person to want to argue that there is no connection between our morals and our bodies, between our wills and spirits and our heritage and background, including our genetic makeup. We are whole beings; all parts interact together. But it is very difficult to imagine people volunteering to sacrifice their lives for the sake of others, taking pain in their place, in order to improve the race. For instance, a person in Auschwitz concentration camp who pretends that he or she did some forbidden deed in order to be hanged so that some other inmate could go free is not readily explained by sociobiology. So nowadays books and essays have begun to respond to the pretensions of sociobiology, arguing that this discipline cannot possibly explain certain kinds of conduct.

Pete Lowman has written a book with the title *A Long Way East of Eden*. (Recall how when they left the garden Adam and Eve went east of Eden.) Lowman's purpose is to show that the account of the fall makes much more sense of the moral dilemmas and twisted living in the world than any other explanation. The sociologist Christian Smith makes much the same case in his *Moral, Believing Animals: Human Personhood and Culture.*

A second point of note is that Genesis 3 does not think of evil primarily in horizontal terms but in vertical terms. When we do think of evil, we tend to think of evil at the horizontal level. Probably none of us would want to deny that Auschwitz was evil. Probably we do not want to deny that raping a little child is evil. Probably we do not want to deny that operating a huge Ponzi scheme that rips off billions of dollars from people is evil. Certainly the Bible says many condemning things about horizontal evils, that is, evils we perpetrate among ourselves. But what the Bible most frequently says makes God angry is idolatry. This is evil's vertical dimension. The person who is most offended in this chapter is God. The chief problem is not that Eve is really ticked because Adam has blamed her. The primary guilt is guilt before God. Yes, you could read passages from the prophet Isaiah, who condemns horizontal evils such as vicious money-grabbing owners who will not pay fair wages, but pages and pages of the biblical text are devoted to idolatry. That is the supreme evil.

Third, seen in this light, Genesis 3 shows what we most need. If you are a Marxist, what you need are revolutionaries and decent economists. If you are a psychologist, what you need is an army of counselors. If you think that the root of all breakdown and disorder is medical, what you really need is large numbers of Mayo Clinics. But if our first and most serious need is to be reconciled to God—a God who now stands over against us and pronounces death upon us because of our willfully chosen rebellion—then what we need the most, though we may have all of these other derivative needs, is to be reconciled to him. We need someone to save us.

You cannot make sense of the Bible until you come to agreement with what the Bible says our problem is. If you do not see what the Bible's analysis of the problem is, you cannot come to grips with the Bible's analysis of the solution. The ultimate problem is our alienation from God, our attempt to identify ourselves merely with reference to ourselves, this idolatry that de-gods God; and what we must have is reconciliation back to this God, or we have nothing. It is in the light of this analysis that this chapter, Genesis 3, looks forward to the coming of the woman's seed.

Not long ago I attended a funeral. On the card that was handed out at the door, my wife and I found these words from this neighbor: "May those that love us love us, and those that don't love us, may God turn their hearts, and if he doesn't turn their hearts, may he turn their ankle and we shall know them by their limping." Cute. I couldn't help thinking how tragic this was. The man had just gone to meet his Maker, and his last words for us at the funeral were scoring points on people who did not like him—still thinking on a horizontal level.

In the seventeenth century, the great thinker Blaise Pascal wrote, "What sort of freak then is man? How novel, how monstrous, how chaotic, how

paradoxical, how prodigious, judge of all things, feeble earth worm, reposi-
tory of truth, sink of doubt and error, glory and refuse of the universe."[4] He
understood Genesis 1, 2, and 3.

Or in the words of a contemporary thinker and writer, Daniel L.
Migliore:

> We human beings are a mystery to ourselves. We are rational and irrational,
> civilized and savage, capable of deep friendship and murderous hostility, free and
> in bondage, the pinnacle of creation and its greatest danger. We are Rembrandt
> and Hitler, Mozart and Stalin, Antigone and Lady Macbeth, Ruth and Jezebel.
> "What a work of art," says Shakespeare of humanity. "We are very dangerous,"
> says Arthur Miller in *After the Fall*. "We meet . . . not in some garden of wax
> fruit and painted leaves that lies East of Eden, but after the Fall, after many,
> many deaths."[5]

Now you begin to understand the plotline of the whole Bible: who will
fix that?

3

The God Who Writes
His Own Agreements

Ḥow shall we think of the relationship between God and human beings? What kind of mental model do we have when we think of such relationships?

In the various cultures around us, many options are proposed. It might be useful to describe three of them.

Model 1: The Super-Soft Grandfather

God is a benevolent gentleman with a long, flowing beard whose primary job is to be nice. When I was a student in Britain many years ago, I went for a while to Germany to improve my German. While I was there in the language school, a young engineering doctoral student from French West Africa was also there to learn German. Because I was reared in French and he was from French West Africa, every once in a while—twice a week or so—we would go out for a meal together and talk in a language in which we were more comfortable, French rather than German, which was giving both of us headaches. As I got to know him a bit, I discovered that he was married, and while he was in Germany studying German to go back to finish his doctoral studies at a German university in mechanical engineering, his wife was studying medicine in London. It wasn't too long before I discovered that once a week or so he would go to the red-light district in town and pay his money and have his woman. By this time I had gotten to know him pretty well, so one evening

43

when we were out for a meal, I asked him, "I don't mean to be too intrusive, but what would you say if you discovered that your wife were doing something similar in London?"

"Oh," he said, "I'd kill her."

I said, "That sounds like a bit of a double standard."

"Yes," he replied, "but you have to understand. From the part of the world I come from—in our tribal structure—she would be dishonoring me. It would be a matter of honor. I would have to kill her."

I said, "But you told me that you were brought up in a mission school. You were taught the Bible. You know that the God of the Bible doesn't grade on a curve—one set of standards for men and one set of standards for women."

"*Le bon Dieu,*" he replied, "*il doit nous pardonner. C'est son métier.*" "God is good. He's bound to forgive us. That's his job." Now in fact my friend was quoting the words of Catherine the Great. It's a great line to get us off the hook and slither away from any sort of guilt, isn't it? That is one kind of model of the relationship between God and human beings. He is a super-soft grandfather whose only job is to be nice and forgive us.

Model 2: Deism

God is spectacularly great. Think of the unmeasured eons necessary to travel from galaxy to galaxy at the speed of light. And how many galaxies are there? Where is the end? And God made it all! He is bigger than all of it, incalculably huge, transcendently glorious. So of course you cannot expect him to concern himself with your two-bit existence down here. You have as much significance to him as a nanoparticle has to us. Even if you have some genuine concern for the creatures on your farm, you do not usually give a lot of thought to the earthworms. Why should God give a snap about you? He may have wound the entire universe up like a big old-fashioned watch, but now it is running down without any input from him, doing its own thing.

Neither deism nor the grandfather model squares very well with the Bible. True, according to the Bible God really did make it all. Moreover, he is "big" all right, transcendentally glorious. But he is also portrayed as personal, interacting with and talking to the creatures he made in his image, intimately interested in their affairs, and certainly holding them to account. We shall discover that God as he is described in the Bible is incalculably loving yet simultaneously utterly holy, such that when he confronts rebellion, sin, and all that is tawdry and evil, he is—there is no other word for it—angry. So the God of the first model, which is very common, cannot be squared with Scripture because he is merely nice: there is nothing of justice in him, no moral fiber or judgment, no passion simply to be God and be recognized as such. The grandfather model leaves us at the center of the universe, and God's role is to coddle us there.

That is called idolatry. The second model cannot be squared with Scripture because its picture of God makes him out to be too distant, too unconcerned, too impersonal. God as he is depicted in the Bible is as intensely personal as he is utterly sovereign.

We might consider another model of the relationship between God and human beings.

Model 3: Mutual Back-Scratching

This model is very common in the world of polytheism, that is, in religions where there are multiple gods. These gods are all finite. They all have personalities, and many of them have their quirks, weaknesses, evils, eccentricities, sins, and needs. They also have their spheres of interest, their domains of operation. So the way such pagan religion works is that you go to the temple of the particular god in question, and you give the god the kind of thing that the god wants. You scratch the god's back (metaphorically, of course) by offering a specified sacrifice, or making a donation to the god's temple, or engaging in some prescribed ritual. Then maybe that god will give you what you want. So you want to make a nice safe sea voyage in the first century in the Mediterranean world? You go to the temple of Neptune, the god of the sea. You offer the appropriate sacrifices, and you hope and pray that Neptune will keep the sea calm and you will have a safe trip. You have to give a major speech to your stockholders? Then you go to the god of communication, Hermes in the Greek world and Mercury in the Latin world. You offer the appropriate sacrifices. You scratch the god's back, and the god scratches your back. So this form of religion is a kind of tit-for-tat arrangement: you scratch my back, I scratch yours. Under this sort of regime you may live in a certain kind of fear that you have not paid enough or scratched appropriately, or maybe that the god in question is particularly bad-tempered.

We must acknowledge that some people who think of themselves as Christians also think that their relationship with God is of this "you scratch my back, I scratch your back" sort. Provided you are good enough, you will get married happily. Provided you read your devotions every day, you will live a long life and will not get cancer until you are at least ninety-six. Provided you are honest at work, you will not lose your job as has happened to others, who deserve to lose them a lot more than you do. Provided you always say your prayers, your kids will never rebel. And one day you will go to heaven. You scratch my back, I scratch your back.

The problem with this model, of course, is that it presupposes that the God of the Bible has needs and, therefore, you really can offer him something that he needs and therefore wants. That is why the mutual back-scratching approach to religion is a barter system. That is why the system works in theory in polytheism. The gods are all finite, and they all have needs. But suppose you deal with a God who has no needs. What are you going to offer him?

God Cannot Be Manipulated (Acts 17:24)

The apostle Paul understands these matters. Paul was a first-century preacher who appeared on the scene shortly after Jesus was crucified and came back to life again. He wrote about one quarter of the New Testament. He was especially gifted when it came to announcing the God of the Bible to the polytheists who dominated the culture of the Roman imperial world. So we find him, for example, in the great city of Athens, carefully explaining what a difference it makes to see that there is but one God and that he cannot be manipulated. At the time Athens had the reputation of being the most learned city in the Roman world, followed by Alexandria in Egypt.

When Paul gives his address to some philosophers and teachers in Athens, he explains what he holds to be the truth. Theirs is a world of gods, and the very nature of their religion is "you scratch my back, I scratch your back." But Paul says, "The God who made the world and everything in it [thus you find him articulating the Bible's teaching about creation from Genesis 1–2] is the Lord of heaven and earth and does not live in temples built by hands" (Acts 17:24). Paul does not mean that God may not disclose himself in a temple if he chooses to do so. What he means is that God cannot be reduced to the temple where he is manipulated and domesticated by a priestly class. You cannot get him into a position where you can manipulate him to do your will by providing cash to a certain class of priests, connected with a temple, who are allegedly experts in figuring out what the gods want. The God of the Bible is too big for that; he made everything, he is sovereign over the whole lot, and he cannot be manipulated.

God Does Not Need Us (Acts 17:25)

Then Paul says this: "And he is not served by human hands, as if he needed anything" (Acts 17:25). Isn't that remarkable? God does not need you. He certainly does not need me. He does not need our praise bands. It is not as if God gets to Thursday afternoon and starts saying, "Oh boy, I can hardly wait until Sunday when they crack out those guitars again. I'm feeling pretty lonely. I need to be stroked up here." He does not need our worship. He does not need our money. He does not need us. He does not need anything. In eternity past, before there was anything else, God was, and he was entirely full of joy and contentment. Even then he was a loving God because in the complexity of God's oneness (in categories we will see in due course), the Father loved the Son (we'll come to those categories). There was an otherness right within God himself. He did not create human beings because he was lonely and thought, "You know, my job as God will be a little more palatable if I make an image-bearer or two who strokes me once in a while." He simply does not need us. In this respect God as he is disclosed in the Bible cannot be compared to the finite and needy gods of polytheism.

Do not misunderstand: the truth that God does not need us does not mean that he does not respond to us, that he cannot delight in us, that he might not be pleased with us. He does respond to us, but he responds not out of some intrinsic need in his own being or character but out of the entire volition of his perfections and will. He interacts with us not because he does not foresee the future, not because he has let things get out of control, not because he has abandoned his sovereignty, not because he never was sovereign, not because he is psychologically damaged, not because he *needs* something—but out of the perfections of all that he is with all of his characteristics and attributes. He always responds in line with all of his attributes. He is never less than God.

Can you imagine how hard it was for Paul to get that point across to so-phisticated academics whose entire notion of religion was bound up with a form of "you scratch my back, I scratch your back" polytheism?

We Need God (Acts 17:25)

To make the distinction between God and the gods of the Athenians even sharper, Paul adds another line: "Rather, he himself gives everyone life and breath and everything else" (Acts 17:25). God does not need us, but we need him. Paul's point comes directly out of Genesis 1–3: we are dependent on him for "life and breath and everything else."

When the Lord Jesus was on earth, he taught that not a sparrow falls from the heavens without God's sanction and that the very hairs of your head are numbered (see Matt. 10:29–30). In my case that means God is keeping a rapidly subtracting account, and he knows them all, even the disappearing ones. And every breath I draw is by his sanction. I am dependent upon him, Paul reminds us, for life and breath and everything else—for food, for health. I am an utterly dependent creature. I am not the Creator.

So how are you going to have a relationship with a God like that? He is not some soft-hearted grandfather; moreover, he is not safely distant. He is intensely personal, but he has no needs. That means you have nothing to barter with. The only reason you are still around is because God sanctions it.

Last week one of my friends who taught at a seminary in Dallas—a good man, a teacher of the New Testament, author of major books, father of three children, one a missionary in Siberia, one a missionary in Russia, and one a missionary in Afghanistan—was out jogging. He came home, lay down, and died. Not a thing he could do about it. If your heart keeps beating, it is because

God sanctions it. And if he says, "Come home, my child. Now is the time. Your work is done," you go. Or if he ever says, "You fool, tonight your soul will be required of you," you die. How are you going to barter with a God like that? "God, I'll give you ten percent." But he owns *you* and all you are and have. "Lord, I'll become a missionary." "I'll become a deacon in church." Are you trying to bribe God? Will that make you a better person?

No, there is only one way you are going to have a relationship with this kind of God, and that is if he displays sovereign grace to you. We have nothing with which to barter.

The way sovereign grace—God's decision to be gracious to some people—works out in the Bible lies in a number of different structures. Sometimes God graciously promises what he is going to do so that people learn to believe what he says, to trust his Word, and to look forward to what he is going to do. Sometimes God enters into formal agreements with them. These formal agreements are called "covenants." We might, I suppose, think of them as a kind of contract, a legal agreement—except that modern contracts are negotiated by both parties. The covenants in the Bible often mirror covenants that were well known in the ancient world. In some cases a regional superpower would impose a "covenant" on a vassal state: it was all top-down. Similarly with God: he is the God who writes his own agreements, his own covenants, and here his grace is spectacularly displayed.

The Bible speaks of several covenants that God draws up. We begin with God's covenant with Abraham.

Genesis 12

What has taken place in the intervening chapters—that is, between Genesis 3 and Genesis 12—is not particularly pretty. Abominations have multiplied until God has wiped out nearly all on the planet with a flood. Just a handful of people are spared, but the leader, Noah, promptly gets drunk. By chapter 11, a rebellion is towering through the land again, defying God. And now in Genesis 12 we are told, "The LORD had said to Abram [his name is later changed to Abraham—I'll keep calling him Abraham], 'Go from your country, your people and your father's household to the land I will show you'" (12:1). At the time, Abraham had been in a place called Ur in ancient Babylon; then he moved to a city called Haran. Now God is telling him to go to what would eventually become the land of Israel. God promises him these things:

> [2]I will make you into a great nation
>   and I will bless you;
> I will make your name great,
>   and you will be a blessing.

> [3]I will bless those who bless you,
>   and whoever curses you I will curse;
> and all peoples on earth
>   will be blessed through you.

Genesis 12:2–3

That's a promise. Later on the promise is further elaborated on. Abraham's descendants would be as numerous as the sand of the sea. A son was promised to him, and this promised son through whom all of these blessings would spring would be born in Abraham's old age. At this point Abraham is already seventy-five years old. His wife is getting up there too, but nevertheless, the promise is that this child will come from the union of Abraham and his wife Sarah. Abraham goes through periods of doubt and uncertainty. He tries to short-circuit things by sleeping with somebody else. It is a pretty messy story. But ultimately God keeps his promise. They have a child, a son named Isaac.

Isaac eventually marries, and his wife gives birth to twins. Before the twins are born, God says to the mother, "You have twins inside you. Let me tell you: the older will serve the younger" (see 25:23). In that culture such ordering was not the normal way of things, but God in his sovereignty chose the younger one before either child had done anything good or evil. Out of sovereign grace God chose one above the other and predicted what would happen. God then preserved a certain line down through the years, generation after generation, until the tribes multiplied and eventually possessed the land.

In the midst of all of these promises, this one stands out: "all peoples on earth will be blessed through you" (12:3). God is not only choosing Abraham and his descendants but insisting that through these tribal descendants *all peoples* on earth will be blessed. This is God graciously, sovereignly *promising* something, unconditionally.

Genesis 17

But then comes not only promise but covenant. In Genesis 17 we read,

[1]When Abram was ninety-nine years old, the LORD appeared to him and said, "I am God Almighty; walk before me faithfully and be blameless. [2]Then I will make my covenant between me and you and will greatly increase your numbers."

[3]Abram fell facedown, and God said to him, [4]"As for me, this is my covenant with you: You will be the father of many nations. [5]No longer will you be called Abram; your name will be Abraham, for I have made you a father of many nations. [There's a pun in the Hebrew.] [6]I will make you very fruitful; I will make nations of you, and kings will come from you. [7]I will establish my covenant as *an everlasting covenant* between me and you and your descendants after you

for the generations to come, to be your God and the God of your descendants after you. ⁸The whole land of Canaan, where you now reside as a foreigner, I will give as an everlasting possession to you and your descendants after you; and I will be their God."

⁹Then God said to Abraham, "As for you, you must keep my covenant, you and your descendants after you for the generations to come. ¹⁰This is my covenant with you and your descendants after you, the covenant you are to keep: Every male among you shall be circumcised.

Genesis 17:1–10, emphasis added

This is all very remarkable. This is not simply promise but *covenant*—a covenant imposed by God but leaving both parties with some obligations. God will be the God of Abraham and his descendants; he will secure the land for them and guarantee that entire nations will spring from him. For their part, Abraham and his descendants are to keep the covenant—that is, they are to maintain allegiance to God and seal their acceptance of this covenantal arrangement with the rite of circumcision. At the end of the chapter, we are told, "On that very day Abraham took his son Ishmael and all those born in his household or bought with his money, every male in his household, and circumcised them, as God told him" (17:23).

Genesis 15

So here is first a promise (Genesis 12) and then a covenantal structure (Genesis 17). In between Genesis 12 and 17 is another chapter that speaks of the covenant: Genesis 15. At the beginning of the chapter, God says, "Do not be afraid, Abram. I am your shield, your very great reward" (15:1). Then later in the chapter, Abraham falls into a deep sleep (15:12), and he experiences a spectacularly weird vision. The setup for it comes when Abraham asks God a question:

⁸"Sovereign Lord, how can I know that I will gain possession of [the land]?"

⁹So the Lord said to him, "Bring me a heifer, a goat and a ram, each three years old, along with a dove and a young pigeon."

¹⁰Abram brought all these to him, cut them in two and arranged the halves opposite each other; the birds, however, he did not cut in half.

Genesis 15:8–10

So now you've got a heifer cut into two halves, a ram cut into two halves, a goat cut in two halves, one bird on one side, and one bird on the other.

¹¹Then birds of prey came down on the carcasses, but Abram drove them away.

[12]As the sun was setting, Abram fell into a deep sleep, and a thick and dreadful darkness came over him. [13]Then the LORD said to him, "Know for certain that for four hundred years your descendants will be strangers in a country not their own and that they will be enslaved and mistreated there. [14]But I will punish the nation they serve as slaves, and afterward they will come out with great possessions. [15]You, however, will go to your ancestors in peace and be buried at a good old age. [16]In the fourth generation your descendants will come back here, for the sin of the Amorites has not yet reached its full measure."

[17]When the sun had set and darkness had fallen, a smoking firepot with a blazing torch appeared and passed between the pieces. [18]On that day the LORD made a covenant with Abram.

Genesis 15:11–18

What's going on? This strikes the modern reader as bizarre. When we speak today of writing our own agreements, this is not usually what happens at the final signing ceremony.

Covenants in the Ancient World

There were different kinds of covenants in the ancient world. As I've already indicated, sometimes covenants were established between a sovereign regional superpower and small vassal states. The regional superpower—the Hittites at some points in time, the Assyrians at others, the Babylonians at still others—would arrange an agreement, a covenant. Basically, the covenant said, "We will look after you. We will secure your borders. We will make sure that you are protected against enemies. And you—you will pay your taxes and show allegiance to us," and so on. It was an agreement between the two parties. The covenant specified that if either side did not fulfill the terms, certain disgusting things should happen to the offending party. Obviously, the regional superpower had the power to impose the nasties, not the other way around, but that is the way the covenants were written. Sometimes one of the signs of this covenant agreement and corresponding threat was to take animals, tear them apart, and put them side by side with a kind of bloody alleyway between the two parts, and then the two parties of the covenant would walk between the divided animals so as to signify "May this be done to me if I break this covenant. May I be torn apart. May I be cut in half."

So Abraham prepares the animals. Obviously, however, God is not a human being to walk beside Abraham between animals. Abraham falls into a deep sleep, and in his sleep he sees a firepot, something to represent the presence of God. What is so stunning is that instead of the firepot moving between the animals *side by side with Abraham* (so that the two of them are saying, in effect, "May it be done to us if either of us breaks the covenant"), God goes down this bloody alleyway *all by himself*. He takes the full responsibility for the fulfillment of the covenant all by himself. That is grace.

Abraham will sin. Isaac, his son, will be a wimp. The next son, Jacob, learns some lessons on the long haul, but he is a trickster and a deceiver all the way through. Jacob has twelve sons: one of them sleeps with his father's concubine; another sleeps with his daughter-in-law; ten of those sons cannot figure out whether to murder the eleventh or to sell him into slavery. And these are the patriarchs! And still God does not wipe them out. He has sworn in this symbolic act that whatever curses fall, they are to fall on him. Of course, the descendants of Abraham, later called Israelites, are to practice the sign of the covenant to show that they are the children of the covenant—and so they practice circumcision generation after generation. But then as the years go by and the moral tide swings up and down, one marvels at how much damage and destruction are done, while God still forbears because he promises to keep his covenant. He will protect them. He will bring them into this land. And from their seed will come someone through whom all the nations of the earth will be blessed.

There is one more chapter in Genesis to think about.

Genesis 22

Genesis 22 takes place after the favored son Isaac has been born. There we are told:

> [1]Some time later God tested Abraham. He said to him, "Abraham!"
>
> "Here I am," he replied.
>
> [2]Then God said, "Take your son, your only son, whom you love—Isaac— and go to the region of Moriah. Sacrifice him there as a burnt offering on a mountain I will show you."
>
> Genesis 22:1–2

So he gets there. The son, who is about thirteen, says,

> [7]"Father?"
>
> "Yes, my son?" Abraham replied.
>
> "The fire and wood are here," Isaac said, "but where is the lamb for the burnt offering?"
>
> [8]Abraham answered, "God himself will provide the lamb for the burnt offering, my son." And the two of them went on together.
>
> Genesis 22:7–8

But in a horrendous scene, Abraham eventually stretches his own son out on this altar and is about to kill him—to sacrifice his own son.

[11]But the angel of the LORD called out to him from heaven, "Abraham! Abraham!"

"Here I am," he replied.

[12]"Do not lay a hand on the boy," he said. "Do not do anything to him. Now I know that you fear God, because you have not withheld from me your son, your only son."

[13]Abraham looked up and there in a thicket he saw a ram caught by its horns. He went over and took the ram and sacrificed it as a burnt offering instead of his son. [14]So Abraham called that place The LORD Will Provide. And to this day it is said, "On the mountain of the LORD it will be provided."

[15]The angel of the LORD called to Abraham from heaven a second time [16]and said, "I swear by myself, declares the LORD, that because you have done this and have not withheld your son, your only son, [17]I will surely bless you and make your descendants as numerous as the stars in the sky and as the sand on the seashore. Your descendants will take possession of the cities of their enemies, [18]and through your offspring all nations on earth will be blessed, because you have obeyed me."

Genesis 22:11–18

Now, you might begin by asking, "What kind of God wants someone to sacrifice his own son?" In the pagan religions of the time, it was not all that uncommon for parents to sacrifice their own sons. One particular pagan god called Moloch was pictured as holding a big stone pot in its hands, and a fire would be built under the pot until it was glowing red. Parents would sometimes throw their screaming children into this pot. That was not all that uncommon. It was a mark of devotion. But the whole point of this account is that this is *not* what God wants. How can you possibly please God, the God of the Bible, by destroying your children?

In one sense we should see this as a kind of test in line with the cultural norms of the day: "Do you have the kind of trust in me that the pagans seem to have in their gods—their false, murderous gods to whom they are willing to sacrifice their own sons?" But when push comes to shove, God says, in effect, "Don't you understand? *I* provide the sacrifice! How can you ever please me by sacrificing your son?" Just as in Genesis 15 God alone walks down the bloody alleyway and takes the curse of the covenant on himself, so here he provides the sacrifice. Prohibition of child sacrifice was in due course enshrined in law in the Old Testament. Child sacrifice was to be seen as an idolatrous crime, regardless of the cultural pressures of the day. The God who is there does not demand that we sacrifice our children; instead, in sovereign grace he provides a sacrifice. What he wants of us is that we turn to him wholly and say in effect, "You are God. You are Lord. You are sovereign. I am dependent upon you. I need you. I will trust you. I will obey you."

For all the failures in Abraham's life and in your life and mine, God provides the sacrificial lamb. The stories and the accounts begin to multiply through the Old Testament pages in anticipation of the time when God would provide a sacrifice that far exceeds the value of some ram caught in a thicket.

Concluding Prayer

We confess, Lord God, that in a digital world full of countless material blessings, in a world of nuclear physics and an astonishingly fast pace, it takes an effort to think our way through these passages. But we begin to glimpse that you are the sovereign God to whom we owe everything. The very heart of our rebellion is the desire to be God instead of you, to run things ourselves, to barter with you. We make messes that are damaging to ourselves, to our family, to the culture at large, and to the relationships among nations, everything from petty one-upmanship to racism and genocide and everything in between. Yet at the heart of all of it, we confess, is this horrendous rebellion, this idolatry that demands that we be our own gods.

Open our eyes, Lord God, that we may see your sovereign independence, your glory, your patience with us so that we are not destroyed, the way you took time across countless generations to show what a gracious sovereign God you are until in the fullness of time you sent your own Son to be the Lamb of God who really does take away our sin. Open our eyes and our hearts, Lord God, that we may be drawn inescapably to him. In Jesus's name, Amen.

4

The God Who Legislates

I suspect that one of the most common objections raised against Christians and against Christianity in the West today is that Christians are intrinsically narrow and bigoted. They hold that certain things are true and that their opposites are not true. They distinguish between orthodoxy and heresy. They have their own rules of conduct, of morality. Some things they approve, and some things they disapprove. This is arrogant; worse, it is divisive. Instead of building up civic community so as to establish a genuinely tolerant society, these unyielding lines have the inevitable result of generating divisiveness. For those who are brought up in some of the strongest postmodern trends under the influence of, say, Michel Foucault, all claims to speak the truth are really claims to power; they are forms of manipulation. Instead of fostering freedom, they merely engender constraint and coercion.

Yet when you look at the charges more closely, they are problematic. No community is completely inclusive. Tim Keller, a pastor in New York City, likes to give this example: Suppose you have a gay-lesbian-transgender committee plugging away in some big city, working on inclusiveness. The committee members get along pretty well together. Then suppose that one of them comes to one of the committee meetings and says, "You know, this is a bit embarrassing, but I've had this strange religious experience. I've met this odd bunch of people—they're Christians—and my whole life has been changed. I just do not view things the same way. I am not quite convinced anymore that homosexuality is merely an alternative lifestyle." The others say to him, "Well, we think that you are dead wrong on that score, but you are welcome to your views. We still want to cherish you." As the weeks go by, however, the tensions build up because the committee as a whole is not heading in the same direction as this particular member. Eventually the people on the committee will say to this committee member, "You know, you really do not share our views anymore. You are heading in another direction. Your perception of right and wrong is different from our perception of right and wrong. We are not sure that you belong on this committee anymore. We think it would be a good thing for you to resign."

They have just engaged in excommunication.

It is impossible to be completely, endlessly open because even that endless openness is based upon the assumption that such endless openness is a good thing—so if somebody then says, "It is not a good thing to be endlessly open," those committed to endless openness feel they must reject that person precisely because they cannot be endlessly open to the person who does not hold their view of being endlessly open. In other words, in a finite world there are inevitably boundaries. There are inevitably inclusions and exclusions.

Moreover, even an appeal to truth is inevitable. In an earlier generation, often truth was analyzed to death under the rubric of psychiatry and psychology. That's changing again now. A generation ago the popular lyricist Anna Russell gently mocked this "me generation" with its forms of explaining away all strange behavior:

> I went to my psychiatrist to be psychoanalyzed
> To find out why I killed the cat and blacked my husband's eyes.
> He laid me on a downy couch to see what he could find,
> And here is what he dredged up from my subconscious mind:
> When I was one, my mommy hid my dolly in a trunk,
> And so it follows, naturally, that I am always drunk.
> When I was two, I saw my father kiss the maid one day,
> And that is why I suffer now from kleptomania.
> At three, I had the feeling of ambivalence towards my brothers,
> And so it follows naturally I poisoned all my lovers.
> But I am happy; now I've learned the lesson this has taught:
> Everything I do that's wrong is someone else's fault.

That was a generation ago. Now we handle things a wee bit differently. Now we say that truth is shaped by community. Truth is merely what some particular group or any individual in the group perceives. There was a time when skeptics rejected Christianity because (they argued) it isn't true. Today they are more likely to reject it because it *claims* to be true, because they believe there are no absolutes. In the 1960s, many students on our campuses pursued the individual existentialism of Albert Camus or Jean-Paul Sartre; today they are likely to believe that notions of morality and truth are socially constructed and that no social construct has any legitimate claim to be superior to any other socially constructed perspective.

But of course, if you hold that view to be true, then you believe that view itself is merely socially constructed, so it cannot legitimately claim any superiority. At the end of the day we simply cannot escape the notion of truth. Moreover, freedom itself cannot be endlessly open-ended. Would you like to be free to play the piano extremely well? Then inevitably you must learn a lot of discipline, that certain chords sound right and certain chords do not sound right. There are principles in the way music works. Do you want to be free to have a really excellent, trusting, joyous marriage? If you do, then you are not free to do certain things. In other words, an endless openness toward freedom becomes a kind of slavery.

All of these things have to be kept in mind when we come to the Bible and discover that God legislates. He lays down laws. Unless we are willing to think outside our own Western cultural box, we may find that somewhat offensive. Yet within the Bible's storyline, we discover that God's law is actually bound up with the joyous freedom of life lived under the God who made us.

The Bible's Storyline from the Patriarchs to the Giving of the Law

Let me pick up the Bible's storyline from where we left off in the last chapter. We ended with the patriarchs (Abraham, Isaac, Jacob), who had been called by God to constitute a kind of new humanity that would enter into a covenant relationship with him. They continued in the land of Canaan (later called Israel) as nomads looking after their vast herds until the time came when because of famine they moved down in a block to Egypt. As the centuries slipped by and their numbers multiplied, eventually they became serfs and slaves to the Egyptians. They still had a heritage of faith that had been fostered by the God who had disclosed himself to Abraham the patriarch. This band of Hebrews multiplied. This band of people who would later be known as Israelites and still later as Jews flourished, and yet they flourished under slavery and captivity.

In due course God raised up a man named Moses. Moses himself was a Hebrew, but through strange circumstances he had been brought up in the Egyptian royal court. As a young man, he thought he would side with his own oppressed ethnic people and ended up killing an Egyptian and fleeing for his life. He spent most of his life as a shepherd on the back side of the desert, but at the age of eighty he heard the voice of God telling him to go back and lead the people out of slavery, out of Egypt. In Exodus 3, Moses gives all the reasons that he really shouldn't go: he is too old, and he does not speak in public very well. Somebody else should go. He is still a wanted man in Egypt.

[13]Moses said to God, "Suppose I go to the Israelites and say to them, 'The God of your fathers has sent me to you,' and they ask me, 'What is his name?' Then what shall I tell them?"

[14]God said to Moses, "I AM WHO I AM. This is what you are to say to the Israelites: 'I AM has sent me to you.'"

[15]God also said to Moses, "Say to the Israelites, 'The LORD, the God of your fathers—the God of Abraham, the God of Isaac and the God of Jacob—has sent me to you.'"

Exodus 3:13–15

In other words God does give himself a name ("I AM WHO I AM. . . . I AM has sent me to you"), but it is not a name that puts himself in a box. He is what he is. "I AM WHO I AM." He then further defines himself, as it were; he further reveals himself, for people like Moses, for people like us, as he progressively discloses himself across the centuries. He is the eternal subject. He is not somebody else's object that can be categorized and defined. He is what *he* says he is. He is what he discloses of himself. He is. "[Tell them,] 'I AM has sent me to you'" (3:14). And eventually, then, Moses does lead the people out of slavery. You may have heard of the ten plagues and the crossing of the Red Sea: Moses does lead them out.

Eventually the escaping Israelites come to a mountain in the desert: Mount Sinai. They have not arrived at the promised land. On Mount Sinai, God constructs another covenant; he writes another agreement with them. God's agreement or covenant with Abraham (as we saw last chapter) was grounded in the promise of what God would do conditional merely on God being God. God put himself symbolically through the parts of those animals to say, "This is what *I* will do. It is unthinkable that anything else could be done. *I* will bless you. *I* will secure you. *I* will raise up your seed, make you a great nation, and ultimately through your seed all the nations of the earth will be blessed." Now God enters into a covenant with the entire nation. We sometimes call it the Mosaic covenant (after the man who mediated it) or the Sinai covenant (after the mountain where God disclosed it) or the law covenant (since it contains many laws, just as the covenant with Abraham is characterized by promise). In the New Testament it is once or twice referred to as the "old covenant" because it precedes the covenant Jesus himself introduces, the covenant referred to as the "new covenant"—which of course makes the preceding one, the one given through Moses, "old." This is the origin of the titles given to the two parts of the Christian Bible: "Old Testament" and "New Testament" are alternative ways of referring to the old covenant and the new covenant.

The old covenant laid out in the second book of the Bible, the book of Exodus, specifies forms of religion, how the nation is to organize itself, who the priests are, and so forth, and above all discloses more of God.

The Ten Commandments (Exodus 20)

Right at the heart of this covenant is a group of verses that provide us with the Ten Commandments. They are given in two places in the Old Testament. The place we'll look at is Exodus 20:1–19:

> ¹And God spoke all these words:
>
> ²"I am the LORD your God, who brought you out of Egypt, out of the land of slavery.
>
> ³"You shall have no other gods before me.
>
> ⁴"You shall not make for yourself an image in the form of anything in heaven above or on the earth beneath or in the waters below. ⁵You shall not bow down to them or worship them; for I, the LORD your God, am a jealous God, punishing the children for the sin of the parents to the third and fourth generation of those who hate me, ⁶but showing love to a thousand generations of those who love me and keep my commandments.
>
> ⁷"You shall not misuse the name of the LORD your God, for the LORD will not hold anyone guiltless who misuses his name.
>
> ⁸"Remember the Sabbath day by keeping it holy. ⁹Six days you shall labor and do all your work, ¹⁰but the seventh day is a sabbath to the LORD your God. On it you shall not do any work, neither you, nor your son or daughter, nor your male or female servant, nor your animals, nor any foreigner residing in your towns. ¹¹For in six days the LORD made the heavens and the earth, the sea, and all that is in them, but he rested on the seventh day. Therefore the LORD blessed the Sabbath day and made it holy.
>
> ¹²"Honor your father and your mother, so that you may live long in the land the LORD your God is giving you.
>
> ¹³"You shall not murder.
>
> ¹⁴"You shall not commit adultery.
>
> ¹⁵"You shall not steal.
>
> ¹⁶"You shall not give false testimony against your neighbor.
>
> ¹⁷"You shall not covet your neighbor's house. You shall not covet your neighbor's wife, or his male or female servant, his ox or donkey, or anything that belongs to your neighbor."
>
> ¹⁸When the people saw the thunder and lightning and heard the trumpet and saw the mountain in smoke, they trembled with fear. They stayed at a distance ¹⁹and said to Moses, "Speak to us yourself and we will listen. But do not have God speak to us or we will die."

These are the Ten Commandments. They are often said to be divided into two parts: the first four have to do with the people's relationship with God, and the second six have to do with relationships among each other (not committing adultery, telling the truth, and so forth). We shall run through some of them quickly.

Commandment 1: God's Exclusiveness

The first of the Ten Commandments directs us to recognize the exclusiveness of God: "You shall have no other gods before me" (20:3). Notice the context in which this command is given. "I am the LORD your God, who brought you out of Egypt, out of the land of slavery" (20:2). Up to this point in the Bible's storyline, God is disclosed as the Creator, the one who has made everybody and everything. As the Creator, he is the God to whom we give an account, the God on whom we are dependent, the God who gives us life and breath and health and strength and everything else. That is true for all human beings. Here, however, the focus is on what God has done for some specific human beings, the descendants of Abraham. God has brought them out of slavery. In the wake of this liberation, God says, "You shall have no other gods before me" (20:3).

This is a constantly reiterated theme in the Bible. Both because of creation and because of God's liberation of his covenant people, there is a repeated demand for allegiance to the God who is there. Two chapters farther on: "Whoever sacrifices to any god other than the LORD must be destroyed" (22:20). A chapter after that: "Do not invoke the names of other gods; do not let them be heard on your lips" (23:13). Eleven chapters later: "Do not worship any other god, for the LORD, whose name is Jealous, is a jealous God" (34:14). Or again: "I am the LORD, and there is no other" (Isa. 45:5). "Surely God is with you, and there is no other; there is no other god" (Isa. 45:14).

Initially we might be a bit worried about the notion of a jealous God. Do you want your mate to be constantly jealous? Yet even within the context of marriage, surely you want some element of jealousy, don't you? Or is it going to be the kind of open marriage where both parties are allowed to sleep around with no repercussions—everybody's happy with that? Isn't there a sense in which if you really are committed to each other, a certain kind of jealousy to preserve the relationship is seen to be a good thing, a healthy thing, a wise reaction? And that reaction is among pairs, between peers. Now you have God, the one God who made everything. We have returned to the situation we discovered in Genesis 3. The very nature of the first rebellion was idolatry. What is God supposed to say? "Ah, make up your spirituality as you go along. Invent your own god. I don't really care." That sort of response would deny who he is. It denies his role as Creator; it denies his exclusive function as sovereign sustainer of all of life. In the passage before us, he is the God who rescued his covenant people from slavery. Shall he now say, "But you can pretend that some other power saved you if you like. You can make your own gods"?

He is the LORD, whose name is Jealous.

The truth of the matter is that this is also for their good. If he were to say, "You can do what you want," they would simply slide into endless self-justification, self-love, self-focus. They would become indistinguishable from the pagans all around them. Pretty soon they would be offering their children to Moloch, the god I described in chapter 3. Why not? The neighbors are doing it. This God-centeredness that God insists upon is for their good. It is in fact an act of love, of great generosity. "I am the LORD your God, who brought you out of Egypt, out of the land of slavery. You shall have no other gods before me" (Exod. 20:2–3). The first of the Ten Commandments enjoins us to recognize the exclusiveness of God.

Commandment 2: God's Transcendence

The second enjoins us to recognize the transcendence of God. "You shall not make for yourself an image in the form of anything in heaven above or on the earth beneath or in the waters below" (Exod. 20:4). The prohibition preserves the distinction between Creator and created thing. As soon as you start saying "God looks like this" (whether a fish or a mountain or a human being), somehow God gets reduced. He becomes something that we can encapsulate, domesticate, and thus in some measure control. But we saw that from the beginning, that is not the way God wants us to understand him. There is but one Creator, and he is to be distinguished from all of the created order. God must not be domesticated.

Commandment 3: God's Importance

The third of the Ten Commandments enjoins us to recognize the importance of God. "You shall not misuse the name of the LORD your God, for the LORD will not hold anyone guiltless who misuses his name" (Exod. 20:7). In the ancient world, the name of a person was tightly tied to the identity and character of the person. For a person to misuse God's name was in some sense to disrespect him, to slur him. Thus, when the Bible tells us to give glory to his glorious name (as in Ps. 72:19), it means to give glory to God. It means to praise God himself.

The reason that we are not to say "Oh, God!" when we hit our thumb with a hammer or say "Jesus!" when we are disappointed is precisely because it diminishes God. If you were to be so bold as to turn to the person who has just used Jesus's name because he has hit his thumb with a hammer and say, "I wish you wouldn't use my Savior's name like that," he would probably reply, "I do not mean anything by it." But that is the point: he does not mean anything by it. That is precisely why the usage is "profane," that is, common. Using the name of God or of Jesus when you "mean nothing" by it is not profane because you have spoken a magic word that you are not really allowed to use, as if only priests can say the right abracadabra. The usage is profane because it is common, cheap. We are dealing with God, and we must say and do nothing that diminishes him or cheapens him. It is at best disrespectful, ungrateful, and demeaning; at worst it de-gods him and thus sinks again to the level of idolatry.

Commandment 4: God's Right of Reign, Including over Our Use of Time

The fourth of the Ten Commandments enjoins us to recognize God's right of reign over every domain of life, including our use of the time in which we live and move and have our being.

> [8]Remember the Sabbath day by keeping it holy. [9]Six days you shall labor and do all your work, [10]but the seventh day is a sabbath to the LORD your God. On it you shall not do any work, neither you, nor your son or daughter, nor your male or female servant, nor your animals, nor any foreigner residing in your towns. [11]For in six days the LORD made the heavens and the earth, the sea, and all that is in them, but he rested on the seventh day. Therefore the LORD blessed the Sabbath day and made it holy.
>
> Exodus 20:8–11

This pattern was established in creation. God did his creative work in the six days of creation week and then stopped on the seventh day, and that pattern here establishes a cycle of time in the human order. There is a place for rest. The primary motive is not only to live to the pattern that God has established but to preserve a day devoted "to the LORD your God" (20:10).

Further Observations

We could work through the rest of the Ten Commandments, but instead I shall restrict myself to several brief observations:

1. The chapter begins, "God spoke all these words" (Exod. 20:1). He is still being presented as a talking God, not only with the kind of speech that calls the universe into existence (Genesis 1–2) and with the kind of speech that interacts with his image-bearers (Genesis 3) and writes a covenant with them (Genesis 15), but with the kind of speech that commands them. Later on we are told, "These are the commandments the LORD proclaimed in a loud voice to your whole assembly there on the mountain from out of the fire, the cloud and the deep darkness; and he added nothing more" (Deut. 5:22). He spoke.

2. These Ten Commandments have a central place in the old covenant. They are cited by later prophets (Hosea in the eighth century BC and Jeremiah at the end of the seventh and into the sixth century) and in the Psalms, and they are sometimes referred to in the New Testament.

3. These first four commandments lead to the next six. *Because* God is who he is, *because* he is to be honored and revered, therefore we are to behave in a certain kind of way among ourselves.

4. Above all, the Ten Commandments are related to God's self-disclosure in a gracious redemptive act, the liberation of his people from slavery. He is

the God who called the people out of slavery, and then he says, "And therefore you shall act in this way."

5. For the most part, the Ten Commandments do not so much introduce new standards of behavior as codify the relationship that God's covenant people are supposed to have with him. To put this another way: After creation, what goes wrong first is the betrayal of the relationship between the Creator and his created image-bearers. It is not long before human beings are so lost that one of them kills another (see Genesis 4)—even before there is a law in place that says, "You shall not murder." The introduction in the Ten Commandments of the law prohibiting murder does not make committing murder a sin for the first time, as if committing murder before the introduction of the Ten Commandments was acceptable. Rather, murder was already wicked, a wretched betrayal of the kind of relationships we should have had with God and with each other—but the Ten Commandments formalize some of what is required and what is forbidden. For exactly this reason, the laws of God, not least the Ten Commandments, do not have the power to transform us; they do not have the power to liberate us from our addiction to sin. They lay out the standards, and thus in a sense they underscore our failures and faults—they expose our bad behavior for what it is and make it more than idolatrous self-centeredness: it is now also transgression of specific commands.[1] We lusted and fornicated without a law that says, "You shall not commit adultery," but now in addition to the betrayal and broken relationships intrinsic to lust and fornication, they are also a breach of a specific command.

The Most Holy Place (Leviticus 16)

We have glanced at the Ten Commandments, but these commandments are not the only kinds of laws that God gives. God also sets up an entire structure of ritual.

It is not possible to summarize the entire ritual structure God establishes in this law, but it will be helpful to grasp one big part of it. God ordains that a tabernacle (a big tent, a kind of predecessor to the temple) be built, and it is to be built a certain way. He provides the exact dimensions and the design, and the people go ahead and build it.

The tabernacle is basically a room three times as long as it is wide. Two thirds of it is set off from the last third, which is thus a perfect square. In fact, it is a perfect cube; the dimensions of its length, height, and width are all exactly the same. The first room, the larger one, is called the Holy Place; the second room, hidden from the first room by a veil or curtain, is called the Most Holy Place. Outside of the tent is a place for sacrificing animals; inside this tent, this tabernacle, is a variety of accoutrements: a lampstand, a place where bread is set out week by week, and other matters that we shall not go into. Outside of this tabernacle are also various courtyards where people gather. In many ways the basic layout is very simple—not exactly the kind of cathedral you'd find in Rome or Canterbury, some massive structure. It is, after all, a finely designed tent.

Inside the Most Holy Place is a box. It is called the ark of the covenant, or the ark of the agreement, and it holds certain things, including a copy of the Ten Commandments. Something special takes place with this box once a year. God ordains a special class of people to carry out this activity, namely, some priests. All of these priests are drawn from one of the tribes of the ancient Hebrews, called the Levites, and the high priest must be a Levite who descends from one particular line, the line of Aaron, who is Moses's brother. Once a year, the high priest is supposed to take the blood of a slaughtered goat and a slaughtered bull, take it behind the veil into the Most Holy Place, and sprinkle it on the top of that ark of the covenant. That happens on the day that is called "the Day of Atonement." Meanwhile, outside the tabernacle another goat has been taken out into the desert to wander away.

Given our largely secular world, some of us cannot help but think, "What sort of religion is this with its bloody animals and wandering goats?" These too are parts of what God ordains in his law. In this case the description is found in the third book of the Bible: Leviticus 16. Leviticus is a book that describes many of the priestly sacrifices and what they signify, but here we take a moment to find out a little more precisely what happens on the Day of Atonement as prescribed by God, the God who legislates.

> [1]The LORD spoke to Moses after the death of the two sons of Aaron [i.e., Moses's brother] who died when they approached the LORD. [2]The LORD said to Moses: "Tell your brother Aaron that he is not to come whenever he chooses into the Most Holy Place behind the curtain in front of the atonement cover on the ark, or else he will die. For I will appear in the cloud over the atonement cover.
>
> [3]"This is how Aaron [who is the high priest] is to enter the Most Holy Place: He must first bring a young bull for a sin offering and a ram for a burnt offering. [4]He is to put on the sacred linen tunic, with linen undergarments next to his body; he is to tie the linen sash around him and put on the linen turban. These are sacred garments; so he must bathe himself with water before he puts them on. [5]From the Israelite community he is to take two male goats for a sin offering and a ram for a burnt offering."
>
> Leviticus 16:1–5

Then the entire ritual is described. On the head of one goat—the one that is not to be killed—he puts his hand. This is a way of signifying that the sins of the priest himself, of his family, and of the entire people are being transferred, as it were, to this goat that then symbolically takes the sin away. The animal is released into the desert, never to return. The other two animals, a ram and a bull, are slaughtered, and their blood is captured in a little pan, taken into the Most Holy Place behind the veil, and sprinkled on top of the ark of the covenant, which is a way of saying that someone has died—someone has paid the price of death—for the sins of the priest and his family and for the sins of the people. That is to happen once a year every year, on the Day of Atonement. That is the only time that the high priest is allowed into the Most Holy Place, that perfect cube of a room.

I am mentioning these details because you will see by the end of this book that all of these details are picked up later in the Bible. The fact that the room is a cube is picked up later; the ark of the covenant is picked up later. This blood of bulls and goats is picked up a little later too. So also the high priest's role.

But do you see where we are in the developing storyline of the Bible? God has displayed himself as a God who holds his people to account. He has already sent Adam and Eve away from his presence. How do you get back into the presence of this God? How can you be reconciled to this God? What you discover is that all of these sacrifices are mandated under this law-covenant, under this covenant of Moses, to indicate that death is still going to prevail, apart from sacrifice, because there is still so much sin even among the covenant people. Abraham was a sinner. Isaac and Jacob were sinners. The patriarchs were sinners. And now the people of God—this covenant community, this people with whom God establishes his covenant—are terrible sinners too. This brings us to another passage in this collection of books. It is one of the most shocking.

Exodus 32–34

What is depicted in these chapters is the descent of Moses from Mount Sinai when he first brings down the Ten Commandments chiseled onto tablets of stone. He is accompanied by a young man named Joshua, who will ultimately become Moses's successor. As they approach the camp, they hear a lot of noise, and Joshua does not know what is causing it. Is this a happy sound? Moses is the first to discern what it is: "It is not the sound of victory, it is not the sound of defeat; it is the sound of singing that I hear" (Exod. 32:18). They discover that while Moses was away for a period of time (some weeks), this people who had just been saved from slavery and who had repeatedly been exposed to God's gracious self-disclosure, this people who were on the edge of moving into a promised land and being established as a nation—this people somehow reduced God, who had brought all this liberation about, to an image of a calf. They say, in effect, "We don't know where this Moses is. He's been away for several weeks now. And we're not convinced that this God is so transcendent a being. We would like some image that portrays him. Can't we have a god that we can look at and touch like the neighbors all around us?"

Aaron, Moses's brother who has been left in charge, is frightened by what is going on, not least the potential for mob violence, so he says, "Well, give me your gold earrings and gold bracelets, and we'll see what we can do." Eventually he produces a lovely little gold calf, the kind of image that was known in idol circles in Egypt. The people are having a wild party around this god, a kind of pagan worship that becomes more and more enthusiastic. It is indeed the sound of singing that Moses hears as he comes down the mountain—but not singing to worship the God who is there, but singing to a domesticated god that can be touched and kissed and fawned over. "This is the god that brought you out of the land of Egypt," they sing. In the horrible scenes that follow, God threatens to wipe out the entire nation and start over again, perhaps with Moses. Moses intercedes with God in prayer (see Exodus 33). Moses feels terribly alone and let down by his own brother.

> [12]Moses said to the LORD, "You have been telling me, 'Lead these people,' but you have not let me know whom you will send with me [i.e., God has sent his brother with him, and now Aaron's not there]. You have said, 'I know you by name and you have found favor with me.' [13]If you are pleased with me, teach me your ways so I may know you and continue to find favor with you. Remember that this nation is your people."
>
> Exodus 33:12–13

That is, Moses says in effect, "I didn't choose them. I didn't take them out of the land of Egypt. I'm just your spokesperson. *You* have to do what needs to be done with them. I can't change their hearts. I can't finally save them. I can't redeem them. They're *your* people. They're not mine. Meanwhile, who will you send with me?" In fact, God had threatened that he would not go with Moses anymore. If he did, the people's sin in proximity to his transcendent holiness would simply mean that he would end up destroying them. But instead,

> The LORD replied, "My Presence will go with you, and I will give you rest."
>
> Exodus 33:14

Rest. Where have we heard that language before? Do you remember that at the end of creation week, God rests? Going into the promised land is often depicted as going into the land of rest. Now God promises that despite the people's sin, he will go with them. He will be forbearing. He will lead them into rest.

> Then Moses said to him, "If your Presence does not go with us, do not send us up from here."
>
> Exodus 33:15

What any people must have is the presence of the living God. It is not enough in any church simply to have the right rituals and the right sermons and the right kind of music. If God does not manifest himself in some way, if he is not present, then what is the point of the whole exercise? Is religion merely some sort of structured ritual heritage? Or is it bound up with being reconciled to the God who made us, who holds us to account? "If your presence does not go with us, what is the point in the exercise?" Moses continues,

> How will anyone know that you are pleased with me and with your people unless you go with us? What else will distinguish me and your people from all the other people on the face of the earth?
>
> Exodus 33:16

There's no point in merely being different because we have rules. We must have God.

> [17]And the LORD said to Moses, "I will do the very thing you have asked, because I am pleased with you and I know you by name."
> [18]Then Moses said, "Now show me your glory."
>
> Exodus 33:17–18

It's one thing to walk by faith, to know that God has spoken, but "Please," Moses says, "can't I see something of the manifestation of your transcendence? How spectacular you are—can't I see that? Can't I have more of that?"

> [19]And the LORD said, "I will cause all my goodness to pass in front of you [i.e., God's glory manifested somehow in his goodness—pay attention to those words; we'll come back to them when we study Jesus later on], and I will proclaim my name, the LORD, in your presence. I will have mercy on whom I will have mercy, and I will have compassion on whom I will have compassion. [20]But," he said, "you cannot see my face, for no one may see me and live."
>
> Exodus 33:19–20

We have already noted that when the word "LORD" occurs in small capital letters in our English Bibles, it reflects the Hebrew four letters YHWH (often pronounced Yahweh) by which God has disclosed himself: "I AM WHO I AM." God proclaims his own name. He names himself amidst all the many gods in the neighborhood. God is saying, "This is who I am. This is the God who is there. I will proclaim my name, the LORD (Yahweh), in your presence. I will have mercy on whom I will have mercy, and I will have compassion on whom I will have compassion." How do you deal with a God with whom you cannot barter, who has no needs? It must be a work of sovereign grace: "I will have mercy on whom I will have mercy, and I will have compassion on whom I will have compassion" (33:19). But if what you are really asking for is that you may see me up close and personal, face-to-face, then God says, "you cannot see my face, for no one may see me and live" (33:20).

> ^{21}Then the LORD said, "There is a place near me where you may stand on a rock. ^{22}When my glory passes by, I will put you in a cleft in the rock and cover you with my hand until I have passed by. ^{23}Then I will remove my hand and you will see my back; but my face must not be seen."
>
> Exodus 33:21–23

The spectacular account of what then takes place is found in Exodus 34. Moses hides himself. The Lord goes by while Moses hides in the cleft in the rock. God speaks certain words. After the Lord has gone by, Moses is permitted to peek out and see something of the trailing edge of the afterglow of the glory of the Lord. That is all he is allowed to see. As the Lord goes by, the words that he utters are these:

> ^{6}And he passed in front of Moses, proclaiming, "The LORD, the LORD, the compassionate and gracious God, slow to anger, abounding in love and faithfulness, ^{7}maintaining love to thousands, and forgiving wickedness, rebellion and sin. Yet he does not leave the guilty unpunished; he punishes the children and their children for the sin of the parents to the third and fourth generation."
>
> Exodus 34:6–7

We could easily spend the rest of this book unpacking all the things that God says of himself. As the Bible's storyline unfolds, God progressively reveals just who and what he is.

God says he "punishes the children and their children for the sin of the parents to the third and fourth generation" (34:7). This is because sin is social. Sin is never merely individualistic. You cannot commit any sin, no matter how private, without it having repercussions not only in your own life but in the community where you live. Maybe the addiction is as private as looking at porn in secret: surely that is not doing any damage to anybody but you (if it is doing any damage at all). But in reality, if you focus in secret on porn, the way you view the opposite sex will gradually be changed, and that will reshape family dynamics, which will in turn influence your children. Your sin has social implications to the second, third, and fourth generation: that is what God here says. God transcends time and space, and he can see the ramifications that you cannot see.

But I shall focus on the one profound paradox in God's self-depiction. *On the one hand*, he is compassionate and gracious. If he had not been compassionate and gracious, the human race would have ended at the end of Genesis 3. There would have been only judgment. Death was the promise, and instead

God was forbearing. He abounds in "love and faithfulness,[2] maintaining love to thousands, and forgiving wickedness, rebellion and sin" (Exod. 34:6–7). *On the other hand*, although he is a God of forgiveness, he does not fit into that first model that we saw in the last chapter where God is really like a super-granddaddy with a long white beard, whose sole business is forgiving and being nice. He is also the God who does not leave the guilty unpunished. How do we put these two themes together? We have just been told that he *does* forgive sin, and now we are also told that he cannot pretend sin is not there: God does not leave the guilty unpunished. The closest you get to resolving this tension in the old covenant, in the Mosaic covenant, is in the Day of Atonement: once a year a high priest places his hands on the head of a goat and sends it off to symbolize sin being removed, taken away. Then he takes the blood of another goat and of a bull and carries it into the very presence of God in the Most Holy Place and sprinkles it over the ark of the covenant. The priest says, in effect, "We deserve to die. These animals died in our place. Will this do? It is what you have commanded. Will this do? Will you not have mercy on us in our sin, in our rebellion and defection?"

We have already seen that the law of God, as important as it is, cannot save us. It is powerless to do so, for we have the power to disobey it. The most remarkable demonstration in the Bible to show that the law cannot finally save us and reconcile us to God is found at the end of the first five books. What are the first five books? Genesis, Exodus, Leviticus, Numbers, Deuteronomy. They're often called the "Pentateuch" or the five books of Moses. At the very end of the last one, Deuteronomy, in the last chapter, Moses himself does not get into the promised land. Moses is called the meekest man who ever lived; he is the one who mediates this covenant; he is the hero who in his old age is organizing the nation, setting up a system of priests and a judicial structure; he is a man of justice and integrity, leading the people again and again through tormented times. But he blows it here and there. He sins too and does not make it into the promised land. The law cannot finally save.

But what the law has provided is the vehicle—a sacrificial structure—in which God has disclosed himself as the one who pursues his own people. This includes the paradox before us: God's desire to forgive is paired with his insistence that sin be punished. These poles will not come together to glorious resolution until a millennium and a half later. After the death and resurrection of Jesus another book is written, a book in the New Testament. We call that book the letter to the Hebrews. The writer of that book, in chapters 9 and 10, invites his readers to look back on the old sacrificial system and say, "Do you not understand? That sacrifice of a bull and a goat cannot ever deal finally with sin! How can it deal finally with sin when the priests have to offer the same sacrifices again and again, year after year? How can the blood of a bull and a goat pay for sin in any case? In what sense does the bull itself offer a sacrifice? Does the bull come up and say, 'All right, I'll die for you. Slit my throat'? Where precisely is the moral value in this sacrifice?"

The old Day of Atonement, once held every year in accordance with the Mosaic covenant, has been superseded, because we have the ultimate sacrifice for sin: Jesus himself, who shed his blood on our behalf, a perfect moral sacrifice. He offers up his life, takes our death, and bears our sin away in a fashion that no animal ever could. The law pointed forward to that sole means of God reconciling rebels to himself and brings together in Jesus the poles of Exodus 34: God abounds "in love and faithfulness" (34:6), and he forgives "wickedness, rebellion and sin" (34:7), not because he leaves the guilty unpunished but because another bears their punishment.

Here is the God who legislates, and even in his legislation he points us to Jesus.

5

The God Who Reigns

What do we conjure up in our minds when we hear a word like "king" or "monarch"? Doubtless it depends in part on where we live in the world. The last king that America had, King George III, by and large is not held in very good regard. America is a democratic republic, thank you, and we neither want nor need a monarch. Probably we do not want to go quite as far in our anti-royalty and anti-clerical assessment of things as Voltaire, who said that he would be satisfied when the last king is strangled with the entrails of the last priest. Nevertheless, whatever monarchs there are in the world, we are pretty glad they are not here but over there somewhere. If we are in a more positive mood, we might think of Her Majesty Queen Elizabeth II, and then we concede that royal pomp has its attractions. They sure know how to put on a decent royal wedding, don't they, with prancing horses and gold-encrusted chariots and spectacular crowns and those long trumpets with such a shrill, piercing sound? There is something pretty entrancing about that, isn't there? Mind you, Queen Elizabeth II is a constitutional monarch, which is a polite way of saying that she does not have much real power. She is limited by a constitutional structure, apart from whatever moral influence or advice she might offer to her prime minister.

This is very different from, let us say, the kingdom of Saudi Arabia. Although some constraint comes from the larger family, this is closer to an absolute kingdom. It is different again from the kingdom of Thailand. The Thais love their king. You really cannot speak any word against royalty in Thailand. The people would not have it, even though the limitations on his power are quite significant.

God's Kingdom over All

So perceptions of what we mean by "king" and "monarch" differ in different parts of the world. In biblical times, however, there was no understanding of what *we* mean today by "constitutional monarch." If you are a king, you *reign*! That is what kings do. You have the authority. The fact of the matter is that God is often presented in Scripture as the king. The Psalms say, for example, "The LORD has established his throne in heaven, and his kingdom rules over all" (Ps. 103:19). And Daniel 4:35 says, "He does as he pleases with the powers of heaven and the peoples of the earth. No one can hold back his hand or say to him: 'What have you done?'" This is another way of saying that his sovereignty covers absolutely every domain. That is built into the very creation account: he made everything, it is all his, and he continues to reign. He remains sovereign over the whole lot. In that sense you and I are in the kingdom of God whether we like it or not. You cannot *not* be in the kingdom of God in this sense. If he really does reign over all, even those who disbelieve him, who hate him, and who think that there are other gods are in God's kingdom.

God's Kingdom over Israel

The notion of the kingdom of God—the reign of God—is in fact very flexible in Scripture. You have to pay attention to the context to make sense of what is being said in any particular passage. In the Old Testament, once God has called his people—the Hebrews, the Israelites—to himself, first with the covenant with Abraham and then with the covenant under Moses's leadership, God is still understood to be the king of his people. God himself is to be their ruler, their king. In that sense the Israelites constitute *his* nation. You are under his kingship in that sense only if you belong to this covenant community. This is rather different from the notion of God's reign that is roughly equivalent to the limitless extent of his providential sway. For the moment, however, we shall focus on the small scope—the way God reigns over his covenantal people, the Israelites.

The Book of Judges

After the people finally get into the promised land, they go through cycles that are really depressing. After two or three generations, what they knew of God's kindness in the past—of how he had spared them, how he had secured them, how he had provided for all of their needs—is forgotten, and they become virtually indistinguishable from the pagans all around them. After a time God sanctions earthly judgments of various kinds. For instance, they are attacked and harassed by other tribes living in the area—Midianites or others. Eventually they cry out to God again for mercy, forbearance, and forgiveness.

God then raises up a judge. This judge leads the people in renewal and in small pitched battles against some of their oppressors, and the people reestablish themselves and renew their covenantal vows to be faithful before God. Then in another two or three generations, everybody forgets, and they collectively slide down in disgrace and shame to various forms of really awful debauchery, let alone the idolatry that underlies it. There follows another round of judgment, another desperate appeal to God for help. Then God raises up another judge, and the cycle begins all over again. The downward spirals in the book of Judges are so appalling that in the last two or three chapters it is really difficult to read them in public because they are so grotesque and barbaric. As the book progresses, you begin to hear a sad, repeated refrain: "In those days Israel had no king; everyone did as they saw fit" (Judges 21:25). This is the way the book ends: bloody mayhem. It is as if the book ends by saying, "O God, how we need a king to order our lives and secure our nation."

Saul

Pretty soon you discover that some people want a king not so they can be a little more secure, or so that somebody in authority can hold them to be covenantally faithful, or to police things when the moral and ethical fabric is being torn apart. No, some of the people want a king simply so that they can be more like the pagan nations all around, all of whom have their own petty kings. The cry, in effect, is this: "We want to be like them. They seem to have things in civil order. We would like to have exactly the same sort of constitutional arrangement." God says, "All right, if you really want a king, we'll go ahead, but you will be sorry!" God marks out for them a strapping young man by the name of Saul, who seems suitably humble, diffident (he doesn't really want the job), and careful; he loves the Lord. Yet in a few short years he becomes a corrupt, paranoid, fearful, brutal, and ungodly man who craves more power. Anybody he sees as a threat to his authority, he wants to kill. It's a mess (see 1 Samuel 8–31).

David

But God raises up another king. He says, "Now let me show you, at least in principle, what a good king would be like. Here is a man after my own heart. His name is David." So after Saul is gone, David becomes king. Initially he turns out to be a very good king, an able administrator. He secures the frontier; he unites the tribes. Eventually he moves his capital from the little town of Hebron to Jerusalem—the same site as modern Jerusalem. He establishes himself there and brings a measure of order, peace, and prosperity (see 1 Samuel 16; 2 Samuel 1–5).

2 Samuel 7

"After the king [i.e., King David] was settled in his palace and the LORD had given him rest from all his enemies around him, he said to Nathan the prophet, 'Here I am, living in a house of cedar, while the ark of God remains in a tent'" (2 Sam. 7:1–2).

That "ark of God" is what was described in the last chapter. The ark was a box placed in the Most Holy Place, a box that held certain elements in it, including the stone tablets on which were written the Ten Commandments. The top of the ark of God was where the blood was sprinkled on the Day of Atonement. At this juncture in Israel's history, about 1000 BC, this ark of God still resides in a tent—a tabernacle. "I am living in a cedar palace," David says to Nathan. "The place where God meets with his priests is nothing but a pretty tent."

> [3]Nathan replied to the king, "Whatever you have in mind, go ahead and do it, for the LORD is with you."
>
> [4]But that night the word of the LORD came to Nathan, saying:
>
> [5]"Go and tell my servant David, 'This is what the LORD says: Are you the one to build me a house to dwell in? [6]I have not dwelt in a house from the day I brought the Israelites up out of Egypt to this day. I have been moving from place to place with a tent as my dwelling. [7]Wherever I have moved with all the Israelites, did I ever say to any of their rulers whom I commanded to shepherd my people Israel, "Why have you not built me a house of cedar?"'
>
> [8]"Now then, tell my servant David, 'This is what the LORD Almighty says: I took you from the pasture, from tending the flock, and appointed you ruler over my people Israel. [9]I have been with you wherever you have gone, and I have cut off all your enemies from before you. Now I will make your name great, like the names of the greatest men on earth. [10]And I will provide a place for my people Israel and will plant them so that they can have a home of their own and no longer be disturbed. Wicked people will not oppress them anymore, as they did at the beginning [11]and have done ever since the time I appointed leaders over my people Israel. I will also give you rest from all your enemies.
>
> "'The LORD declares to you that the LORD himself will establish a house for you: [12]When your days are over and you rest with your ancestors, I will raise up your offspring to succeed you, who will come from your own body, and I will establish his kingdom. [13]He is the one who will build a house for my Name, and I will establish the throne of his kingdom forever. [14]I will be his father, and he will be my son. When he does wrong, I will punish him with a rod wielded by human beings, with floggings inflicted by human hands. [15]But my love will never be taken away from him, as I took it away from Saul, whom I removed

from before you. [16]Your house and your kingdom will endure forever before me; your throne will be established forever.'"

[17]Nathan reported to David all the words of this entire revelation.

[18]Then King David went in and sat before the LORD, and he said:

"Who am I, Sovereign LORD, and what is my family, that you have brought me this far? [19]And as if this were not enough in your sight, Sovereign LORD, you have also spoken about the future of the house of your servant—and this decree, Sovereign LORD, is for a human being!

[20]"What more can David say to you? For you know your servant, Sovereign LORD. [21]For the sake of your word and according to your will, you have done this great thing and made it known to your servant.

[22]"How great you are, Sovereign LORD! There is no one like you, and there is no God but you, as we have heard with our own ears. [23]And who is like your people Israel—the one nation on earth that God went out to redeem as a people for himself, and to make a name for himself, and to perform great and awesome wonders by driving out nations and their gods from before your people, whom you redeemed from Egypt? [24]You have established your people Israel as your very own forever, and you, LORD, have become their God.

[25]"And now, LORD God, keep forever the promise you have made concerning your servant and his house. Do as you promised, [26]so that your name will be great forever. Then people will say, 'The LORD Almighty is God over Israel!' And the house of your servant David will be established in your sight.

[27]"LORD Almighty, God of Israel, you have revealed this to your servant, saying, 'I will build a house for you.' So your servant has found courage to pray this prayer to you. [28]Sovereign LORD, you are God! Your covenant is trustworthy, and you have promised these good things to your servant. [29]Now be pleased to bless the house of your servant, that it may continue forever in your sight; for you, Sovereign LORD, have spoken, and with your blessing the house of your servant will be blessed forever."

2 Samuel 7:3–29

The king was supposed to be God's vice-regent, the under-king. God still remained the king, the final sovereign over all the people, but the king was supposed to mediate God's justice to the people, to mediate God and his ways and his laws to the entire people. But here we have a remarkable set of relationships.

1. A King with Religious Initiatives Restrained (2 Samuel 7:1–11)

King David wants to do God a favor. He is now settled. The very first verse says that the nation is enjoying rest. (Notice this theme of rest again: rest from their enemies, rest in the promised land.) David looks around. He has been in the new capital city long enough to obtain a fine palace for himself, yet the center for corporate worship for the entire nation is still this now slightly ratty tent. He may remember that the book of Deuteronomy, back at the time of

Moses, had foreseen a permanent center, so he thinks, "Well, it's about time. Why shouldn't I be the person to build it? That's what I would like to do." And Nathan the prophet says, in effect, "Great idea. God's with you. Go right ahead." Then God intervenes and says to Nathan, "Not quite so fast. This is not the way it is going to happen." And God gives two or three reasons why it will not be so:

1. God alone takes the initiative in these turning points in the story of the Bible (see 2 Sam. 7:5–7). Have we not seen this already? Think back to Abraham. Does he wake up one day and in his devotions say something like this?

> God, quite frankly this world seems to me to be sliding to hell in a teapot. I think we should do something about it. I think we should start some new race among the human race, a kind of subunit. I'd like to head it. I'll be the great-granddaddy of this entire new humanity. We'll call them "Hebrews." You can be our God, and we'll be your people. You tell us what to do, and we'll obey you. And we'll start off this whole new dynastic structure. Isn't that a great idea? And this new race, this new covenant community, will show the world what it's like to be in right relationship with you.

Is that the way it happened? No, God took the initiative: he called Abraham, moved him to the land, and gave him a covenant. Even in that scene in the middle of the night where God puts himself under a kind of covenant vow to look after his people, God himself takes the initiative to walk that bloody alleyway alone (see Genesis 15). God takes the initiative in Genesis 22 to provide a lamb.

Or think of Moses. When he was a young man, Moses did wonder about the possibility of starting a revolution and leading the people out of slavery. In fact, he got caught up in a murder, so he had to run for his life. He lived on the back side of a desert for the next half century or so. In fact, when God did take the initiative, Moses was not too keen on going: "God, I'm getting a bit old now, and I have a speech impediment. I'm not a leader. I'm just a shepherd." But God takes the initiative and in due course uses Moses.

God will not share his glory with anybody else. God is really not open to our suggestions about how to run the universe, and that is in effect his first objection: "Go and tell my servant David, 'This is what the LORD says: Are you the one to build me a house to dwell in? All along I've been living in this tabernacle. Wherever I have moved with all the Israelites, did I ever say to any of their rulers whom I commanded to shepherd my people Israel, "Why have you not built me a house of cedar?"'" (see 2 Sam. 7:5–7). It is not that the temple will not be built. In fact, it is going to be built in the next generation. The task is going to be assigned to David's son, King Solomon. But God will take the initiative.

2. God makes his servants great—not the other way around (see 2 Sam. 7:8–11). God said,

⁸Now then, tell my servant David, "This is what the LORD Almighty says: I took you from the pasture, from tending the flock, and appointed you ruler over my people Israel. ⁹I have been with you wherever you have gone, and I have cut off all your enemies from before you. Now *I* will make *your* name great, like the names of the greatest men on earth."

2 Samuel 7:8–9, emphasis added

Deep down, perhaps David is beginning to think that he is going to do God a favor. If he can build a bigger temple than the neighboring pagans build for their gods, then isn't he showing that the true God is more magnificent than their gods? David is going to magnify God's name and do God a favor. But God says, in effect, "It doesn't work like that. I'm the one who makes your name great."

In certain contexts it is wonderful for believers to try to magnify God's name, but not ever because they succumb to the illusion that they are thereby doing God a favor. Worshiping God, magnifying his name, ought to be the response of gratitude and adoration—not somehow saying, "The pagans worship their gods. We can out-worship them because in a competition we can make your name greater than they can make their gods' names great." God says, "You've got this entirely wrong. I make your name great, not the other way around. You were a shepherd boy. Not only have I made you a king, I'm about to make your name resound down the ages."

Today there are millions of Christians all over the world who know the name of David. Many of them have never heard of Alexander the Great. They do not know much about King Tut. But David's name has come down to us across three thousand years.

The chapter begins, as we have seen, with a king with religious initiatives restrained, and it is in this context that God next gives an amazing promise.

2. A Dynasty with an Unending Promise Disclosed (2 Sam. 7:11–17)

"The LORD declares to you that the LORD himself will establish a house for you" (2 Sam. 7:11). There is a pun here, of course. David wanted to build a "house," that is, a temple for God. God's going to build a "house," that is, a household, a dynasty for David. "You want to build a house for me?" You can almost see God smiling. "*I'm* going to build a house for *you*. Let me tell you how I will do it."

¹²When your days are over and you rest with your ancestors, I will raise up your offspring to succeed you, who will come from your own body, and I will establish his kingdom. ¹³He is the one who will build a house for my Name [i.e., Solomon would build the temple], and I will establish the throne of his kingdom forever. ¹⁴I will be his father, and he will be my son. When he does wrong, I will punish him with a rod wielded by human beings, with floggings inflicted by human

hands. [15]But my love will never be taken away from him, as I took it away from Saul, whom I removed from before you. [16]Your house and your kingdom will endure forever before me; your throne will be established forever.

2 Samuel 7:12–16

Two or three observations clarify what the passage is saying:

1. David is aware that his predecessor, Saul, started well and ended badly, and in consequence, Saul's son Jonathan never got to the throne. No dynasty was ever established. It was a one-generation dynasty (if you can speak of a dynasty in one generation). There was so much wickedness by the end that God said, "This is not going to continue." Even if David remains faithful all his life (and in point of fact, he had his own pretty horrible lapses), who guarantees what happens in the next generation and in the generation after that? If you are royalty, you are concerned with preserving the family line, the dynasty, the house—whether the house of Windsor (for Her Majesty Queen Elizabeth II) or, in this case, the house of David. Reassuringly, God says, "*I'm* going to build a house for you such that even if your son does something wrong—even if he is really wicked—I will not remove him from the throne the way I removed Saul, leaving him without a successor to establish the family dynasty. I will not do that. I will preserve your house, your household."

So there may be some temporal infliction of punishment. There may be some temporary chastening. There may be nations that rise up against your nation. There may be things of that sort. But God will not impose the final sanction that wipes out the line. That is what God promises to David.

2. What does God mean when he says, "I will be his father, and he will be my son" (7:14)?

For us sonship has to do with DNA. How many television shows, not least the various *CSI* series on television, use DNA to discover who the real father is, which person is the real son? Bound up with this science are paternity suits. Sonship is first of all a matter of genetic descent. But the ancient world saw things a bit differently. Physical descent told only part of the story; there was also the descent of work and identity.

How many men today are working in the same vocation as their fathers did at the same age? How many women are doing vocationally today what their mothers did? I have asked this question in many Western contexts, and I have never found that more than five or six percent could answer affirmatively, and often fewer. By contrast, in the ancient world if your father is a baker, you become a baker; if your father is a farmer, you become a farmer; if your father's name is Stradivari, then you make violins. In other words, in an agricultural, tradecraft, preindustrial society, in the overwhelming majority of cases the son ends up doing what his father did, and the daughter ends up doing what her mother did. Today's notions of freedom are such that we go away from home to university or to a technical college and get a job somewhere else and pursue some vocation entirely removed from family tradition. Such freedom was frankly unthinkable a mere three or four hundred years ago, except in rare instances. So as a result you became identified not only by the family name but by the family's profession. That is why Jesus came to be called "the son of the carpenter": Joseph, recognized as his father, was a carpenter. Indeed, in one place Jesus himself is called "the carpenter." Apparently his father, Joseph, has died, and Jesus himself has taken over the family business. Joseph was a carpenter. What do you expect Jesus to be? He's a carpenter.

This vocational pattern meant that in the normal course of events the father taught the boy his trade. Certainly there was no higher education. In later Judaism, local synagogues might teach the sons basic reading and writing. Well-to-do families might hire people to teach basic educational skills, or even more advanced book learning, to a handful of children. But your *trade*, what you learned to make a living, that sort of training you received from your father. If he was a farmer, he taught you when to plant the seed, when to irrigate, how to read the weather, how to build a decent fence, and that sort of thing. Because of the son's identification with the father's vocation, the notion of sonship took on a broader set of associations than it has on *CSI*.

Out of this social matrix come a lot of biblical metaphors. For example, here and there in the Bible someone is called a "son of Belial," which means a "son of worthlessness." This is not saying that the father is Mr. Worthless. What it is saying is that this person's character is so worthless that he must belong to the worthless family; that is the only adequate explanation. Jesus gives us a saying that illustrates these kinds of metaphors: "Blessed are the peacemakers, for they shall be called sons of God" (Matt. 5:9 ESV). The idea is that God himself is the supreme peacemaker, so if you make peace, then in that respect at least you are acting like God; you show yourself to be a son of God. Jesus's saying is not telling you how to become a Christian. It is saying that in this one respect, you are doing what God does, so you are acting like God and show yourself to be his "son."

Elsewhere, when Jesus is debating with some Jewish opponents (see John 8), he claims that his teaching will set them free, and they respond, in effect, "How can this be? We are ourselves the true sons of Abraham. We are the true heritage here, and this heritage sets us free." Jesus replies, "If you sin, you are a slave to sin, and only I can set you free. I know that physically you are Abraham's descendants, but you are not responding to revelation the way Abraham did. You are responding the way your father does." They up the ante and say, "We're not only sons of Abraham. We're sons of God. God himself is our real Father." Jesus replies, in effect, "Can't be. I come from God. God knows me, and I know God. If you do not recognize me, then you cannot be sons of God. Let me tell you who your real daddy is. You are of your father the devil. He was a murderer from the beginning, and you are trying to murder me. He was a liar from the beginning, and you are not telling the truth about me."

Obviously Jesus is not denying that his opponents really are sons of Abraham, genetically speaking. They are. Nor is he suggesting that somehow demons copulated with women to produce some sort of bastard crew. He is saying that at the level of behavior, they are acting like the devil. That makes them sons of the devil.

That is the use of "son" terminology going on here in 2 Samuel 7. It is used to refer to kings. If God is the supreme king over this people, then when the human person comes to the throne in the line of David, he becomes God's "son." This does not mean he literally takes on divine nature or anything of that sort. It simply means that he is now acting as God's son in God's place in the king-family, as it were. God rules over his covenantal people; he is concerned to administer justice and preserve faithfulness to the covenant. If a king in David's line does that, he is acting as God's son. That is the nature of the promise that is given here. "He [i.e., the heir of David] is the one who will build a house for my Name, and I will establish the throne of his kingdom forever. *I will be his father, and he will be my son*" (7:13–14, emphasis added).

But sons can go astray. What then? "When he does wrong," God adds, "I will punish him with a rod wielded by human beings, with floggings inflicted by human hands. But my love will never be taken away from him, as I took it away from Saul, whom I removed from before you" (7:14–15).

3. There is one more thing to understand from this passage: "Your house and your kingdom will endure forever before me; your throne will be established forever" (7:16). In other words, God is not only promising that the Davidic line will endure to the next generation, the generation of Solomon when the temple will be built, even if Solomon turns out to be quite wicked. Rather, God is saying that this dynasty will go on and on; it will be established forever.

Such a promise could be fulfilled in only two ways. One is for every generation to produce a new Davidic heir so that the throne is passed to the next heir and the next heir and the next heir and the next heir, world without end. That's one way this promise could be fulfilled. The only other possible way is not even mentioned here. In theory, however, if you could eventually have an heir in the Davidic line who himself lives forever, the promise could be fulfilled that way.

This promise is given around 1000 BC. It is the precursor to a number of other promises to Davidic kings across the centuries. Most of us, I'm sure, have listened to Handel's *Messiah*, which cites Isaiah 9, which was written late in the eighth century BC, more than two hundred years after the promise to David. Isaiah envisions a coming king: "For to us a child is born, to us a *son* is given. . . . He will reign on David's throne and over his kingdom" (Isa. 9:6–7, emphasis added). In other words, he will be a Davidic son who is thus also a "son of God," standing in under God as God's vice-regent. "Of the increase of his government and peace there will be no end" (Isa. 9:7). "He will be called Wonderful Counselor, Mighty God, Everlasting Father, Prince of Peace" (Isa. 9:6).

The language is extraordinary: a son of David who is to be called "Mighty God" and "Everlasting Father"? I do not imagine that Isaiah himself entirely understood the full extent of his own prophecy, but on the face of it, it seems to be promising that somehow there would be a Davidic descendant, someone in the line and heritage of David, who himself would rightly be addressed as none less than God himself. (We shall shortly see that there are other prophets who make similar promises.) Here is the anticipation of a Davidic descendant who would vastly surpass his esteemed ancestor.

3. A King with Spectacular Privileges Humbled (2 Sam. 7:18–27)

David is hushed and crushed by what has been promised him, and basically his plea now is not, "Let me build a temple for you and do something for *you*." Now it is all gratitude: "I do not deserve this. This is wonderful. All I ask, dear God, sovereign Lord, is that you keep your promise."

From King David to King Jesus

All this takes place, as I've said, about 1000 BC. There are a lot of intervening developments before Jesus appears. After several centuries, the Davidic kingdom itself has become corrupt. A mere two generations later, the kingdom splits into a northern kingdom and a southern kingdom, and David's line rules over only the south. Two and a half more centuries go by, and the northern kingdom never has established a dynasty. Kings come and kings go; the new usurper comes and slaughters all the children of the previous one. It is a brutal mess replete with many forms of idolatry. Eventually the leaders are carted off into captivity under the Assyrian Empire. Another century and a half goes by and the Davidic dynasty itself is so corroded and corrupted, despite occasional times of revival and renewal, that at the beginning of the sixth century (about 587 BC), it is destroyed. The Babylonians have taken over. Many of the leaders are taken into exile, this time under the Babylonian Empire, which has replaced the Assyrian.

In due course God brings some of them back: initially, only about fifty thousand or so. They rebuild the temple that had been burned down, but by comparison with the great temple built in the time of David's son Solomon, this structure is a pathetic little affair. There is still no king. By this time they are living under Persian rule, which gives way to Greek authority and then to the Roman Empire. So we travel all the way down to the turning of the ages from BC to AD, and still there is no restored Davidic king on the throne. The Israelites always find themselves under one authority or another. Now the regional superpower is Rome, and the local monarchs are ruthless petty kings like the Herods.

Then you open up the pages of the New Testament, the part of the Bible that begins by telling us what happens in the time of Jesus. What is the very first line of the very first book of the New Testament? "This is the genealogy of Jesus the Messiah the son of David, the son of Abraham" (Matt. 1:1). Here is the fulfillment of the promise of the Davidic king. (The word "Messiah" is the Hebrew equivalent of "Christ" and refers to someone who is "anointed" or set aside for a particular task.)

When Jesus begins his public ministry, he announces the dawning of the kingdom, and he uses the word "kingdom" in a variety of ways. For example, he says something like this: "The kingdom is like a man who plants wheat in a field, good seed in a field, and then at night some hooligans come by and they plant a lot of weeds. The wheat and the weeds grow up together. The servants of the man say, 'Should we go out and try to pull out the weeds now?' 'No, no, let both grow until the end, and there will be a final separation at the end.' That is what the kingdom is like." In other words, here you have a picture of the kingdom that is embracing this world with both good seed growing and bad seed growing. It includes Billy Graham and Adolf Hitler. There is good seed and there are weeds, and they are both to grow until the end when there will be a final division. That is one perspective on the kingdom.

But elsewhere, in John 3 (in a passage we'll look at later), Jesus says, "No one can enter the kingdom of God without being born of water and the Spirit" (John 3:5). Now according to this notion of the kingdom, not everyone is in it. Everybody is in the other one; you are either wheat or weeds. But in this notion of the kingdom, you now have a subset of God's reign, of God's rule, of God's kingdom, under which there is life. Only those who are born again can enter or see this kingdom.

To mention further variations: sometimes Jesus speaks of the kingdom as already having dawned. It is already here, operating secretly, as it were. It is like yeast that is put into dough; it is already quietly working and having its effect. Yet elsewhere Jesus speaks of the kingdom as what comes at the end when there is a final consummation and tremendous transformation. So the kingdom is already; seen another way, it has not yet come. All these notions of kingdom center on Jesus the king.

After World War II a Swiss theologian named Oscar Cullmann used one of the turning points in the war to explain some of these notions. He drew attention to what happened on D-day, June 6, 1944. By this time the Western allies had already cleaned out North Africa and had started pushing up the boot of Italy. The Russians were coming in from the steppes; they had already defended Stalingrad, and they were pushing their way to and through Poland and other Eastern European countries. And now on D-day the Western allies landed on the beaches of Normandy, and in three days they dumped 1.1 million men and tons and tons of war materiel. There was a second Western front. Anybody with half a brain in his head could see that the war was over. After all, in terms of energy, war materiel, the numbers of soldiers, and the way all of these lines and trajectories were converging, the war was over. Does that mean that Hitler said, "Oops, I miscalculated" and pleaded for peace? No. What came next was the Battle of the Bulge where he almost made it right through to the coast of France again, except that he ran out of fuel. There followed the battle for Berlin, which was one of the bloodiest of the entire war. So the war was not over yet. A year later the war finally ended in Europe, after the combatants had navigated this massive gap between D-day and VE-day (Victory in Europe).

Cullmann says that the experience of Christians is like that. The promised king came. That is our D-day: the coming of Jesus and his cross and resurrection. After rising from the dead, Jesus declares, according to the last verses of Matthew's Gospel, "All authority in heaven and on earth has been given to me" (Matt. 28:18). He is the king. But does that mean that the devil says, "Oops, I miscalculated. I think I had better plead for peace"? Does it mean that human beings will say, "Okay, okay, you've risen from the dead. You've won. We'd better bow the knee"? No, what it means is that you have some of the fiercest fighting left because Jesus has not yet defeated all of his enemies. He reigns. All of God's sovereignty is mediated through king Jesus. The kingdom has dawned. It is here. And you are either in this kingdom in the new-birth sense or you are not. Alternatively, if you conceive of Jesus's total reign (all authority is already his), you are in this kingdom whether you like it or not. The question is whether you bow the knee now, cheerfully in repentance and faith and thanksgiving, or wait until the end to bend the knee in holy terror. The end is coming; the Christian VE-day is coming, and there is no doubt who will be seen to be king on the last day.

When Paul writes to Christians in the city of Corinth in about the middle of the first century, he describes Jesus as the king with all of God's sovereignty mediated through him: "For he must reign until he has put all his enemies under his feet. The last enemy to be destroyed is death" (1 Cor. 15:25–26). Death will die. This, of course, picks up exactly what happened in Genesis 1, 2, and 3. Over against this massive rebellion that tried to de-god God, a rebellion that brought only death and decay, stands Jesus Christ. King Jesus has already beaten death, and he continues as God's own king in David's line. Yet though he is a man in David's line, he is the one who is called "Mighty God, Everlasting Father" (Isa. 9:6). And he will reign until he has destroyed the last enemy: death itself. This is why the church stands up and sings, again and again, "Hail, King Jesus." We need a king—one who is perfectly righteous, who cannot be corrupted, who is entirely good, in whom there is never any taint of evil. He powerfully saves and transforms his people, who come to him and gladly acknowledge his Lordship.

Hail, King Jesus.

6

The God Who Is
Unfathomably Wise

In this chapter we focus on two types of literature in the Old Testament. One is the book of Psalms, and the other is an array of quite diverse books often collectively called wisdom literature. For reasons I shall mention shortly, even some of the psalms are rightly said to belong to wisdom literature.

Neither of these categories—psalms and wisdom literature—brings the story forward very much. They are not part of the sequence of narrative books that tell us what happens next to the Israelites or refer to what is going on in world history at the time. Sometimes individual psalms can be shown to spring from a particular period in Old Testament history. By and large, however, these materials contribute something a little different. They reflect the experiences, the insight, the revelation of God that his people turn over in their minds during these times. Even though this material does not, by and large, bring the narrative forward, the contribution it makes is so substantial that it cannot be ignored. We must say something about these books to understand what they contribute to our grasp of God as he has disclosed himself in the Bible.

The God Who Makes His People Sing: Psalms

Some wag has said, "Let me write the songs of a nation, and I care not who makes its laws."[1] Given some of the things being sung today, that is a pretty scary thought. Yet the notion is understandable enough. If people are walking around with iPods, regardless of what people in Washington decide, the most fundamental shaping of the public mind, including the public mind represented in Washington, will take place via iPods (or some other delivery system).

In the Old Testament the book that incorporates most of this song-like—or hymn-like—material is the book of Psalms, virtually in the middle of the Bible, containing 150 of them. It was written over a period of about 1200 years; the collection was not the result of somebody sitting down to make it their writing project in a particular year. For example, one of the psalms is a psalm of Moses, taking you all the way back to the first part of the Bible. Many psalms were written by David, who was a musician who used his royal authority to help organize the choirs and public worship connected with the ancient tabernacle, patterns of worship and song then improved by his son Solomon to be used in the new temple whose construction Solomon oversaw. Then there are psalms that depict the experiences of the people of God as they are going into exile four hundred years later. There are even some psalms that reflect the thoughts of the people of God as they come back from exile, which brings you down to about 400 BC. The psalms cover a very broad period of time.

Obviously we can't possibly survey 150 psalms. What I would like to do is drop in on a few of them so that you can overhear what the people were singing. The psalms are very diverse.

Those of you who have been Christians for some time or who have gotten to know some elderly believers have discovered that elderly Christians are usually the ones who love the book of Psalms. Not a lot of people know the book of Psalms well at twenty-five. This is because the book of Psalms resonates with people who have had a lot of experiences. You have to have quite a lot of different experiences under your belt before you resonate easily with a lot of the things that are said in the book of Psalms: lament, loss, shame, death, triumph, the exaltation of informed and godly God-centered praise, and prophecy anticipating what is still to come. If instead you have a very limited experience, most of these things just sound a bit over the top or a bit extravagant or even alien to you. I have been by the beds of enough people who were dying to discover that if I ask, "What would you like me to read to you?" many will say, "Psalm 23. The Lord is my shepherd" or "Psalm 42" or "Psalm 40, about how he lifts me out of the miry bog and sets my feet on a safe, stable place." But until you have been through experiences where you feel as if you are wallowing in a miry bog, that psalm is probably not going to speak powerfully to you.

So let me drop in on a few psalms to overhear the kinds of things they say about God and his people. We'll begin at the beginning.

Psalm 1

> [1]Blessed are those
>   who do not walk in step with the wicked

> or stand in the way that sinners take
>> or sit in the company of mockers,
> 2but who delight in the law of the LORD
>> and meditate on his law day and night.
> 3They are like a tree planted by streams of water,
>> which yields its fruit in season
> and whose leaf does not wither—
>> whatever they do prospers.
> 4Not so the wicked!
>> They are like chaff
>> that the wind blows away.
> 5Therefore the wicked will not stand in the judgment,
>> nor sinners in the assembly of the righteous.
> 6For the LORD watches over the way of the righteous,
>> but the way of the wicked will be destroyed.
>
> Psalm 1

If you look at the psalm closely, you discover that it is broken into three unequal parts: verses 1–3 describe the righteous; verses 4–5 describe the unrighteous; and verse 6 is a final summarizing contrast.

The Righteous (Ps. 1:1–3)

Psalm 1:1 describes the righteous negatively: what they are *not* like, what they *do not* do. "Blessed are those who do *not* walk in step with the wicked"; that is, they avoid walking along with them, marching beside them. They do not want to be coordinated with them. For if they do that long enough, they might begin to "stand in the way that sinners take." To "stand in the way" of people is not an appropriate translation (almost all of our English translations say something like that). The trouble is that in Hebrew to stand in someone's way does not mean what we mean in English when we use the same words. To stand in someone's way in English means to impede them, to block their path, like Robin Hood and Little John on the bridge, each standing in the other's way, guaranteeing that one of them ends in the stream. But in Hebrew to stand in someone's way means to have your feet in their moccasins, to do what they do, to be indistinguishable from them. You are not blocking them; you are where they are. You stand in their way. This is why this version renders it in somewhat of a paraphrase, "stand in the way that sinners take." You're now where they are.

If you do that long enough, you might "sit in the company of mockers." Now you are in your recliner, you pull the lever, you look down your self-righteous nose at the ignorant, stupid, right-wing, bigoted Christians, and every comment you make is a mocking sneer. The very first verse of the very first psalm says, in effect, "Blessed are those who do not do these things." It describes the righteous negatively.

Psalm 1:2 describes the righteous positively. They "delight in the law of the LORD and meditate on his law day and night" (1:2). This is what they think about. And it changes them.

When I first started teaching at Trinity Evangelical Divinity School, we had a lecturer there—already an old man—who loved to utter any number of one-liners born out of fifty years of ministry. Some of them were really good. One of his best was "You are not what you think you are, but what you think, you are." We are not just what we say or what we do, because we can say and do things to cover up what is really going on inside. But what we think, we are. So this text says that the righteous person learns to think God's thoughts after him. He delights in the law of the Lord. He meditates on God's Word day and night. It is not a question of quasi-magic: "a verse a day keeps the devil away." This is much more than having a Bible verse handy or mechanically making sure that you have your "devotions." It is such a love affair with all that God says that it feeds your mind. You go for a lunch break, or the light turns red ahead of you, and you sit in your car and your mind naturally gravitates toward thinking through what God has said. This sort of meditation is going on all the time. You meditate on God's Word day and night, and that means that you are now *not* listening to the advice of the wicked or developing paths that are indistinguishable from theirs or slinking down into sly mockery.

Psalm 1:3 describes the righteous metaphorically: "They are like a tree planted by streams of water, which yields its fruit in season and whose leaf does not wither—whatever they do prospers." The land of Palestine—the land of Israel— is a semi-arid land, a bit like the American Southwest, so during some seasons of the year there is no rain at all. The dry arroyos in the Southwest look like death warmed over. Then sudden rains come and gullies flood with water and host quite dangerous flash floods. These arroyos are often called wadis in Israel. When the rains come, the land that seems like death suddenly blooms; it comes to life with desert flowers. But only where there is a confluence of streams, not intermittent water, do you find trees whose leaves *never* wither, trees that bring forth fruit in season. In that sense such trees always prosper. This is not promising what some people today call "a prosperity gospel": follow Jesus and become filthy rich. The language of Psalm 1:3 is lodged in the metaphor of this tree, which "prospers" even when there is heat and blight because it is well watered; it is evergreen. In due course it produces fruit.

This metaphor is not uncommon in the Bible, precisely because the people who wrote the Bible experienced these sorts of things all the time, observing the cycles of the seasons. Hence Jeremiah 17, written about 600 BC or a little later, reads:

> [5]Cursed are those who trust in mortals,
>   who depend on flesh for their strength
> and whose hearts turn away from the LORD.

> ⁶They will be like a bush in the wastelands;
>   they will not see prosperity when it comes [i.e., the prosperity of life
>   and growth].
> They will dwell in the parched places of the desert,
>   in a salt land where no one lives.
> ⁷But blessed are those who trust in the LORD,
>   whose confidence is in him.
> ⁸They will be like a tree planted by the water
>   that sends out its roots by the stream.
> It does not fear when heat comes;
>   its leaves are always green.
> It has no worries in a year of drought
>   and never fails to bear fruit.

Jeremiah 17:5–8

So here in Psalm 1:1–3, the righteous person is described negatively, positively, and metaphorically.

The Unrighteous (Ps. 1:4–5)

In verses 4–5, the focus shifts to the unrighteous. The contrast is very strong: "Not so the wicked!" (1:4). "Not so," as if everything of significance that you care to affirm of the righteous you have to negate with respect to the unrighteous. Are the righteous those who avoid the counsel and the patterns of life of rebels and ungodly people? Not so the wicked, not so. Are the righteous those who delight in the law of the Lord and think about it day and night? Not so the wicked, not so. Are the righteous those who can be likened to a tree planted by streams of water that yields fruit in its season and whose leaf never withers? Not so the wicked, not so.

Well, what are *they* like? "They are like chaff that the wind blows away" (1:4). The image is of the ancient grain harvest where someone beats the heads of grain with a winnowing shovel. The chaff falls off and the wind blows it away, leaving the grain to fall to the threshing floor to be gathered and turned into flour and bread and all the rest. The chaff blows away or is burned up: it is rootless, lifeless, fruitless, useless. That is how the psalmist describes the wicked.

A Final Summarizing Contrast (Ps. 1:6)

This final contrast, strictly speaking, is not between the righteous and the wicked but between the *way* of the righteous and the *way* of the wicked: "For the LORD watches over the way of the righteous" (1:6); that is, he owns it as his; he protects it. "But the way of the wicked will be destroyed" (1:6) like tracks made on the seashore when the tide is out. The tide rolls in and the tide rolls out; you no longer see the tracks. Fifty billion years from now, if I may dare to speak of eternity in the categories of time, no one will be talking about the significance of Stalin or Pol Pot, but every cup of cold water given in the name of Jesus will still be remembered and celebrated, because the Lord watches over the way of the righteous; the way of the wicked will perish.

That is the first psalm: two ways to live, and there is no third. There are a lot of psalms like that. They are sometimes called "wisdom psalms." These psalms and wisdom literature sometimes get tied together because in wisdom literature the way of wisdom is cast against the way of folly in a simple and absolute polarity. Wisdom literature regularly offers you a choice between two ways. That is what this psalm does and therefore why it is sometimes called a wisdom psalm.

In the New Testament, the most remarkable wisdom preacher is Jesus. In fact, Jesus is an astonishingly flexible preacher, using many different modes of speech: apocalyptic imagery, one-liners, parables, and much more. But in more than a few of his addresses he uses this basic wisdom polarity: two ways. At the end of the Sermon on the Mount (Matthew 5–7), for instance, Jesus offers a number of vignettes that are exactly along this line. He says, in effect, "Picture two people: one builds a house on rock; the other builds a house on sand. The house on sand is not stable. The storms come in, the water rises, the winds lash the place, and it collapses. The house that is strongly built on rock endures" (see Matt. 7:24–27). Note well: there are just two houses. You're rather missing the point if you say, "Jesus, suppose you try hardpan clay." You cannot respond to wisdom preaching in that fashion. In the same context, Jesus says, "Wide is the gate and broad is the road that leads to destruction, and many enter through it. But small is the gate and narrow the road that leads to life, and only a few find it" (Matt. 7:13–14). Once again it misses the point to long for a medium-sized gate. You cannot do that; this is wisdom literature, wisdom preaching. There are only two ways.

Now you see what is scary about wisdom literature in general and Psalm 1 in particular. If we are really honest, we must face the fact that we never quite fit the good way. Oh, there may be times when we delight in the law of the Lord and meditate on it day and night. There are other times, quite frankly, when it is a real struggle to delight in the law of the Lord. There are times when the counsel of the ungodly sounds very attractive. If there are only two ways, where does that leave us?

What wisdom literature does is clarify our thinking and show us that there are some absolute polarities out there that must not be fudged over, even though most of us find ourselves in the middle, sometimes acting this way, sometimes acting that way. This is true of a man like King David himself, who is responsible for some of these psalms. King David can be described as a man after God's own heart, yet he also committed adultery and even arranged for a murder. One wonders what he would have done if he hadn't been a man after God's own heart. If there are only two ways, where does that leave David?

Wisdom literature clarifies the polarity between holiness and unholiness, between righteousness and unrighteousness. But although it clarifies, it cannot save us. If all we had were wisdom literature, it would tend to puff us up when we are doing well and drive us to despair when we are not. Like the law studied in the last chapter, wisdom literature cannot save us, even though it is a powerful teacher.

But Psalm 1 is not the only psalm in the Bible, of course. We must quickly survey a few others.

Psalm 8

Psalm 8 not only praises God for his power in creation ("You have set your glory above the heavens" [8:1]) but also marvels that God has a peculiar relationship with human beings, with mere mortals: "what are mere mortals that you are mindful of them, human beings that you care for them?" (8:4). God has actually set them above the rest of the created order.

> ⁵You have made them a little lower than the heavenly beings
>   and crowned them with glory and honor.
> ⁶You made them rulers over the works of your hands;
>   you put everything under their feet:
> ⁷all flocks and herds,
>   and the animals of the wild,
> ⁸the birds in the sky,
>   and the fish in the sea,
>   all that swim the paths of the seas.
> ⁹Lord, our Lord, how majestic is your name in all the earth!
>
> Psalm 8:5–9

Do you hear how adoring this is? This is a hymn that has been composed as a reflection on Genesis 1–2. Quite a few psalms are meditative reflections used in the corporate worship of the people of God, reflections based on earlier Scriptures. God's people reflect on God's truth and join together to sing these truths—that is, they do not just recite certain truths or merely read them, but instead sing them.

Psalm 19

This is another psalm that is a reflection on how the created order reflects who God is.

[1]The heavens declare the glory of God;
    the skies proclaim the work of his hands.
[2]Day after day they pour forth speech;
    night after night they display knowledge.
[3]They have no speech, they use no words;
    no sound is heard from them.
[4]Yet their voice goes out into all the earth,
    their words to the ends of the world.
In the heavens he has pitched a tent for the sun,
    [5]which is like a bridegroom coming out of his chamber,
    like a champion rejoicing to run his course.
[6]It rises at one end of the heavens
    and makes its circuit to the other;
    nothing is deprived of its warmth.

                                                    Psalm 19:1–6

Then after talking about how the Lord has disclosed himself in this created order, the psalmist talks about how the Lord has disclosed himself in Scripture.

Psalm 14

To change the pace entirely, take a look at the opening line of Psalm 14: "Fools say in their hearts, 'There is no God'" (14:1). I have a friend in Australia who has a bit of a reputation for talking about Christ with a bluntness that other cultures might find more than a little aggressive. He once gave an address titled "Atheists Are Fools, and Agnostics Are Cowards." Whatever you may think of the approach, there is a sense in which my friend is in line with this psalm, which begins: "Fools say in their hearts, 'There is no God'" (14:1). That is so out of line with contemporary perceptions. In some circles shaped by the contemporary "new atheism," the fool is the idiot who believes that there *is* a God.

But look at it from God's perspective. Just grant for a moment that the God of the Bible is the God who is there: who is the fool? This is not written from the point of view of someone who sets himself up in the heritage of René Descartes, a sort of Cartesian independence, saying, "I think I'm in the place where I can evaluate whether God exists and which God it will be." This is the God who is there, who has named himself and disclosed himself. In his mercy he has come back again and again to save his people, and he keeps promising an even greater deliverance to come. He insists that the reason people do not see this reality is that this side of the fall we human beings suffer from such a deep moral and spiritual corruption that we are blind to the obvious. It is the *fool* who says in his heart, "There is no God."

This does not mean that no Christian is a fool. What it means is that everyone who has become a Christian started off a fool, and if in this respect we are no longer fools, that too, in the Bible's storyline, is a mark of singular grace. Christians never have the right to say, "I am smarter than you are," because Christians deep down know that they can never be more than fools who have been shown forgiveness and grace. We are never more than poor beggars telling other poor beggars where there is bread. But it does us a world of good to hear the Bible's perspective on who is the real fool.

Psalm 40

Here is a psalm with quite a different flavor. This is a psalm of personal experience that develops into something more. I do not have space to go through all of it, but we shall try to pick up its main points. The superscription informs us that this psalm was written by David.

> ¹I waited patiently for the LORD;
>> he turned to me and heard my cry.
> ²He lifted me out of the slimy pit,
>> out of the mud and mire;
> he set my feet on a rock
>> and gave me a firm place to stand.
> ³He put a new song in my mouth,
>> a hymn of praise to our God.
> Many will see and fear the LORD
>> and put their trust in him.
>
> Psalm 40:1–3

We do not know what this miry bog is, what this slimy pit is. It was obviously something so awful in David's experience that he felt the way you do in a slimy pit: desperate, unable to get out, sliding into oblivion, sucked down. And God pulled him out.

Much of the rest of the psalm talks about how the psalmist will respond by devoting himself to the living God and how he will give testimony to this in the community of God's people. Then in the last part of the psalm he openly acknowledges that just because he has been through this sort of experience, it does not follow that he will not go through other bleak experiences. Just because you have been through a divorce does not mean that you are therefore going to be spared cancer. Just because you have had cancer does not mean that you will not lose your spouse. Just because you have had a kid go off the rails does not mean that you will not be in a car accident. Life in this fallen and broken world brings many kinds of heartaches, defeats, and discouragements. David gives thanks to God for God's help and release from this particular miry bog, but he is realistic enough to look into the future and say, in effect, "There are so many other things, Lord God, where I'm going to need your help."

> [11]Do not withhold your mercy from me, LORD;
>   may your love and faithfulness always protect me.
> [12]For troubles without number surround me;
>   my sins have overtaken me, and I cannot see.
> They are more than the hairs of my head,
>   and my heart fails within me.
> [13]Be pleased to save me, LORD;
>   come quickly, LORD, to help me.
>
> Psalm 40:11–13

"The worst thing that I face," David says in effect, "is not this slimy pit experience through which I have passed, but my own sins, sins which cripple me and crush me and take me down because I look at my own heart and I cannot fit into the good side of Psalm 1." "My sins have overtaken me, and I cannot see" (40:12).

But there are still other troubles David must face, not least those who mock him and give him difficulties:

> [15]May those who say to me, "Aha! Aha!"
>   be appalled at their own shame.
> [16]But may all who seek you
>   rejoice and be glad in you;
> may those who long for your saving help always say,
>   "The LORD is great!"
>
> Psalm 40:15–16

So here is a psalm of huge intensity as a believer looks at how God has helped him and anticipates the way he is going to need God's help in the future.

Psalm 51

Before thinking through this psalm it is very important to read the superscription: "A psalm of David. When the prophet Nathan came to him after David had committed adultery with Bathsheba." This refers to the account where he seduces a young woman next door who is the wife of one of David's own soldiers fighting on the front in one of David's wars. How callous is that? It transpires that Bathsheba becomes pregnant by David, and she lets the king know. So he arranges to have her husband, Uriah, shipped back from the front. He sends a message that Uriah is to bring back a message to the king, ostensibly to communicate between the officers in the field and the commander-in-chief.

In fact, this is David's way of getting the bloke home, for if Uriah comes home, surely he will sleep with his wife. As for the timing of the birth—well, it is not unheard of for that to be off a month or two. As it turns out, however, Uriah is so concerned for his mates at the front that he cannot even bring himself to go home, so he sleeps in the open courtyard of the palace, prepared to return to the front the next day.

King David knows he is snookered. So he sends back a message by this young man's hand—a sealed message—for the unit commanders on the front. They are to arrange a skirmish, and everybody else in the platoon will receive some sort of code or signal to know when to fall back—everyone except this young man Uriah. They find themselves in a skirmish, the signal is given, everybody falls back except Uriah, and he is killed.

David thinks that he has gotten away with it. Then the prophet Nathan confronts him. David is in the depths of public humiliation and shame. His actions are all out in the open. What a mess! Nevertheless, David has been broken, and in the midst of his deep repentance he writes Psalm 51. That is what is meant by the superscription: the psalm was written "when the prophet Nathan came to him after David had committed adultery with Bathsheba."

> ¹Have mercy on me, O God,
>   according to your unfailing love;
> according to your great compassion
>   blot out my transgressions.
> ²Wash away all my iniquity
>   and cleanse me from my sin.
> ³For I know my transgressions,
>   and my sin is always before me.
>
> Psalm 51:1–3

Haven't you felt like that when you have awakened in the middle of the night and remembered some insanely evil or stupid thing you have done, and you break out into a cold sweat and squirm and wish you could undo it but can't?

"My sin is always before me. Against you, you only, have I sinned and done what is evil in your sight" (51:3–4). That is a stunning comment. At one level you want to say that it is not true. David sinned against Bathsheba: he seduced her. He sinned against Bathsheba's husband: he had him bumped off after sleeping with his wife. He sinned against his own family: he betrayed them. He sinned against the military high command: he corrupted them. He sinned against the people: he was not acting as a righteous king. It is hard to think of anybody that he did *not* sin against.

Yet he has the cheek to say, "Against you, you only, have I sinned and done what is evil in your sight" (51:4). At the deepest level, David's words speak the exact truth. What makes sin so heinous, what makes sin so wretched, is precisely that it defies God. Certainly it is awful when we hurt our friends. It is awful when we wound one another, so when we wake up in the middle of the night with those feelings of huge shame, it is not surprising that we are embarrassed because of what our friends will think of us now on account of what we have said or done that was so insensitive or cruel. But beyond all of this horizontal shame lies a much bigger guilt that we are rarely aware of and rarely squirm over: guilt before the living God. David, however, gets this right. He is squirming over his sin because he sees what it is in God's sight: "Against you, you only, have I sinned and done what is evil in your sight." What gives sin its most horrendous odor, its most heinous aspect, is precisely that it is defiance of the God who made us and who judges us on the last day. David understands this because he understands the opening chapters of Genesis. The heart of Eve's problems or Adam's problems is not that they broke a little rule or betrayed each other's trust; rather, they de-god-ed God.

In any sin that we commit, whether it's genocide or cheating on our income taxes, the most offended party is always God. "Against you, you only, have I sinned and done what is evil in your sight." That is why, as we have seen from the beginning of the Bible's storyline, what we must have—whatever else we have—is *God's* forgiveness, or we have nothing.

Other Psalms

There are many other psalms, of course. Psalm 110 looks to a coming one who is simultaneously a king and a priest. It's the chapter most frequently quoted in the New Testament. Psalm 119, the longest chapter in the Bible, is full of thanksgiving to God and is a meditation on the nature of God's words, of God's self-disclosure in words, of his law, his decrees, his judgments, his teaching, his truth. It is all about what we would call the Bible. It provides us with ways to think about the fact that God is a talking God, a God who speaks and gives us his words. Psalm 139 says something of the same. "How precious to me are your thoughts, God! How vast is the sum of them!" (139:17).

This is the God who makes his people sing in thanksgiving, contrition, petition, lament, and reflection. Taken together, these psalms indicate the kind of relationship that God wants his people to have with him. It is deeply authentic, not the kind of religion characterized by mumbo jumbo, merely formal religious duties, self-importance, and religious arrogance, all of it carefully masking a stinking hypocrisy. The intensity of the psalms conspires to underscore that God cannot be deceived by religious rituals. He wants his image-bearers to enjoy a real relationship with him, the true and living God. Here is wisdom.

Wisdom Literature

Several books make up the wisdom literature of the Bible, and we will glance at some of them.

Proverbs

The book of Proverbs has one kind of literature: many proverbs. Many of these proverbs are not isolated reflections but are linked thematically. For example, many of the proverbs revolve around two metaphorical women: Lady Wisdom and Dame Folly. We are following either one or the other. Wisdom literature forces us to choose "this path" or "that path." It will compare two things and say, "This is the way of wisdom. This is the way of folly. Make sure that what you follow is the way of wisdom."

At the beginning of the book is a proverb that recurs in a variety of ways: "The fear of the LORD is the beginning of knowledge, but fools despise wisdom and instruction" (Prov. 1:7). A little later: "The fear of the LORD is the beginning of wisdom, and knowledge of the Holy One is understanding" (9:10). The fear in view is not the kind of cringing fear that a whipped dog has when you pick up a newspaper, knowing that you are an arbitrary and cruel master who extracts cheap glee out of scaring the poor little thing to death. This is the fear of God that recognizes that he is matchlessly holy, righteous, and just—and we are not. God is our judge as well as our only hope. There lies the beginning of wisdom. This is the opposite of what we found in Psalm 14:1: "Fools say in their hearts, 'There is no God.'" A right sense of how to live under the sun must begin with God and his self-disclosure. There is the beginning of wisdom.

Job

One of the most remarkable books in the wisdom collection of the Bible is the book of Job. We do not know when it was written, though it is probably very old. It depicts a man who is not perfect but is an astonishingly good man: filthy rich but generous, caring, and loving. He even prays preemptively for his own ten children lest they should commit any sins and do something bad. He is generous with the poor. He could testify, "I made a covenant with my eyes not to look lustfully at a virgin" (Job 31:1). He is an astonishingly pious man, and his piety is genuine.

What Job doesn't know is that behind the scenes the devil, whom we met as the serpent in Genesis 3, makes a wager with God: "The only reason that Job likes you is that he is filthy rich and you protect him. You take away all the good things that he possesses, and he will turn around and curse you to your face." God says, "Go ahead. Just don't hurt him" (see Job 1:9–12). Successive waves of marauders invade his property: his cattle are stolen, his herds are decimated, a windstorm blows down the house where his ten children are having a party and kills them all. Job responds by saying, "Naked I came from my mother's womb, and naked I will depart. The LORD gave and the LORD has taken away; may the name of the LORD be praised" (1:21).

Satan says to God, "Skin for skin. Just take away this chap's health, and he'll curse you to your face." God replies, "Go ahead, but spare his life." Pretty soon you find Job on an ash pit using pieces of broken pottery to pick his scabs. When three friends come to visit him, they sit down for a week and do nothing but keep quiet—the wisest thing they could do.

The rest of the book is set out as a drama. These friends think they have mastered theology and can give Job all the correct answers he needs. They say, in effect, "Job, do you believe that God is sovereign?"

"Yes."

"Do you believe that God is just?"

"Yes."

"So if he is sovereign and just, and you're suffering, then the implication is . . . ?"

Job says, "I know that God is sovereign and just, but quite frankly I do not deserve this. I am an innocent sufferer. I should not be suffering this."

"Job, do you hear what you are saying? Are you implying that God is making a mistake or that God is unjust to you?"

"Oh, no. I am not saying that. I know that God is sovereign. I know that he is just. But I still have to say that what I am going through isn't fair."

The discussion gets hotter and hotter until eventually the friends begin to say, "Job, you do not understand. You have committed more sins than you can possibly recognize—sins that you have committed that you don't even know about, more than you can possibly imagine. Otherwise, you are really saying that God is unjust. What you ought to do is confess them in any case, even if you cannot name any specific sins. Just confess them generally to God, and God will forgive you and everything will get better."

Job replies, "How can I possibly do that? How can I repent of something that I do not know that I have done wrong? How can I possibly repent and claim that I am asking for God's mercy and forgiveness when I don't think that I deserve this? That would actually be making me a liar, and I would be sinning against God. What I really need is a lawyer. I wish I had somebody who would go between God and me; that is what I need."

The tension in the drama mounts and mounts. I shall not unpack all of the levels of argumentation, but eventually God speaks. He addresses Job with a series of rhetorical questions: "Job, have you ever designed a snowflake? Where were you when I made the first hippopotamus? Did you give me any advice on how to cast the constellation Orion into the heavens, Job?" At the end of two chapters of these rhetorical questions, Job says, in effect, "I'm sorry. I spoke foolishly, claiming that I know more than I do." And do you know what God says? "Prepare to defend yourself; I will question you, and you shall answer me" (Job 40:7)—followed by two more chapters of rhetorical questions.

God's chapters are stunning because at the end of the day he provides no systematic answer that will sort out the entire problem of innocent suffering. All of his rhetorical questions combine to mean one thing: we human beings are not always going to get explanations, but God is bigger than we are and sometimes we just have to trust him. At the end, Job repents (see 42:1–6)—not of imaginary sins that his "friends" think he needs to confess in order to win back God's favor, but of his rather presumptuous tendency to insist on answers rather than to trust.

God nevertheless insists that Job basically got the account right. Doubtless Job was becoming a bit pushy toward the end, but God's displeasure is reserved for the three "friends" who think they have God all figured out.

At the end of the story God restores the fortunes of Job. This should not be surprising. After all, at the end of time, according to the Bible, not only will justice be done, but it will be seen to be done. The restoration of Job's fortunes is a kind of microcosm of the bigger story of world history under God: justice will prevail in the end. That too is wisdom.

Ecclesiastes

In Ecclesiastes, Solomon sets out to find meaning in life. He engages in vast public works and discovers that is ultimately meaningless, for none of them is finally enduring. He devotes himself to wisdom, literature, scholarship, and meditation, and after a while he discovers that these are not very satisfying either. Then he devotes himself to generosity or asceticism or hedonism and then something else and something else. Nothing finally satisfies; nothing finally endures. Everything done here is still "under the sun." At the end of the book, when he looks back over his life at all the things he has attempted to do in his effort to seek pleasure, meaning, and fulfillment, he concludes,

> [1]Remember your Creator
>   in the days of your youth,
>   before the days of trouble come
> and the years approach when you will say,
>   "I find no pleasure in them". . . .
> [13]Now all has been heard;
>   here is the conclusion of the matter:
> Fear God and keep his commandments,
>   for this is the duty of every human being.
> [14]For God will bring every deed into judgment,
>   including every hidden thing,
>   whether it is good or evil.
>
>   Ecclesiastes 12:1, 13–14

That is to say, what he finally comes up with is a teleological vision, a vision of what happens at the end. You have to live in light of the end. That is wisdom because we will give an account to this God.

Conclusion

When we feel in our hearts and minds, as we grow older, that there has to be something more—there has to be something more satisfying, there has to be something bigger—we are right to listen to that brooding voice, because we were made for God and our souls will be restless until we know him. Those are the kinds of things that wisdom books teach us as the Old Testament barrels along in anticipation of the day when Wisdom incarnate—that is, Wisdom in the flesh—will come, when there is some final resolution between the perfections that God demands in Psalm 1 and the compromise of misconduct of our own lives, between David as a man after God's own heart and David as a wretched sinner in desperate need of God's mercy. A resolution is still coming, and his name is Jesus.

7

The God Who Becomes
a Human Being

So far in this book I have referred only infrequently to that block of books that boast the name of their prophetic authors. I have mentioned Isaiah once or twice, and a couple of others, but that's about all.

I wish there were space to unpack them for at least a couple of chapters. For although these books contain sections that are obscure, many parts of these prophecies are among the most brilliant and intense writings anywhere in the Bible. Without me commenting on them or explaining their contexts, the following brief quotations amply illustrate the point:

> [8]I am the LORD; that is my name!
>   I will not yield my glory to another
>   or my praise to idols. . . .
> [14]For a long time I have kept silent,
>   I have been quiet and held myself back.
> But now, like a woman in childbirth,
>   I cry out, I gasp and pant.
> [15]I will lay waste the mountains and hills
>   and dry up all their vegetation;
> I will turn rivers into islands
>   and dry up the pools.
> [16]I will lead the blind by ways they have not known,
>   along unfamiliar paths I will guide them;
> I will turn the darkness into light before them
>   and make the rough places smooth.
> These are the things I will do;
>   I will not forsake them.

[17]But those who trust in idols,
    who say to images, "You are our gods,"
    will be turned back in utter shame.

Isaiah 42:8, 14–17

[2]When you pass through the waters,
    I will be with you;
and when you pass through the rivers,
    they will not sweep over you.
When you walk through the fire,
    you will not be burned;
    the flames will not set you ablaze.
[3]For I am the LORD your God,
    the Holy One of Israel, your Savior. . . .
[4]Since you are precious and honored in my sight,
    and because I love you,
I will give nations in exchange for you,
    and peoples in exchange for your life.
[5]Do not be afraid, for I am with you;
    I will bring your children from the east
    and gather you from the west.

Isaiah 43:2–5

Oh, that my head were a spring of water
    and my eyes a fountain of tears!
I would weep day and night
    for the slain of my people.

Jeremiah 9:1

[2]It is my pleasure to tell you about the miraculous signs and wonders that the Most High God has performed for me.

[3]How great are his signs,
    how mighty his wonders!
His kingdom is an eternal kingdom;
    his dominion endures from generation to generation!

Daniel 4:2–3

There are those who turn justice into bitterness
    and cast righteousness to the ground.

Amos 5:7

[2]How long, Lord, must I call for help,
    but you do not listen?

> Or cry out to you, "Violence!"
>   but you do not save?
> ³Why do you make me look at injustice?
>   Why do you tolerate wrongdoing?
> Destruction and violence are before me;
>   there is strife, and conflict abounds.
> ⁴Therefore the law is paralyzed,
>   and justice never prevails.
> The wicked hem in the righteous,
>   so that justice is perverted.
>
>   Habakkuk 1:2–4

¹⁰"Oh, that one of you would shut the temple doors, so that you would not light useless fires on my altar! I am not pleased with you," says the LORD Almighty, "and I will accept no offering from your hands. ¹¹My name will be great among the nations, from where the run rises to where it sets. In every place incense and pure offerings will be brought to me, because my name will be great among the nations," says the LORD Almighty.

                                                        Malachi 1:10–11

Sometimes these prophetic books preserve the spiritual wrestling of the prophets themselves. Sometimes they predict the immediate future: Assyria will invade Moab but will not succeed in taking Jerusalem; Judah's alliance with Egypt is irresponsible and will backfire. Sometimes they predict a renovation of everything at the end of history, a new heaven and a new earth. And between these two predicted ends there are prophecies that anticipate the coming of God, or the dawning of a new covenant that he will inaugurate, or the coming of a new Davidic king, or the coming of God's unnamed Servant.

We must pause for a moment. The chapter you are now reading has the frankly amazing title, "The God Who Becomes a Human Being." It presupposes that this God keeps telling us, throughout the Old Testament, that he is coming. And now he does come—by becoming a human being.

In one sense, of course, the Old Testament narrative establishes that God comes to Abraham and calls him on his pilgrimage. He comes to Moses and gives him certain tasks. He comes to David and establishes a dynasty. In the Old Testament, through large swaths of the biblical books, God is repeatedly said to come.

Sometimes the coming of God means judgment. People would speak of "the day of the Lord," the time when the Lord would come, as something wonderful, a time of revival and blessing. But sometimes God says, "Why do you long for the day of the LORD? That day will be darkness, not light" (Amos 5:18). The coming of the Lord may bring with it the fiercest judgment. This judgment extends beyond his own covenant people to all the nations, for God is sovereign over all. "Righteousness exalts a nation, but sin condemns any people" (Prov. 14:34). So in the major prophets of the Old Testament, God promises to come visit the Babylonians with judgment, or the pagan cities of Tyre and Sidon with judgment, and so forth.

He also keeps promising to come with forgiveness and hope. In some of these passages there is a confusion—in retrospect, an intentional confusion—about *who* is coming. Is it God himself, or is it the ultimate Davidic king? We saw one of those passages briefly in the prophecy of Isaiah 9, in words with which many of us are familiar because of Handel's *Messiah*. This promised king will reign on David's throne—yet, as we saw, this is said of him:

> ⁶For to us a child is born,
>   to us a son is given,
>   and the government will be on his shoulders.
> And he will be called
>   Wonderful Counselor, Mighty God,
>   Everlasting Father, Prince of Peace.
> ⁷Of the increase of his government and peace
>   there will be no end.
>
> Isaiah 9:6–7

In this passage, of course, we start with the Davidic king, and then suddenly he is being called "Mighty God." In other passages the direction is reversed: we begin by reading about the coming of God himself, only to learn that the coming of the Davidic king is in view. One of the most remarkable passages in this respect is by the prophet Ezekiel:

> ¹The word of the LORD came to me: ²"Son of man, prophesy against the shepherds of Israel [that does not mean the people who keep the sheep literally but the rulers, the nobles, the monarchs as they come and go, the leaders, the priests]; prophesy and say to them: 'This is what the Sovereign LORD says: Woe to you shepherds of Israel who only take care of yourselves! Should not shepherds take care of the flock? ³You eat the curds, clothe yourselves with the wool and slaughter the choice animals, but you do not take care of the flock. ⁴You have not strengthened the weak or healed the sick or bound up the injured. You have not brought back the strays or searched for the lost. You have ruled them harshly and brutally. ⁵So they were scattered because there was no shepherd, and when they were scattered they became food for all the wild animals. ⁶My sheep wandered over all the mountains and on every high hill. They were scattered over the whole earth, and no one searched or looked for them.'"
>
> Ezekiel 34:1–6

Then what God says in many different ways through verse after verse is, in effect, this: "I will not only judge the false shepherds. I myself will become the shepherd of my people."

This is what the Sovereign LORD says: I am against the shepherds and will hold them accountable for my flock. I will remove them from tending the flock so that the shepherds can no longer feed themselves.

Ezekiel 34:10

Then he goes on to say,

[12]As shepherds look after their scattered flocks when they are with them, so will I look after my sheep. I will rescue them from all the places where they were scattered on a day of clouds and darkness. [13]I will bring them out from the nations and gather them from the countries, and I will bring them into their own land. I will pasture them on the mountains of Israel, in the ravines and in all the settlements in the land. [14]I will tend them in a good pasture, and the mountain heights of Israel will be their grazing land. There they will lie down in good grazing land, and there they will feed in a rich pasture on the mountains of Israel. [15]I myself will tend my sheep and have them lie down, declares the Sovereign LORD. [16]I will search for the lost and bring back the strays. I will bind up the injured and strengthen the weak, but the sleek and the strong I will destroy. I will shepherd the flock with justice.

Ezekiel 34:12–16

In other words, "All these false shepherds are just ruining the flock. I myself will be their shepherd." Then after saying again and again—about twenty-five times—that God himself is going to shepherd his people, that he is going to do the job himself, he then says,

[23]I will place over them one shepherd, my servant David, and he will tend them; he will tend them and be their shepherd. [24]I the LORD will be their God, and my servant David will be prince among them. I the LORD have spoken.

Ezekiel 34:23–24

So somehow this promise of God himself coming and a Davidic king coming get merged into one.

Other promises dot the Old Testament prophetic literature. For example, six centuries before Jesus, the prophet Jeremiah reports that God will make a new covenant with his people (see Jer. 31:31–34). That means the covenant already in force, the covenant established at Sinai, has become the old covenant. If the Sinai covenant has been declared *old*, in some sense or other it is becoming obsolete, as it will be replaced by the *new* covenant.[1] People steeped in such Scriptures could not help but wonder when this new covenant would dawn, and in what ways it would preserve the emphases of the old covenant, and in what ways it would outstrip them. But we can imagine the excitement, confusion, uncertainty, and hope when, on the very night Jesus was betrayed and went to the cross, he took a cup of wine during the meal he was having with his most intimate followers, and said, "This cup is the new covenant in my blood, which is poured out for you" (Luke 22:20). We shall have occasion a little later to ponder Jesus's words. For the moment it is enough to recognize some of the patterns of Old Testament prophecies that point to Jesus.

One more: in several places in the prophecy of Isaiah, God announces someone he refers to simply as "my servant." For instance:

> ¹Here is my servant, whom I uphold,
>   my chosen one in whom I delight;
> I will put my Spirit on him,
>   and he will bring justice to the nations.
> ²He will not shout or cry out,
>   or raise his voice in the streets.
> ³A bruised reed he will not break,
>   and a smoldering wick he will not snuff out.
> ⁴In faithfulness he will bring forth justice;
>   he will not falter or be discouraged
> till he establishes justice on earth.
>   In his teaching the islands will put their hope.
>
> Isaiah 42:1–4

> ⁴Surely he took up our pain
>   and bore our suffering,
> yet we considered him punished by God,
>   stricken by him, and afflicted.
> ⁵But he was pierced for our transgressions,
>   he was crushed for our iniquities;
> the punishment that brought us peace was on him,
>   and by his wounds we are healed.
> ⁶We all, like sheep, have gone astray,
>   each of us has turned to our own way;
> and the LORD has laid on him
>   the iniquity of us all.
> ⁷He was oppressed and afflicted,
>   yet he did not open his mouth;
> he was led like a lamb to the slaughter,
>   and as a sheep before its shearers is silent,
>   so he did not open his mouth.
> ⁸By oppression and judgment he was taken away.
>   Yet who of his generation protested?
> For he was cut off from the land of the living;
>   for the transgression of my people he was punished.
> ⁹He was assigned a grave with the wicked,
>   and with the rich in his death,
> though he had done no violence,
>   nor was any deceit in his mouth.

> [10]Yet it was the LORD's will to crush him and cause him to suffer,
>   and though the LORD makes his life an offering for sin,
> he will see his offspring and prolong his days,
>   and the will of the LORD will prosper in his hand.
> [11]After he has suffered,
>   he will see the light of life and be satisfied;
> by his knowledge my righteous servant will justify many,
>   and he will bear their iniquities.
>
> Isaiah 53:4–11

It is a rather stunning fact that before the coming of Jesus, more than seven hundred years after the prophecy of Isaiah, no one clearly understood that the promised servant of the Lord would also be the Davidic king, whose coming would also simultaneously be the visitation of God. In retrospect it is easy to see that the pieces are there. One suspects that one of the reasons why people did not put it together was that it was hard to imagine how a conquering and victorious king of David's line could also be a suffering servant, somehow suffering the torments of the damned so that the damned might be justified.

Old Testament strands are coming together.

The New Testament

So we come to the New Testament. The first four books of the New Testament are often called "Gospels": Matthew, Mark, Luke, and John. They all begin a little differently, but they all begin in some way with the coming of Jesus.

Luke's Gospel, for example, depicts an angelic visitation to a young woman named Mary, promising her a virginal conception, such that the child born in her would be called the Son of God. Then the familiar Christmas story occurs in Luke 2.

In Matthew's Gospel, the situation is looked at less from Mary's perspective and more from Joseph's perspective. Mary was engaged to be married to Joseph, and then he discovers that she is pregnant. Do not forget that in that society they could not go off in a corner somewhere and have a little chitchat so that she could try to convince him that it was a miracle brought about by the power of God and she was still a virgin. In those days you simply did not have that kind of easy conversation about sexual matters before you were married. Chaperones and guardians were around all the time. But God visited Joseph as well and insisted that this was God's own doing; Mary was still a virgin.

> [20]But after he had considered this, an angel of the Lord appeared to him in a dream and said, "Joseph son of David, do not be afraid to take Mary home as your wife, because what is conceived in her is from the Holy Spirit. [21]She will

give birth to a son, and you are to give him the name Jesus, because he will save his people from their sins."

Matthew 1:20–21

So when the baby came, Joseph was to give the baby the name Jesus. Jesus is simply the Greek form of Joshua, and Joshua means "Yahweh saves." Yahweh, you will recall, is the name of God in the Old Testament, connected to "I AM WHO I AM." This God saves; Yahweh saves. From what? Joseph was to give this baby the name Jesus, meaning "Yahweh saves," because Jesus will save his people from their sins. Occurring as it does in the first chapter of Matthew's Gospel, this crucial name announces that the rest of this Gospel is to be read as the book in which Yahweh saves his people from their sins. Every chapter of that book can be fit under this theme. The accumulated sins from the time of the fall (Genesis 3) are about to be addressed.

What shall we make of this Jesus?

John 1:1–18

John's Gospel begins a slightly different way. It does not begin with the historical developments (Joseph, Mary, Bethlehem, the visit of the shepherds, and so forth). It begins by thinking about what the coming of the eternal Son, the coming of God, *means*. It is worth taking the time to read carefully John's first eighteen verses, sometimes called John's prologue:

> [1]In the beginning was the Word, and the Word was with God, and the Word was God. [2]He was with God in the beginning. [3]Through him all things were made; without him nothing was made that has been made. [4]In him was life, and that life was the light of all people. [5]The light shines in the darkness, and the darkness has not overcome it.
>
> [6]There was a man sent from God whose name was John. [7]He came as a witness to testify concerning that light, so that through him all might believe. [8]He himself was not the light; he came only as a witness to the light.
>
> [9]The true light that gives light to everyone was coming into the world. [10]He was in the world, and though the world was made through him, the world did not recognize him. [11]He came to that which was his own, but his own did not receive him. [12]Yet to all who did receive him, to those who believed in his name, he gave the right to become children of God—[13]children born not of natural descent, nor of human decision or a husband's will, but born of God.
>
> [14]The Word became flesh and made his dwelling among us. We have seen his glory, the glory of the one and only Son, who came from the Father, full of grace and truth.
>
> [15](John testified concerning him. He cried out, saying, "This is he of whom I said, 'He who comes after me has surpassed me because he was before me.'")
> [16]Out of his fullness we have all received grace in place of grace already given.

[17]For the law was given through Moses; grace and truth came through Jesus Christ. [18]No one has ever seen God, but the one and only Son, who is himself God and is in closest relationship with the Father, has made him known.

John 1:1–18

We must now run through the thought of this prologue—rather too quickly, no doubt, but in enough detail to begin to sense the wonder and power of who this Jesus is and why he has come.

The Word: God's Self-Expression (John 1:1)

The one who is coming is simply called "the Word": "In the beginning was the Word, and the Word was with God, and the Word was God" (1:1). We might say, "In the beginning was God's self-expression [for that is what "Word" here suggests], and this self-expression was with God [that is, God's own peer], and this self-expression was God [that is, God's own self]." Already your heart begins to flutter; your mind wonders, "What is going on here? How can you think in these terms?" But that is what the text says. This "Word" who, as we'll see in a moment, becomes a human being, is described both as God's own peer (he is already with God in the beginning!) and God's own self (he *is* God!).

Even the term "Word" is an interesting choice. What title or metaphorical expression should be applied to Jesus in the opening verses of John's Gospel? I can imagine various possibilities going round and round in John's head. But at some point John remembers, for example, that in the Old Testament we frequently read expressions like this: "The *word of the Lord* came to the prophet, saying. . . ." So God has disclosed himself by his *word* in revelation. Then perhaps he remembers Genesis 1: God *spoke*, and the world came into being; otherwise put, by the *word of the Lord* the heavens and earth were made (see Ps. 33:6). So here we have God's *word* in creation. Elsewhere, biblical writers speak of God sending forth his *word* to heal and help and transform his people (see for example Ps. 107:20). All these things God's *word* accomplishes: by his word, God reveals, he creates, he transforms, and John thinks to himself, "Yes, that's the appropriate expression that summarizes all who Jesus is." He is God's self-expression, God's revelation; he is God's own agent in creation; and he comes to save and transform God's people.

We are now on the edge of something massive, something extraordinarily important about the God who is there, the God who discloses himself in the Bible. All along the Bible has insisted on the fact that there is but one God, the God who is the Creator, Sustainer, and Judge of all. But here in the first verse of John's Gospel, we are told that the Word was with God in the beginning, so he is as eternal and as self-existent as God; that he is God's own peer, "with God" from the beginning, an astonishing equivalence granted what the Bible says about the uniqueness of God; and he is God's own self, for "the Word was God." Somehow this Word is differentiable from God (he was "with" God), yet he is identified *as* God ("the Word was God"). A little farther down, we will be told how this Word becomes a human being, the human being we know as Jesus. That is why Christians hold that Jesus is simultaneously differentiable from God (as God's own peer) yet fully identified with God. Our minds boggle at the paradox.

In fact, to leap ahead a little, Christians have invented a word to refer to God. This one God, we say, is the *Trinity*, the three-in-one God. Not only is the Father God, and Jesus the Son is God, but the Holy Spirit is God (as we shall see). No Christian, no matter how learned or thoughtful, pretends to understand all of this completely. Historically, Christians have found ways to speak about these things without falling into silly contradictions. They say, for instance, that the Word shares one "substance" with the Father, but is a distinguishable "person." But Christians have also learned not to pretend we understand more than we do.

The evidence for thinking about God as Trinity depends on more than the first verse of John's prologue, of course. For example, in John's Gospel alone, we find an array of passages that support this understanding of God. In John 5:19, Jesus insists that he does "whatever" the Father does—something no sane *mere* human could ever say. In the same chapter, God shows he is resolved that all should honor the Son "just as they honor the Father" (5:23)—something that makes no sense if Jesus is not himself God. In John 8:58, in a context where he is involved in a difficult dispute about who he is, Jesus insists, "Before Abraham was born, *I am*" (emphasis added). Since Abraham had been dead for two thousand years, Jesus's claim is that he has existed for about two thousand more years than the thirty years or so of his own physical existence; more importantly, he has taken on his lips the name by which God himself is known: *I am* or *I am what I am*.

On the night he is betrayed, Jesus says to one of his followers, "Don't you know me, Philip, even after I have been among you such a long time? Anyone who has seen me has seen the Father" (John 14:9)—which is either arrogant blasphemy of the highest order, a sick joke, or the sober truth: the closest human beings get to "seeing" God in this broken world is the Word-made-flesh, the Lord Jesus himself. Also on the night he was betrayed, Jesus insists that after he has risen and returned to his heavenly Father, he will send the Holy Spirit as a stand-in for himself, another Advocate (see John 14:15–17; 14:25–27; 15:26; 16:7–15). This Spirit, this Advocate sent from the Father, discharges a range of personal functions: he teaches, reminds people of Jesus, bears witness, convicts people, and is himself the very presence of the Father and the Son. After Jesus has risen from the dead, one of his followers, a man called Thomas, is so overwhelmed that he says to him, "My Lord and my God!" (John 20:28). That Thomas, a first-century Jew, addresses Jesus this way says something very remarkable about Thomas's increasing grasp of how the one God is nevertheless a complex God, what later Christians would call the Triune God. No less remarkable is that Jesus accepts the homage as his due—something no devout first-century Jew would do *unless he were God*.

In fact, that brings us to two more observations. First, since the time of Jesus's resurrection, Christians have worshiped Jesus as they worship God; indeed, while Christians address the Father and Jesus as distinct persons, Christians worship the Father as God and Jesus as God, and, for that matter, the Spirit as God. Second, this complex view of God as the Trinity helps us to grasp what we glimpsed earlier in this book: this is why, even in eternity past, before there was a universe, the God of the Bible, the God who is there, can be thought of as a *loving* God. For the nature of love is that there must be an "other" to love! Somehow in the very being of this one God lies the complexity that preserves love: the Father loves the Son (see John 3:35; 5:20) and the Son loves the Father (see John 14:31). Indeed, the love among the persons of the Godhead (as God the Trinity is sometimes called) becomes the controlling model that mandates how Christians should love one another (see John 17:24–26).

But now we are getting ahead of ourselves. We need to flesh out the rest of John's prologue.

What John Says about the Word (John 1:2–13)

The opening verses of John are packed with intertwined reflections on the Word, but we can easily isolate some of the most important of these.

First, the Word creates us; he is God's own agent in creation. "Through him all things were made; without him nothing was made that has been made" (John 1:3). That means that if we human beings are God's dependent creatures, we are no less the dependent creatures of the Word.

Second, the Word gives us light and life. "In him was life, and that life was the light of all people. The light shines in the darkness, and the darkness has not overcome it" (John 1:4–5).

Some books you read only once. You have a flight, let's say, to Los Angeles, so you pick up a whodunit at the bookshop in the airport, and by the time you get to LA, you have found out "who done it." You decide that this is not a book you are going to keep in your library, so you put it in the seat pocket in front of you. The cleaners take it out and you will never read it again.

Other books, of course, you want to read more than once. They are books you may even pore over, perhaps for the quality of the English prose or the brilliance of the descriptions or the characterizations. You may read such a book once for the plot and then reread it again for the pleasure of all the other touches. Any really good author of narrative writes in such a way that additional layers are peeled back when the book is reread.

The question is this: did John write his book as a throwaway tract to be read once, or is it the sort of book where he wanted it to be read again and again, with additional insight coming each time? I think it can be shown that he wrote it in such a way that he expected readers to see new things as they keep rereading his work. The first piece of evidence is found in verses 4–5 of the first chapter. If you read those verses without ever having read the rest of the book (that is, all you have read so far are verses 1–3), how will you understand verses 4–5? Verse 3: "Through him all things were made; without him nothing was made that has been made." This is surely talking about creation. Verse 4: "In him was life, and that life was the light of all people." That is, he had life in himself, and he gave life to all human beings. That was their light. Before him, there was darkness, and then he introduced light; there was the darkness of nothingness before he created everything, and after creation there was light and life. In other words, you can understand verses 4–5 entirely with respect to verse 3, and I suspect that if you were reading them for the first time, this is the way you would understand them.

But then you read verses 6 and following:

> [6]There was a man sent from God whose name was John. [7]He came as a witness to testify concerning that light, so that through him all might believe. [8]He himself was not the light; he came only as a witness to the light.
>
> John 1:6–8

You start seeing how "light" now has overtones not of physical light over against the nothingness that existed before the creation. Now light has some sort of overtone of revelation or truth—light that is revealed. As you read on in the book, the same sort of moral or revelatory association with light becomes clearer and clearer. Thus we read, "people loved darkness instead of light because their deeds were evil" (3:19). People choose the darkness because they are afraid to come to the light: "All those who do evil hate the light, and will not come into the light for fear that their deeds will be exposed. But those who live by the truth come into the light, so that it may be seen plainly that what they have done has been done in the sight of God" (3:20–21). In this context, light is not the light of creation; it is the light of revelation, of truth. By the time you get to John 8, Jesus says, "I am the light of the world" (8:12).

Now go back and re-read John 1:4–5: "In him was life, and that life was the light of all people. The light shines in the darkness [i.e., of corruption and rebellion], and the darkness has not overcome it." Now you have another set of overtones. Here the light is revelation and truth from God, truth that is overcoming the darkness of moral corruption and ignorance.

So should verses 4–5 be read in the light of verse 3 or in the light of verses 6–8? Which is true: the Word as the agent of physical life and light at the time of creation, or the Word as the one who brings revelation and transformation, overcoming moral darkness?

The answer, of course, is both. We are *supposed* to read it both ways. That is the way the Gospel of John has been written: the more we read it, the more we see new connections that are there in the text. The same light that brought life to the creation brings eternal life to this world of corruption and death.

Third, the Word confronts and divides us:

> [9]The true light that gives light to everyone was coming into the world. [10]He was in the world [i.e., the world that he had made], and though the world was made through him, the world did not recognize him. [11]He came to that which was his own [i.e., his own home], but his own [i.e., his own people] did not receive him.
>
> John 1:9–11

Most people did not look on Jesus and say, "Ah, you are finally here: the light of the world." Many were puzzled by him. Some were repulsed by him because even if they did see the light, they were ashamed in his presence and preferred the darkness to the light. So his very coming did not guarantee a universal revival with everybody turning to him.

Some did receive him; they believed in his name:

> [12]Yet to all who did receive him, to those who believed in his name, he gave the right to become children of God—[13]children born not of natural descent [it's not just natural children who are in view], nor of human decision [from sexual intercourse] or a husband's will [assuming he's taking some sort of primary role in the conception], but born of God.
>
> John 1:12–13

These people are not simply humanly born. They are also born of God. (That is a theme we will come back to in the next chapter.) They are different because God has done something new in them. There is a new creation. There is a new birth. He is starting something over in them, and they truly believe who Jesus really is.

The Word Becomes Flesh (John 1:14–18)

"The Word became flesh" (John 1:14). That means the Word became a human being. This is what Christians mean when they speak of the *incarnation*, literally "the infleshing."

This Word became something that he wasn't. He already existed; he was God's own agent in creation, but now he becomes a human being. And this human being, as the rest of the chapter shows, is Jesus. John's Gospel does not tell us that the Word merely clothed himself in animal humanity, or pretended to be human, or coexisted with a man called Jesus. Nor does it imagine that all of God is exhausted in Jesus (for then Jesus would not have had a heavenly Father to whom to pray!). The language is exquisitely precise: the Word became flesh; the Word, without ceasing to be the Word (and therefore God's own peer and God's own self, as we have seen), became a human being. Small wonder that Christians across the ages have referred to Jesus as the God-man.

Yet John's interest in the incarnation is not abstract or merely theoretical. Immediately he adds a few more lines to make us recall an Old Testament passage we have already read. Recalling that Old Testament passage will enable us to understand a little better the *significance* of the truth that the Word became flesh. The Old Testament passage is Exodus 32–34, which we looked at in chapter 4. Those chapters from Exodus detail what happens when Moses comes down from the mountain and the people are in an orgy of idolatry. Moses prays before God and wants to see more of God's glory:

> [18]Then Moses said, "Now show me your glory."
>
> [19]And the LORD said, "I will cause all my goodness to pass in front of you, and I will proclaim my name, the LORD, in your presence. I will have mercy on whom I will have mercy, and I will have compassion on whom I will have compassion. [20]But," he said, "you cannot see my face, for no one may see me and live."
>
> Exodus 33:18–20

The verses before us in John 1:14–18 pick up five major themes from these chapters in Exodus. You know what happens if you quote a line or two from a book or film that everyone around you knows: the entire scene comes back to mind. For whatever reason, my son has a formidable memory when it comes to movies, and so you simply drop in one line and he will happily describe the entire scene. For people steeped in the Bible, as many of the first readers were, something similar takes place when you quote a line from the Bible. So if you know the Bible like that, then when you read through John 1:14–18, your mind is going to go back to Exodus 32–34 because of five specific allusions in the John passage to the Exodus passage. *And that is what unpacks the significance of the truth that the Word became flesh.* Let me show you.

> [14]The Word became flesh and made his dwelling among us. We have seen his glory, the glory of the one and only Son, who came from the Father, full of grace and truth. [15](John testified concerning him. He cried out, saying, "This is he of whom I said, 'He who comes after me has surpassed me because he was before me.'") [16]Out of his fullness we have all received grace in place of grace already given. [17]For the law was given through Moses; grace and truth came through Jesus Christ. [18]No one has ever seen God, but the one and only Son, who is himself God and is in closest relationship with the Father, has made him known.
>
> John 1:14–18

1. TABERNACLE AND TEMPLE

"The Word became flesh and *made his dwelling* among us" (1:14)—the expression I have italicized is literally "he tabernacled among us." You cannot help but remember that the tabernacle is what God set up at the time of Sinai, a tabernacle with this special Most Holy Place where only the high priest could enter on behalf of himself and everybody else once a year with the blood of the sacrifices. It was the place where sinners met God, the great meeting place that brought together a holy God and rebellious human beings. That is what the tabernacle was, until the temple superseded it. Now we are told that when the Word became flesh, "he *tabernacled* among us." Again, in John's next chapter, Jesus insists that he himself is the ultimate temple of God (see John 2:19–21), the ultimate meeting place between human beings and God. It is as if he were saying, "If rebels are going to be reconciled to this holy God, they must come to him by means of the temple that God has ordained—and I am the temple."

2. GLORY

"We have seen his glory," John writes, "the glory of the one and only Son, who came from the Father, full of grace and truth" (1:14). "We have seen his *glory*"? What was it that Moses asked for?

> [18]Then Moses said, "Now show me your glory."
> [19]And the LORD said, "I will cause all my goodness to pass in front of you."
>
> Exodus 33:18–19

John plays with this theme of glory right through his book. In John 2, for example, when Jesus performs his first miracle—he turns water into wine at a wedding in Cana of Galilee—we are told at the end of the account that the disciples saw his glory: "What Jesus did here in Cana of Galilee was the first of the signs through which he revealed his glory" (2:11). The others saw the miracle; the disciples saw Jesus's glory. In other words, they saw that this was a *sign* that signified something about who Jesus was; they saw his glory. This kind of use of "glory" is repeated in John's Gospel. Then eventually you get to John 12, where Jesus is to manifest God's glory by going to the cross (see 12:23–33). So where is God's glory most manifested? In God's goodness— when Jesus is "glorified," lifted up and hung on a cross, displaying God's glory in the shame, degradation, brutality, and sacrifice of his crucifixion, and by this means returning to the glory he shared with the Father before the world began (see 17:5).

The most spectacular display of God's glory is in a bloody instrument of torture because that is where God's goodness was most displayed.

It is good to sing the "Hallelujah Chorus," but we must also sing, "On a hill far away stood an old rugged cross, the emblem of suffering and shame"—

because there God displayed his glory in Christ Jesus, who thus became our tabernacle, our temple, the meeting place between God and human beings.

3. Grace and Truth (Love and Faithfulness)

We are still reading John 1:14: "The Word became flesh and made his dwelling among us. We have seen his glory, the glory of the one and only Son, who came from the Father, *full of grace and truth*" (emphasis added).

When he intones who he is before Moses, who is hiding in that cave in Exodus 34, God describes himself in a variety of ways. Included among them are the words "abounding in [or full of] love and faithfulness" (34:6). In Hebrew, the pair of nouns translated "love and faithfulness" are equally appropriately rendered "grace and truth," which is the way John renders them. God displays himself not only as the God who will punish sinners but as the one who is "full of grace and truth" and forgives. Now John, reflecting on who Jesus is, this Jesus who manifests God's goodness, his glory in the cross, says that Jesus is "full of grace and truth," the grace and truth that brought him to the cross and paid for our sins.

4. Grace and Law

John adds, "Out of his fullness we have all received grace in place of grace already given" (1:16). That is exactly what the text says—but what does it mean? It does not mean "grace on top of grace" or "one grace after another," like Christmas presents piled up under a Christmas tree, one blessing after another. It means we have all received a grace in place of a grace already given. What does that mean? The next verse tells us: "For the law was given through Moses [which takes us back to Exod. 32–34]; grace and truth came through Jesus Christ" (1:17). In other words, the gift of the law was a gracious thing, a good and wonderful gift from God. But grace and truth par excellence came through Jesus Christ, not in the display of glory to Moses in a cave but in the display of Jesus and the bloody sacrifice on the cross. The law covenant was a gracious gift from God, but now Jesus is going to introduce a new covenant, the ultimate grace and truth. This is a grace that replaces that old grace. It is bound up with a new covenant.

5. Seeing God

"No one has ever seen God," John reminds us (1:18). Isn't that what God said in Exodus 33? "You cannot see my face, for no one may see me and live" (Exod. 33:20). Now John adds an exception: "But the one and only Son, who is himself God and is in closest relationship with the Father, has made him known" (John 1:18). Do you hear what this text is saying? Do you want to know what God looks like? Look at Jesus. "No one has ever seen God," and God in all of his transcendent splendor we still cannot see until the last day. But the Word became flesh; God became a human being with the name of Jesus; and we can see him. That is why Jesus later says to one of his own disciples (as we saw earlier in this chapter), "Don't you know me, Philip, even after I have been among you such a long time? Anyone who has seen me has seen the Father" (John 14:9).

Do you want to know what the character of God is like? Study Jesus. Do you want to know what the holiness of God is like? Study Jesus. Do you want to know what the wrath of God is like? Study Jesus. Do you want to know what the forgiveness of God is like? Study Jesus. Do you want to know what the glory of God is like? Study Jesus all the way to that wretched cross. Study Jesus.

Concluding Story

It may bring things together if I conclude with a story I have told on a number of occasions. My first degree was in chemistry and mathematics at McGill University in Montreal. Somewhere along the line I befriended a wonderful Pakistani gentleman. He was twice as old as I was. He had come to McGill to do a PhD in Islamic studies. (McGill had, and still has, a very fine Islamic institute.) He had left his wife and two children behind in Pakistan, so he was lonely. Over time I befriended him. After a while it dawned on me that he was trying to convert me to Islam. I thought that I should return the favor, but I soon found myself out of my depth in debate, for he was a trained Muslim theologian while I was studying chemistry.

I remember walking with him one night down Mount Royal along University Avenue to Pine Avenue to catch a bus. He had agreed to come to church with me. He wanted to see what it was like. As we walked, he asked me, "Don, you study mathematics, yes?"

"Yes."

"If you have one cup and then you add another cup, how many cups do you have?"

Well, I was taking some mathematics courses, so I said, "Two."

"If you have two cups and you add another cup, how many cups do you have?"

I said, "Three."

"If you have three cups, and you take away one cup, how many cups do you have?"

I said, "Two." So far I was hitting on all cylinders.

So he said, "You believe that the Father is God?"

"Yes." Uh oh, I could see where this was going.

"You believe that Jesus is God?"

"Yes."

"You believe that the Holy Spirit is God?"

"Yes."

"So if you have one God plus one God plus one God, how many gods do you have?"

I was studying chemistry, not theology. How was I supposed to answer that? The best I could do was say, "Listen, if you are going to use a mathematical model, then let me choose the branch of mathematics. Let's talk about infinities. Infinity plus infinity plus infinity equals what? Infinity. I serve an infinite God."

He laughed good-naturedly. That was the level of our discussion and friendship. About November it suddenly dawned on me that he had never read the Christian Bible. He did not own one; he had never held one in his hands. So I bought him a Bible. He asked, "Where do I start?"

He did not know how it was put together. He did not know about the Old Testament and the New Testament; he did not know about the Gospels. And I did not know what to suggest to him. So I said, "Well, why don't you start with John's Gospel?" I showed him where it was, right after Matthew, Mark, and Luke.

Coming, as he did, from Asia, he did not read books the way I would read a book. (How many pages can I get through tonight? The more the better!) No, he had a style of reading that proceeded slowly with many pauses for reflection, rereading, and wondering. And the passage he was beginning to think about was John's prologue.

That Christmas I brought him home to my parents' home, who at that point lived on the French side of our capital city, Ottawa, in a place called Hull. It transpired that my father had heart problems, and my mother and I spent most of our time in the hospital. My dear friend Muhammad was largely left on his own. By the end of that Christmas break, Dad was recovering nicely, so I asked to borrow the car so I could take Muhammad to see some of the sights in the capital city. We went here and there, and we ended up at our Parliament buildings. In those days there was much less security than there is now. We joined one of the guided tours—thirty of us being led around the buildings—to the rotunda at the rear where the library is, to the Senate chambers, to the House of Commons, to the rogues gallery of Canadian prime ministers from Sir John A. McDonald down, and so forth.

We finally returned to the central foyer, which is circled by some large pillars. At the top of each pillar is a little fresco where there is a figure, and the guide explained, as he pointed from one figure to the next, "There is Aristotle, for government must be based on knowledge. There is Socrates, for government must be based on wisdom. There is Moses, for government must be based on law." He went all the way around. Then he asked, "Any questions?"

My friend piped up, "Where is Jesus Christ?"

The guide did what guides do under such circumstances. They simply say, "I beg your pardon?"

So Muhammad did what foreigners do under such circumstances. They assume that they have been misunderstood because of their thick accent, so he articulated his question more clearly and more loudly: "Where is Jesus Christ?"

Now there were three groups in the foyer of the Canadian Parliament listening to a Pakistani Muslim ask where Jesus was. I was looking for a crack in the ground to fall into. I had no idea where this was coming from.

Finally the guide blurted out, "Why should Jesus be here?"

Muhammad looked shocked. Picking up a line from the Bible verses he had been reading, he said, "I read in the Christian Bible that the law was given through Moses but that grace and truth came through Jesus Christ. Where is Jesus Christ?"

The guide said, "I don't know anything about that."

And I muttered under my breath, "Preach it, brother."

Do you see how it looked to Muhammad? He was a Muslim. He understood about a God who has laws, who has standards, who brings terror, who sits in judgment over you, a God who is sovereign and holy and powerful. He understood all of that. But he had already been captured by Jesus, full of grace and truth, who displays his glory profoundly in the cross and becomes the meeting place between God and sinners because he dies the sinner's death.

8

The God Who Grants
New Birth

The Bible's storyline, we have discovered, has, from the opening chapters of Genesis, set up a massive tension—cosmic in scope but descending all the way down to the level of the individual. The tension is grounded in the fact that God made everything good. God himself, the Creator, is different from the creation, but all that he made was initially God-centered and good. The nature of evil is tied to revolution against this God. In Genesis 3, we saw how this is depicted as obsessive desire to challenge God—to become God ourselves, to usurp to ourselves the prerogatives that belong only to the Creator. Out of this idolatry come all of the social evils, the horizontal evils that we know.

With everybody wanting to be at the center of the universe, there can only be strife. I know full well that nobody goes around chanting, "I'm at the center of the universe." Yet if I were to hold up your high school or college graduation class photo and say, "Here's your graduation class photo," whose face do you look for first? Or suppose you have a really good knock-down, drag-out argument (a one-in-ten-years type). You go away from it seething. You remember all the things you could have said, all the things you should have said and would have said if only you had thought of them fast enough. Then you deploy all of these things as you replay the whole thing in your mind. Who wins?

In my time I have lost many arguments; I have never lost a rerun.

These sorts of reflections are the small indexes of how we want to prevail, how we want to control, how we want to be at the center. Even God—if he, she, or it exists—jolly well better serve me or I'll find another one, thank you. In other words, here is the beginning of all idolatry.

But if our life has come from God and now we view him as our enemy, what do we have but death? Yet instead of instantly wiping out rebels, the God of the Bible, in his sovereign mercy, acts in a variety of ways to restore large numbers of them. He calls out one man, Abraham, and his family. Although they are flawed through and through, God begins the process of starting a new humanity through them, establishing a covenant or agreement with Abraham and his descendants that anticipates what God is going to do to save men and women drawn from every tongue and tribe and nation around the world. In due course he shows what good law should be and how there needs to be sacrifice for sin. If the inevitable result of our revolt against God is death, then does not God's justice require some kind of death, even while this God forgives the sinner? So we witness the beginning of the sacrificial system as it was set up under the old covenant. Eventually God promises in due course a Redeemer, a Messiah, someone from the royal Davidic line. As the promises unfold in the Old Testament, this ultimate Davidic king is portrayed as more than just one more person with David's genes. For we are given glimpses that we recite with pleasure at Christmas:

> ⁶For to us a child is born,
>   to us a son is given,
>   and the government will be on his shoulders.
> And he will be called
>   Wonderful Counselor, Mighty God,
>   Everlasting Father, Prince of Peace.
> ⁷Of the increase of his government and peace
>   there will be no end.
>
>   Isaiah 9:6–7

The Lord God will give him the throne of his father David.

                                   Luke 1:32

An array of biblical texts promises a Davidic king who is nevertheless identified with God himself. So we glanced at some of the Old Testament promises that look forward to the time when the Word, God's own self-expression, becomes a human being, living for a while among us. He became flesh. In becoming flesh he ultimately became the one who is the perfect locus of grace and truth. No one has seen God at any time, but we have seen Jesus. Here is God as he has disclosed himself to us. He is the God who is there and who has disclosed himself. This Word made flesh is named—and his name is Jesus, Yahweh saves, for he came to save his people from their sins.

But so what? Precisely how does this help? So he comes. The God who is there has disclosed himself. How, precisely, does his coming help us? Granted the sweep of the Bible's storyline so far, this is what we need:

1. We need to be reconciled to God.
2. We need to be morally transformed, or else we will just keep on rebelling again and again.
3. We need all the effects of sin somehow to be reversed and overcome. That includes not only our relationships with one another but death itself. Otherwise death just keeps on winning. This is still a decaying universe. There is still betrayal, disappointment, pain, sorrow, and death.

All these things Jesus directly confronts. In other words, the Bible holds out the prospect of utter transformation. Biblical Christianity is much more than simply making a decision for Jesus so that we can live happy lives. We must be genuinely reconciled to the holy God who is there. We ourselves must be transformed—in measure right now, and for the rest of our lives, and ultimately with the kind of thorough transformation that leaves no hint of self-centeredness and death behind and leaves us swamped in sheer delight at the glory and centrality of God.

In large measure, that is where we are going in the rest of this book. We got as far as what Christians call the "incarnation"—the "in-fleshing" of the Word, God becoming a human being, a first-century Jewish human being by the name of Jesus. How, then, in line with the Bible, does he address the needs we have listed?

At least in part, he does so by granting us new birth.

Introduction to the New Birth

There are several passages in the New Testament that talk about the new birth, but I shall focus on John 3. John's Gospel is the fourth book of the New Testament. We should begin by reading the first fifteen verses of his third chapter.

> [1]Now there was a Pharisee, a man named Nicodemus who was a member of the Jewish ruling council. [2]He came to Jesus at night and said, "Rabbi, we know that you are a teacher who has come from God. For no one could perform the signs you are doing if God were not with him."
>
> [3]Jesus replied, "Very truly I tell you, no one can see the kingdom of God without being born again."
>
> [4]"How can anyone be born when they are old?" Nicodemus asked. "Surely they cannot enter a second time into their mother's womb to be born!"
>
> [5]Jesus answered, "Very truly I tell you, no one can enter the kingdom of God without being born of water and the Spirit. [6]Flesh gives birth to flesh, but the

Spirit gives birth to spirit. [7]You should not be surprised at my saying, 'You must be born again.' [8]The wind blows wherever it pleases. You hear its sound, but you cannot tell where it comes from or where it is going. So it is with everyone born of the Spirit."

[9]"How can this be?" Nicodemus asked.

[10]"You are Israel's teacher," said Jesus, "and do you not understand these things? [11]Very truly I tell you, we speak of what we know, and we testify to what we have seen, but still you people do not accept our testimony. [12]I have spoken to you of earthly things and you do not believe; how then will you believe if I speak of heavenly things? [13]No one has ever gone into heaven except the one who came from heaven—the Son of Man. [14]Just as Moses lifted up the snake in the wilderness, so the Son of Man must be lifted up, [15]that everyone who believes may have eternal life in him."

John 3:1–15

This language of new birth: what does it mean? I am old enough to remember when people drove Datsun automobiles. They were produced by the Nissan Motor company, but the base model was the Datsun. Then somewhere along the line they decided that they would change Datsun to Nissan, and all over America there were slogans about the "born-again Datsun." So what does born again mean? A name change?

Or sometimes a Democrat becomes a Republican, or the reverse; a liberal becomes a conservative or vice versa. Someone in the media will start chiding this "born-again" Republican or whatever.

Not too long ago a pollster by the name of Barna polled many self-described "born-again" folk. Of course, to conduct such a poll you have to define what born again means. He defined a born-again person as someone with a personal commitment to Jesus Christ that is still important to them today. To be admitted to the polling group they had to affirm things like "I have a personal commitment to Jesus Christ. It's important to me" and "I believe that I will go to heaven when I die. I have confessed my sins and accepted Jesus Christ as my Savior." When he had his group, Barna discovered, rather sadly, that the morals and way of life of these self-identified born-again people are not substantially different from those of the general public. He found that 26 percent of them did not think premarital sex is wrong. They are just as likely to divorce as are non-Christians. Research of this sort has generated book titles such as Ron Sider's *The Scandal of the Evangelical Conscience: Why Are Christians Living Just Like the Rest of the World?*[1]

So what is "new birth" or "regeneration" really about? Does it mean that you have changed your name? Your party affiliation? Undergone some sort of religious experience?

Not for a moment am I suggesting that the research of these pollsters is wrong. At the purely phenomenological level, it is doubtless disturbingly accurate. But to reach its conclusions it has horribly abused the "new birth" or "regeneration" language used by New Testament writers. The pollsters reason something like this: We'll find those who make a certain evangelical profession of faith; those who make such a profession we'll acknowledge to be born again. We'll plot their morals or lack of morals, and if we discover that their morals are no different from the morals of the broader culture, we will be forced to conclude that the new birth does not radically change people.

By contrast, the reasoning of the New Testament writers is something like this: The new birth is a powerful regeneration, by God himself, in the human life, such that those who have been born again are *necessarily* transformed. It follows that professing Christians whose lives are indistinguishable from those of unbelievers have no biblical ground for thinking they have been born again. The pollsters are running their logic in exactly the wrong direction.

Indeed to talk about the new birth as if it is primarily a metaphor for a specific religious commitment is slightly bizarre. The child about to be born does not make a commitment to come out of his mother's womb. As far as I know, it is the mother who is doing all the work and pushing the little tyke out. The source of new birth comes from the parents. New birth language is strangely chosen if it is primarily a way of referring to the commitment of the one so born.

As far as we know, born-again language was not used (as far as our sources show) in the Jewish world of Jesus's day until he invented the term. So it is important to try to find out what *he* meant by it if we are going to embrace some kind of born-again-ism or born-again theology. We shall proceed in three quite uneven points.

What Jesus Actually Said about Being Born Again (John 3:1–10)

We are introduced to a chap called Nicodemus, who is identified as a Pharisee. That means that he was from a conservative branch of first-century Judaism, a branch known and largely respected in the community for discipline, good deeds, and a certain kind of orthodoxy, though sometimes given to excessive rules. On top of his religious affiliation, he was a member of the Jewish ruling council; almost certainly that is referring to the Sanhedrin, the top council of seventy or seventy-two people who ruled the country under the Roman government. So this means that he belonged both to a specific religious/political party and to the political elite. This combination of political elite and religious elite put him at the top of a lot of heaps in the country. Jesus calls him "Israel's teacher" (John 3:10): the expression suggests that he was widely regarded as "*the* teacher of Israel," the distinguished professor of divinity. So he is politically and religiously connected, and he is learned and professorial. Later on in the book, it appears that he is probably connected with considerable wealth.

He comes to Jesus "at night" (John 3:2). Why? There have been many suggestions. Perhaps he did not want to show up in the day. He might have been a trifle embarrassed: after all, Jesus was a kind of itinerant teacher from the relatively despised area Galilee, complete with funny accent. How could Jesus stack up beside Nicodemus himself, the distinguished professor of divinity? Why would he approach an itinerant preacher to get some theological advice? But I confess I do not believe that theory for a moment. Nicodemus shows up several times in this book, and every time he doesn't really care what people think. He possesses an extraordinarily independent spirit. So why did Nicodemus come at night?

To understand what John means by faithfully recording that it was night, you have to see how John himself in his book uses the contrasts light and darkness, night and day. Doubtless the interview took place at night. But does John record the time merely to add factual detail? Almost certainly he does so because he likes to play with light/darkness and day/night polarities. Later on, for instance, when Jesus is betrayed, Jesus dismisses Judas, the man who betrays him. And as the man goes out, John comments, "And it was night" (13:30). It is as if John is saying, "He went out into horrible darkness and lostness without light and hope ever again."

If that is what is going on here, then the text is saying that when Nicodemus came to Jesus, doubtless during the night, he came with a certain kind of lostness. He did not even know how to approach Jesus properly. He was a bit baffled by him. That becomes pretty obvious as you read on. On the one hand, he approaches Jesus with a certain kind of respect. It is remarkable that this "teacher of Israel" approaches an itinerant provincial preacher and addresses him with the respectful "Rabbi" (3:2). Nevertheless his approach cannot hide a touch of arrogance. He says, "Rabbi, we know that you are a teacher who has come from God. For no one could perform the signs you are doing if God were not with him" (3:2).

We can start by asking why Nicodemus uses this "we." There is no indication that he has brought his students with him: "My class and I together, we have come to this conclusion." There is no hint that anybody else is there. It can scarcely be a royal "we." An editorial "we," perhaps? Later on we will observe that Jesus himself carefully draws attention to this slightly pretentious "we." It is almost impossible to avoid the conclusion that for all the formal respect Nicodemus displays toward Jesus, there is a little element of self-importance: "Rabbi, we have been examining you, and we have observed that you are not the run-of-the-mill religious teacher. There are all kinds of quacks out there who claim to do miracles, and they are all fraudulent, psychosomatic, or faddish. But we look at the kind of thing that you do, and we cannot deny that this is miraculous. The only explanation is that it is from God. So we have come to the conclusion, we have, that you are a teacher sent from God." That's what it sounds like.

In one sense the comment is commendable. At least Nicodemus is looking honestly at the phenomena; he is not simply dismissing Jesus as some sort of nutcase, one more religious quack. The ancient religious world had their quacks, of course, and we have our share today too. The kinds of things that Jesus did were a cut above, and Nicodemus was not going to deny the evident. And yet this editorial "we," this "we theologians," perhaps, or "we Pharisees," or "we the leaders of the Sanhedrin," does sound a bit pompous.

Then Jesus responds: "Very truly I tell you, no one can see the kingdom of God without being born again" (3:3). How is that in any sense a response to what Nicodemus said? Follow the sequence again: Nicodemus says, "We know that you are a teacher who has come from God. For no one could perform the signs you are doing if God were not with him," and Jesus replies, "Very truly I tell you, no one can see the kingdom of God without being born again" (3:2–3). What's the connection?

Some have suggested we are to assume something was left out, as if the conversation really went something like this: Nicodemus said, "We know that you are a teacher sent from God because nobody could do what you are doing unless God were with him. So tell us: are you the one who is going to bring in the coming kingdom? Are you the one who is going to make David's kingdom finally dawn?" And Jesus answered, "The crucial question is not whether I'm going to make the kingdom dawn *but* whether you're qualified to get in it." But that is an awful lot of material for John to leave out and for us to reinsert to make sense of the flow of the passage.

I suggest the connection is far simpler. You may recall that in one of the earlier chapters, chapter 5, I mentioned that the notion of "kingdom" can be quite diverse, depending on context. In broad terms, God's kingdom has to do with his dynamic reign, with his authority and power. Sometimes the specific reference is to his sweeping sovereignty, and sometimes it refers to the exercise of God's reign over the Israelites of the old covenant. There was a broad anticipation that eventually great David's greater son would come and introduce the long-awaited and restored kingdom. And now what does Nicodemus see? He sees Jesus doing miraculous signs that cannot be explained as the tricks of some quack. He sees this as God's reign, God's power. "We have come to the conclusion," he says, "that God is with you." This must be God's reign operating in some sense. Nicodemus is claiming to see something, to discern, perhaps, the coming of the promised kingdom. And Jesus says, "My dear Nicodemus, let me tell you the truth. You do not see a blessed thing. You cannot see the kingdom unless you are born again. You might see the miraculous signs, but you really do not understand their significance. You do not see the kingdom at all." In other words, what Jesus is doing is actually gently but firmly knocking down Nicodemus's pretentions. To see this kingdom, the kingdom that Jesus is introducing, you have to be born again, he says. That is the logical connection between verse 2 and verse 3.

Nicodemus replies with a bit of a sneer: "How can anyone be born when they are old? . . . Surely they cannot enter a second time into their mother's womb to be born!" (3:4). Some have tried to argue that Nicodemus here shows himself to be a rather thick professor of divinity. Does he really imagine that Jesus is seriously suggesting that you have to crawl back into your mother's tummy and start all over again? This reading means that he cannot see a metaphor when it is leaping out to strike him. He is just slow and literalistic. But that does not make any sense either. Nicodemus was not a stupid man. You do not get to be the teacher of Israel without being able to discern the odd metaphor that comes your way. I think that he is simply replying to Jesus in Jesus's own terms. It is as if Nicodemus is saying, "It is easy to promise a lot of things. You can promise that some will turn over a new leaf; you can promise fulfillment in marriage; you could say, 'If you want to get wealthy, follow me.' You can promise all kinds of things, but what you are promising is frankly over the top. You are promising too much. A new beginning? A new birth? How can anyone possibly start over? Time does not run backwards except in some sci-fi stories. You can't crawl back into your mother's womb and have another go at life. You are promising too much. How can any man be born again?"

In point of fact, hasn't this sentiment been expressed by many writers and poets over the years? The English nineteenth-century poet Alfred Lord Tennyson wrote, "Ah, for a man to arise in me / That the man I am may no longer be." The poet John Clare wrote, "If life had a second edition, how I would correct the proofs." But life does not have a second edition. How can you start over by being born again? Jesus seems to be saying, in effect: "What we need is new men and women, not new institutions. What we need is new lives, not new laws. What we need is new creatures, not new creeds. What we need is new people, not mere displays of power. And so from your vantage point, Nicodemus, you really do not see very much. You see the display of power, but you do not see the kingdom in any saving and transforming sense. You do not really understand what is going on at all."

"Jesus, you are encouraging the impossible. There is no new beginning. There is no new birth. Messianic figure you may be, but you are now promising too much."

But Jesus will not back down: "Very truly I tell you, no one can enter the kingdom of God without being born of water and the Spirit" (John 3:5).

What does Jesus mean by his more extended expression, "being born of water and the Spirit"? Over the generations people have understood this expression "born of water and the Spirit" in a large number of ways.

Some people think it refers to two births: natural birth plus some kind of spiritual birth. "Born of water" perhaps refers to the breaking of the water just before the birth. The two births, then, are natural birth followed by supernatural birth. One has to be born of water and of the Spirit.

I doubt that is what the expression means, partly because I have not been able to find anywhere in the ancient world that people spoke of natural birth as being born of water. Moreover, if you very carefully compare verse 3 with verse 5, you discover a crucial parallelism that helps to explain the passage:

Very truly I tell you, no one can *see* the kingdom of God without being born *again*.

> John 3:3, emphasis added

Very truly I tell you, no one can *enter* the kingdom of God without being born of *water and the Spirit*.

> John 3:5, emphasis added

The two sentences are parallel. Verse 5 exchanges "enter" for "see," but the idea in both cases is similar. More importantly, verse 5 moves from "born again" to "born of water and the Spirit." In other words, "born again" is parallel to "born of water and the Spirit." Thus, "born of water and the Spirit" does not signal two births, but one—that is, the entire expression "born of water and the Spirit" is parallel to "born again" and means the same thing. So what is Jesus adding or explaining about "born again" when he adds "born of water and the Spirit"?

There is one other small detail we must pick up before we conclude what it means. Down in verse 9, after Jesus has given his answer, Nicodemus still does not quite understand: "How can this be?" Jesus replies, "You are Israel's teacher . . . and do you not understand these things?" (3:10). "Israel's teacher," I've suggested, was probably a title. So what things *should* Nicodemus have understood because he was "Israel's teacher"? The focus of his expertise was what we call the Old Testament, the first two-thirds of the Bible, plus a large body of Jewish legal and other tradition. So the question becomes, "Where does the Old Testament talk about new birth? Why is Jesus holding Nicodemus responsible for understanding what Jesus is talking about?"

The reality is that nowhere does the Old Testament *explicitly* talk about "new birth."

Interestingly enough, however, in quite a few places it does talk about water and Spirit. In other words, when Jesus says, "The birth I am talking about is of water and Spirit," he expects Nicodemus to pick up on that sort of language because after all, he is Israel's teacher and is intimately familiar with the text of the Old Testament.

There are a number of Old Testament passages where water and Spirit are linked, but perhaps the most striking is found in the writings of a sixth century BC Old Testament prophet by the name of Ezekiel. In Ezekiel 36, God promises a time when he will transform his people. "I will sprinkle clean water on you, and you will be clean," indicating a moral cleaning (36:25). "And I will put my Spirit in you," indicating life and power from God himself (36:27). So whatever else this new birth is, if it is in line with the promise of a prophet six centuries earlier, it is bound up with the dawning of a new covenant that would be characterized by moral transformation (the water sprinkling the heart) and by the power and life of God to transform and renew. That is what Jesus means by a new birth of water and the Spirit.

Jesus is quick to explain a little further: "Flesh gives birth to flesh, but the Spirit gives birth to spirit. You should not be surprised at my saying, 'You must be born again'" (John 3:6–7). What he means by this is that like produces like: "Pigs give birth to pigs; cockroaches generate cockroaches; bats generate bats; kind produces kind; flesh produces flesh. So how on earth do you take lost, self-centered, human beings, and actually connect them with the life of God? You are not going to produce such transformation by natural selection. You are not going to generate moral revolution by merely trying harder or by selective breeding. What you really must have is what Ezekiel said: an act of God that does truly clean you up and that actually fills you with power from God himself, from his Spirit, so that we are changed, transformed. You must have that, or you cannot possibly be connected with the life of God. 'Flesh gives birth to flesh, but the Spirit gives birth to spirit. You should not be surprised at my saying, 'You must be born again.'"

Then he gives another analogy that depends in part on the fact that the word we translate "spirit" can also mean "wind," depending on the context. So in the original, it is a bit of a pun: "The wind [spirit] blows wherever it pleases. You hear its sound, but you cannot tell where it comes from or where it is going. So it is with everyone born of the Spirit [wind]" (3:8). Perhaps Jesus and Nicodemus are standing on a street corner in Jerusalem, and a sycamore branch is swaying in the evening breeze or a tumbleweed dances down the street. Jesus nods at these phenomena and says, in effect, "Do you see the effect of the wind/spirit? Do you really know where it comes from?" Even then they knew something of meteorology but not all that much—a good deal less than we know today. Nobody was sitting around thinking, "There must be a high in the Arabian desert. Is this cyclonic or anti-cyclonic? Where is the line between the depression and the high pressure air mass?" Nobody was thinking in such terms. But that doesn't mean that people denied the existence and power of wind! They saw the effects. They might not have been able to explain all of the dynamics and all of the physical forces that brought this wind about, but they could not deny the effects.

Then Jesus concludes, "So it is with everyone born of the Spirit" (3:8). Understand this: you and I may not be able to explain all the mechanics of new birth. From the Bible we may study passages like this one and a handful of others that talk about new birth, and doubtless we can infer quite a few things about how this new birth works. But at the end of the day, we will not possess a full analysis of how God works powerfully within us to transform us. *Nevertheless, where there is genuine new birth you always see the results.* You can't deny them. "So it is with everyone born of the Spirit" (3:8). That is why Barna's interpretation of "born again" is so abysmally off base. New birth has not necessarily taken place because "somebody's made a commitment to Jesus." Where there is new birth—where it has genuinely come from God—you will see transformation. You will see change in the life. That does not mean that people have suddenly reached perfection: we shall have more Christian growth and Christian failures in due course. But where new birth takes place, there is a change of direction, of origin. There is a cleaning up in the life. There is a transformation. There is the beginning of life from God himself that shapes our existence in a new direction.

"So it is with everyone who is born of the Spirit. And, my dear Nicodemus, you cannot see the kingdom, the real power of God, and you cannot enter this kingdom unless you are born again. That is what you must have. You must be born again."

This passage is dead-set against those who think that Christianity is a matter of ritual or religious practice or mysticism or conventional morality. The Bible keeps saying these kinds of things. The same writer, John, who reports this exchange between Jesus and Nicodemus, also wrote several letters that have been included in the New Testament. In one of them, the one we call 1 John, he keeps saying things like this: "Unless you obey Jesus's words, you really have no part in it. You are not a Christian. Unless you love the brothers and sisters, you cannot possibly have been born again. Unless you overcome the worldliness around you, your life shows you have never experienced the new birth" (see 1 John 2:29; 4:7; 5:4, 18). The new birth signals more than a profession of faith; it signals transforming power.

In the eighteenth century there was a very famous preacher (probably the most famous preacher in the Western world at the time) named George Whitefield. He was a Brit, but he sailed across the Atlantic thirteen times (taking six weeks to three months), so he became as famous a preacher in the thirteen colonies as he was on the English side. He preached to vast crowds without a PA system. He must have had spectacular lungs and vocal chords. Again and again, he preached from this text, "You must be born again," until finally somebody got really ticked with him, cornered him one day, and asked, "Mr. Whitefield, why is it that you keep preaching again and again, 'You must be born again. You must be born again'?"

"Because, sir," Whitefield replied, "you must be born again."

For unless you are born again, you will not enter into this saving, transforming kingdom of God, this dawning kingdom of David's son. Here is the culmination of the Old Testament's story coming to a focus in Jesus, and if you have not been born again you will not participate in it.

This is what Jesus says about the new birth.

Why Jesus Could Speak about Being Born Again (John 3:11–13)

What gave Jesus the authority to speak like that?

> [11]Very truly I tell you, we speak of what we know, and we testify to what we have seen, but still you people do not accept our testimony. [12]I have spoken to you of earthly things and you do not believe; how then will you believe if I speak of heavenly things? [13]No one has ever gone into heaven except the one who came from heaven—the Son of Man.
>
> John 3:11–13

Now initially this passage may strike us as a bit strange. Have you noticed how Jesus begins with the first person plural: "*we* speak of what *we* know, and *we* testify to what *we* have seen, but still you people do not accept *our* testimony" (3:11, emphasis added)? Then in the next verse he switches to the first person singular: "*I* have spoken to you of earthly things and you do not believe; how then will you believe if *I* speak of heavenly things?" (3:12, emphasis added). Why does Jesus begin with the first person plural?

I suspect it is because he is answering Nicodemus in his own terms. Nicodemus said, "Rabbi, *we* know that you are a teacher who has come from God, we do." Jesus now smiles toward the end of this exchange and comments, "Nicodemus, *we* know one or two things too, we do, because quite frankly no one has been to heaven to describe what goes on in the throne room of God. No one has come back to tell us. But that is where I come from."

Make no mistake: the reason that Jesus can speak so bluntly about the new birth is grounded in a claim to revelation, that is, a claim that what he is teaching is revelation from God himself. This is not one more theologian protecting his corner among theologians who like to squabble and write books. This is the word of someone who claims to have come from the very presence of God, God's own peer, God's own self—which is of course exactly what we saw in the last chapter. He is God's Word, God's own self-expression, one with God, truly God, in this complexity of one God who has become a human being—Jesus has come from there, so he speaks with the authority of revelation.

He says, in effect, "Nicodemus, if I were to try to depict the throne room of God for you in all of its spectacular, transcendent glory, you would not have a clue what I would be talking about. You are having a hard enough time believing anything I say when I describe things that take place on earth—things like the new birth." After all, that is where the new birth takes place. It takes place on earth. That is what Jesus means by "earthly things." "If you do not believe when I talk about earthly things—things that take place down here on earth, like the new birth—how are you possibly going to believe if I start describing to you the glories of the transcendent God?"

At the end of the day, to understand Christianity, sooner or later you must come to grips with Christianity's revelation claims. What do you do with Jesus, who claims to come from God, to be one with God, who gives you information about things that you cannot otherwise have information about? No one has made a trip there, taken notes, come back, and filed a report. This is either true, or it is the most unmitigated garbage, blasphemous silliness. But there is no way that you can walk away from this thinking, "Well, Jesus is a nice, moralizing teacher." The reason why Jesus could speak about being born again with the authority and confidence he displayed is bound up in his identity. To dismiss what he says is to deny who he is.

How Jesus Brings about This New Birth (John 3:14–15)

Clearly in this context the eternal life of which Jesus speaks must be the product of new birth. If you have new birth, you have life, and this life is *eternal* life. How do you get it? What Jesus says in verses 14–15 might have made more sense to Nicodemus than initially it makes to us because Nicodemus, for all his strengths and weaknesses, did know the Old Testament. Jesus here alludes to an Old Testament passage that some of us won't know anything about: "Just as Moses lifted up the snake in the wilderness, so the Son of Man must be lifted up, that everyone who believes may have eternal life in him" (John 3:14–15).

The passage to which Jesus is referring, which of course Nicodemus would have picked up on because he knew his Old Testament, is found in the fourth book of the Bible: Numbers. It is a very short account:

> [4]They [i.e., the Israelites, who had now escaped from slavery in Egypt but had not reached their own land] traveled from Mount Hor along the route to the Red Sea, to go around Edom. But the people grew impatient on the way; [5]they spoke against God and against Moses, and said, "Why have you brought us up out of Egypt to die in the wilderness? There is no bread! There is no water! And we detest this miserable food!"
>
> [6]Then the LORD sent venomous snakes among them; they bit the people and many Israelites died. [7]The people came to Moses and said, "We sinned when we spoke against the LORD and against you. Pray that the LORD will take the snakes away from us." So Moses prayed for the people.
>
> [8]The LORD said to Moses, "Make a snake and put it up on a pole; anyone who is bitten can look at it and live." [9]So Moses made a bronze snake and put it up on a pole. Then when anyone was bitten by a snake and looked at the bronze snake, they lived.
>
> Numbers 21:4–9

That is all that is said, the entire account. The nature of the murmuring and grumbling, the whining and complaining, was bound up with a profound dissatisfaction with God. Once again all the way back in Genesis 3 we find the pattern set: you make your own rules, you become your own god, you decide your own destiny, you do not trust God, you do not delight in God or his sovereign care or depend on him for anything, you merely dictate to God, and if you cannot have your own way, you whine and complain. This spells death all over again. And so they die. If they are to escape this snake-induced death, only God can provide the solution. His solution is a plain, flat-out miracle. God tells Moses to cast a bronze snake and stick it up on a pole. Those who have the venom in them will look at the bronze snake and live. How bizarre! Nothing about, "Make sure you say enough ritual 'Hail Marys.' Make sure you do a lot of penance. Lash yourself with some whips to show that you are really sorry. Fast. Do a lot of good works." None of that.

It is as if God is saying, "Will you not learn? You people provide the sin. I provide life. You provide the death and the destruction. I provide the forgiveness. The only way out of this sentence of death is not by digging yourself out but by the provision that I myself make. You look at my provision, and you live." That is the entire account.

A millennium and a half later, Jesus says, in effect, "Just as Moses lifted up the snake in the desert and as a result people lived, so the Son of Man [one of Jesus's ways of referring to himself] will be lifted up." He is now referring to his crucifixion on another stick, another pole, a cross-shaped pole, that those who look to him, those who believe in him, will live. How could it be any other way? We have already seen that we cannot barter with God. We cannot offer him something and make a trade. If people are healed, if people gain eternal life, it is going to be the result of his sovereign grace: there is no other way. The point is frequently made in the Bible, and it was modeled for them again in the episode of the cast bronze serpent. Now that pattern comes to its climactic fulfillment in Jesus. On his cross Jesus provided the means by which we have new birth. By his death we have life. By his crucifixion on a pole, we begin eternal life. The new birth is grounded in Jesus's death. That is what Jesus is saying. You and I receive the benefit of this not by trying harder or by being ultra-religious but by believing in Jesus.

Conclusion

There is much more to say about what moves God to send his own Son to die our death and bring about our new birth. The following verses in John ground God's motives in his unfathomable love. That is what we must explore in the next chapter.

9

The God Who Loves

Although we shall shortly return to John 3 and the account of Nicodemus, I want to begin this chapter by reflecting a little more generally on the love of God.

Why People Today Find It Easy to Believe in God's Love

If there is one thing that our world thinks it knows about God—if our world believes in God at all—it is that he is a loving God. That has not always been the case in human history. Many people have thought of the gods as pretty arbitrary, mean-spirited, whimsical, or even malicious. That is why you have to appease them. Sometimes in the history of the church Christians have placed more emphasis on God's wrath or his sovereignty or his holiness, all themes that are biblical in some degree or another. God's love did not receive as much attention. But today, if people believe in God at all, by and large they find it easy to believe in God's love.

Yet being comfortable with the notion of the love of God has been accompanied by some fairly spongy notions as to what love means. Occasionally you will hear somebody saying something like this: "It's Christians I don't like. I mean, God is love, and if everybody were just like Jesus, it would be wonderful. Jesus said, 'Judge not that you be not judged.' You know, if we could all just be nonjudgmental and be loving the way Jesus was loving, then the world would be a better place." There is an assumption there about the nature of love, isn't there? Love is nonjudgmental. It does not condemn anyone. It lets everybody do whatever they want. That is what love *means*.

Of course, it is sadly true that sometimes Christians—God help us—are mean. Certainly it is true that Jesus said, "Do not judge, or you too will be judged" (Matt. 7:1). But when he said this, did he really mean, "Do not make any morally discriminating judgments?" Why then does he give so many commands about telling the truth? Don't such commands stand as condemnation of lies and liars? Jesus commanded us to love our neighbors as ourselves: doesn't that constitute an implicit judgment on those who don't? In fact, in the very text where Jesus says, "Do not judge, or you too will be judged," he goes on to say just five verses later, "Do not give dogs what is sacred; do not throw your pearls to pigs" (Matt. 7:6), which means that somebody has to figure out who the swine are.

In other words, when Jesus says something as important as "Do not judge, or you too will be judged," there is a context to be understood. Jesus, after all, cuts an astonishingly high moral swath through his time. So if people think "Do not judge, or you too will be judged" means that Jesus is abolishing all morality and leaving all such questions up to the individual, they have not even begun to understand who Jesus is. Jesus *does* condemn the kind of judgment that is judgmental, self-righteous, or hypocritical. He condemns such judgment repeatedly and roundly. But there is no way on God's green earth that he is condemning moral discernment or the priority of truth. In any case, there is more to God's love, to Jesus's love, than avoiding judgmentalism.

That means that when we think of God's love, we need to think of God's other attributes too—his holiness, truthfulness, glory (his manifestation of his spectacular being and loveliness), and all the rest—and think through how all of them work together all the time. Sadly, precisely because our culture finds it relatively easy to believe that God is a God of love, we have developed notions of God's love that are disturbingly spongy and sentimental and almost always alienated from the full range of the attributes that make God, God.

Five Different Ways the Bible Speaks of the Love of God

My little book *The Difficult Doctrine of the Love of God* tries to lay out (among other things) five different ways the Bible speaks of the love of God. Let me quickly run through them with you. I hasten to insist that these are different ways that the Bible speaks of the love of God, not five different *kinds* of love.

1. There is love of God—I don't know how else to say this—within the Godhead, within the Triune God. The Bible explicitly speaks of the love of the Father for his Son and the love of the Son for the Father. Two chapters back we noted that John's Gospel, the fourth book in the New Testament, says that the Father loves the Son and has placed everything into his hands (see John 3:35) and has determined that all should honor the Son even as they honor

the Father (see John 5:23). Explicitly, then, the Bible says the Father loves the Son. It also tells us, equally explicitly, that the Son loves the Father and always does whatever pleases him (see John 14:31). Why Jesus goes to the cross is first of all because he loves his Father and does his Father's will. This love within the Godhead (what people call God's intratrinitarian love—if God can be referred to as the Trinity, then what we are thinking of is the love that flows among the members of the Godhead, of the Trinity) is a love that is perfect. Each person of the Trinity finds the others adoringly, perfectly lovable. It is not as if the Father says to the Son, "Frankly, you really are a hopeless case, but I love you anyway." The Son is perfectly lovely, and the Father is perfectly lovely, and they love each other perfectly. This is one way the Bible speaks of God's love.

2. God's love can refer to his general care over his creation. God sends his sun and his rain upon the just and the unjust. That is to say, it is providential and nondiscriminating. It is an amoral love (not an immoral love). He sustains both the godly and the ungodly. In fact, in the Sermon on the Mount, Jesus can use God's providential love to draw out a moral lesson. He says, in effect, "If God sends his sun and his rain upon both the righteous and the unrighteous, then why should you be making all these terribly fine distinctions between who is your friend and who is your enemy, choosing to love only your friends while hating your enemies?" (see Matt. 5:44–47). So there is a sense in which God's love generously extends to friend and foe alike. Here is a second way in which the Bible speaks of God's love.

3. Sometimes the Bible speaks of God's love in a kind of moral, inviting, commanding, yearning sense. So you find God addressing Israel in the Old Testament when the nation is particularly perverse, saying, in effect, "Turn, turn, why will you die? The Lord has no pleasure in the death of the wicked" (see Ezek. 18:23, 32; 33:11). He is that kind of God.

4. Sometimes God's love is selective. It chooses one and not another. "I have loved Jacob, but Esau I have hated" (Mal. 1:2–3). This is very strong language. In remarkable passages in Deuteronomy 7 and 10, God raises the rhetorical question as to *why* he chose the nation of Israel. He ticks off the possibilities. Because they are more numerous? No. Because they are more mighty? No. Because they are more righteous? No. He set his affection on them because he loved them—that is, he loved them because he loved them. He did not love all the other nations just the same way. In the context, God sets his affection on Israel as opposed to the other nations because he loved Israel. It is his sovereign choice.

5. Once God is in connection with his own people—usually this means he has entered into a covenant-based relationship with them—then his love is often presented as conditional. Consider, for example, the second-to-last book of the Bible, a little one-page book called Jude. Jude, a half-brother of Jesus, writes, "Keep yourselves in God's love" (Jude 21), which shows that

you might not keep yourself in God's love. In such passages there is a moral conditionality to being loved by God. Indeed there are a lot of passages in both Testaments where God's love or Jesus's love for us is in some sense conditional on our obedience. Even the Ten Commandments are partly shaped by conditionality: God shows his love, he says, "to a thousand generations of those who love me and keep my commandments" (Exod. 20:6). So there are contexts in the Bible where God's love is cast in conditional terms.

Do you see how subtle this necessarily becomes? Inevitably one starts asking how these different ways of talking about God's love fit together. It helps to think of human analogies. I could say with a straight face, "I love riding my motorcycle, I love woodwork, and I love my wife." But if I put all three together in the same sentence too often, my wife, quite understandably, will not be pleased. And they really have different weight. Or again, I can say, "I love my children unconditionally." I have a daughter in California who works with disadvantaged kids. If instead she became a hooker on the streets of LA, I think I'd love her anyway. She is my daughter. I love her unconditionally. I have a son who is a Marine, and if instead he started selling heroin on the streets of New York, I think I'd love him anyway. He is my son. I love him unconditionally. Yet in another context when they were just kids learning to drive, if I said to one of them, "Make sure you are home by midnight," and they weren't, they faced the wrath of Dad. In that sense my love was quite conditional on their obeying me and getting the car home on time.

In other words, despite the fact that we are dealing with the same kids and the same dad, the different contexts change the use of the love language. It was not that my love for them, in one sense, became less unconditional, for there is a framework in which that love remains constant. But there can be another framework where agreements and family responsibilities prevail—or, in biblical terms, covenantal obligations—and here the dynamics change somewhat.

Christians have been known to advance such clichés as "God loves everybody just the same." True or false? It depends! There are contexts in which the Bible casts God's love as amoral. He sends his sun and his rain upon the righteous and the unrighteous: in that context he loves everybody just the same. But there are other contexts where God's love is said to be conditional on our obedience, and still others where it is grounded in God's own sovereign choice. In such contexts, God does *not* love everybody just the same.

"You can't do anything to make God love you any more." True or false? It depends! In some contexts this is gloriously and absolutely true, because at the end of the day you cannot earn God's love. Yet there are different contexts in which God's love is spoken of as conditional. The main lesson to learn at this juncture is that we must be careful not to make silly mistakes as we read the biblical text by taking one verse out of its context, universalizing it, and remaining blind to the wonderful diversity of ways in which the Bible speaks of God's love.

At this juncture we must return to the report of Jesus's encounter with Nicodemus.

John 3:16–21

In the last chapter we worked our way through the exchange between Jesus and Nicodemus over the new birth. We saw that toward the end of it, Christ claimed special revelation: he could speak authoritatively about our need for this new birth and about the powerful, transforming effect it has, reconciling us to God and reorienting our lives, precisely because he himself came from heaven. Moreover, to provide an explanation of the *basis* on which people are reconciled to God, Jesus provided an analogy drawn from the Old Testament—Moses lifting up the bronze snake on a pole—showing that everyone who believes may have eternal life in him. That brings us to John 3:16–21, which tells us of God's own motives in pursuing men and women with such regenerating power:

> [16]For God so loved the world that he gave his one and only Son, that whoever believes in him shall not perish but have eternal life. [17]For God did not send his Son into the world to condemn the world, but to save the world through him. [18]Whoever believes in him is not condemned, but whoever does not believe stands condemned already because they have not believed in the name of God's one and only Son. [19]This is the verdict: Light has come into the world, but people loved darkness instead of light because their deeds were evil. [20]All those who do evil hate the light, and will not come into the light for fear that their deeds will be exposed. [21]But those who live by the truth come into the light, so that it may be seen plainly that what they have done has been done in the sight of God.
>
> John 3:16–21

Let me draw some inferences from this passage and related ones.

1. In the Bible It Is Simply Astonishing That God Loves Us

By and large this is not the way we think, but the Bible delights to marvel at God's love. The reason we do not think this way is twofold: not only do we think that God *ought* to love (it is the one thing widely accepted in our culture) but "he especially ought to love *me* because I'm nice and neighborly and maybe even cute. I don't beat up on people. I'm a pretty decent bloke. Of course God will love me. I mean, there's nothing in me not to love, is there?" But this is already so far removed from the storyline of Scripture that we have to rethink it again. Let me come in from the side door, using an illustration I have sometimes used with university students.

Bob and Sue are walking down a beach. It's the end of the academic year. The sun has made the sand warm. They kick off their sandals and feel the wet sand squish between their toes. He takes her hand, and he says, "Sue, I love you. I really do." What does he mean? He could mean a lot of things. He may simply mean that his hormones are jumping and he wants to go to bed with her. But the least that he means is that he is attracted to her. He certainly does not mean that he finds her unlovely but loves her anyway. When he says "I love you," he is in part saying that he finds her lovable, and if he has any sort of romantic twist, this is when it is likely to come out. "Sue, the color of your eyes—I could just sink into them. The smell of your hair, the dimples when you smile—there's nothing about you I don't love. Your personality—it is so wonderful. You're such an encourager. You've got this laugh that can fill a whole room with smiles, it's so contagious. Sue, I love you." What he does not mean is this: "Sue, quite frankly, you are the most homely creature I know. Your bad breath could stop a herd of rampaging elephants. Your knees remind me of a crippled camel. You have the personality of Genghis Khan. You don't have any sense of humor. You're a miserable, self-righteous, narcissistic, hateful woman, and I love you." When he declares his love for her, in part he is declaring that at that moment he finds her lovely. Isn't that correct?

Now God comes along in John 3:16: "God so loved the world." What is God saying to the world? "World, I love you"? Is he saying, "World, your scintillating personality, your intelligent conversation, your wit, your gift—and you're cute! I love you! I can't imagine heaven without you." Is that what he's saying? In other words, when God says, "I love you," is he declaring the loveable-ness of the world? There are a lot of psychologists who use the love of God in exactly that way. If God says, "I love you," it must be that "I'm okay, you're okay; God says we're okay. He loves us; it must be because we're lovable."

Biblically that is a load of nonsense. The word "world" in John's Gospel typically refers not to a big place with a lot of people in it but to a bad place with a lot of bad people in it. The word "world" in John's Gospel is this human-centered, created order that God has made and that has rebelled against him in hatefulness and idolatry, resulting in broken relationships, infidelity, and wickedness. That is why already in the first verses of this Gospel, in a passage we looked at two chapters back, the so-called prologue of John's Gospel (John 1:1–18), we read, "He was in the world, and though the world was made through him, the world did not recognize him" (1:10). It is why we read in this passage, a little farther on, "This is the verdict: Light has come into the world, but people loved darkness instead of light because their deeds were evil" (3:19). That is, with the coming of Jesus comes God's gracious self-disclosure, his revelation, light that is good and clean and pure—but people love darkness instead of light. People do not want to be exposed to that kind of light. All it does is show the dirt.

But the text says, "God so loved the world"—this broken and fallen world. It is as if God is saying to the world, "Morally speaking, you are the people of the crippled knees. You are the people of the moral bad breath. You are the people of the rampaging Genghis Khan personality. You are hateful and spiteful and murderous. And you know what? I love you anyway—not because you are so lovable but because I am that kind of God." That is why in the Bible, this side of Genesis 3, God's love is always marveled at. God's love is wonderful, surprising, in some ways not the way it ought to be. Why doesn't he just condemn us instead?

2. The Measure of God's Love for Us Is Jesus

"For God so loved the world that he gave his one and only Son" (John 3:16). You must understand that John's Gospel is rich in expressions that talk about the love of the Father for the Son and the love of the Son for the Father. There is a wonderful chapter, John 17, that is sometimes called "Jesus's high priestly prayer," where there is a kind of extended meditation on the fact that in eternity past the Father loved the Son in a perfection of love. And in return, the Son loved the Father in a perfection of love, past our wildest, most generous imaginations.

We have already seen that the God who is there does not need us. He exercised and enjoyed a perfection of love in eternity past. Then when he did make us, we thumbed our noses at him and wanted to become God ourselves. God chooses to love this lost and self-destructing "world" (to use one of John's favored expressions) in a yearning, inviting way. Elsewhere John can talk about God's peculiar relationship with his own people, speaking of them as those the Father has given to the Son (see for example 6:37–40). We have already seen that the Bible can talk about God's love in a variety of ways. In this immediate context, the object of God's love is the "world"—men and women, every ethnicity, Jews and Gentiles, but all lost in our wretched determination to cut ourselves off from the God who is there—and he loves us in any case. It is astonishing. And the measure of this love is Jesus, this Jesus who, before he became Jesus, as the eternal Son, the eternal Word, was already one with the Father in a perfect circle of love in eternity past. Now the Father gives his Son for us. That is how much he chooses to love us. God in essence gives himself.

Indeed, when we say that the measure of God's love for us is Jesus, we really mean two things:

First, what did giving Jesus cost the Father? You who are parents, would you *gladly* give your child so that others might be spared death? Even such love is the exchange of a child for a peer, a fellow human being. But God the Father gives his Son over to death for the benefit of mere creatures, ungrateful and self-centered creatures at that.

Second, what love does Jesus himself show? The measure of God's love for us is Jesus. If you want to see the full measure of God's love, watch Jesus.

Let me remind you of half a dozen instances in Jesus's life, reported in other texts in the New Testament that speak of God's love or Jesus's love.

You find him with a heart as big as eternity as he looks out on a crowd that seems leaderless, spiritually empty, and lost. He calls them sheep without a shepherd, and, the text says, he has compassion on them (see Matt. 9:36).

You find him playing with little children and even setting up little children as a kind of model for what his own disciples should be: childlike in their approach to Jesus. Little children do not come to someone who is angry. Yet in the Gospels we find them playing with Jesus and jumping all over him, and he says, "Let the little children come to me" (Matt. 19:14).

Or there is this wonderful passage in Matthew 12. He quotes some words pertaining to himself from the prophet Isaiah (over seven hundred years earlier):

> [18]Here is my servant whom I have chosen,
>   the one I love, in whom I delight;
> I will put my Spirit on him,
>   and he will proclaim justice to the nations.
> [19]He will not quarrel or cry out;
>   no one will hear his voice in the streets.
> [20]A bruised reed he will not break,
>   and a smoldering wick he will not snuff out,
> till he leads justice to victory.
>   [21]In his name the nations will put their hope.
>
> Matthew 12:18–21

Can you envision these images? A candle: the flame goes out, and instead of squeezing out the smoldering wick, he fans it back into flame. Or we have a reed by the side of a lake, a place where red-winged blackbirds flock, and it is bruised—not very strong; yet he does not snap it off; he builds it up. These are powerful ways of saying that his love is gentle, edifying, compassionate.

Even when he is denouncing people for their sins, sometimes in very strong language (he actually says to some people, "You hypocrites! You blind guides! You snakes! You brood of vipers!" in Matt. 23:15–16, 33), at the end of his denunciation you find him weeping over the city. There are some preachers in literature like Elmer Gantry who are quick to denounce, but they are hypocrites. There is a kind of moralizing preaching that denounces and criticizes and is upset by moral decay, but it is always angry. It is never characterized by tears of compassion. That heartlessness never characterized Jesus.

One of the really wonderful things about the demonstration of Jesus's love is the way he addresses individuals where they are, without some mere one-size-fits-all formula. A rich young man whose money is his god is told he must sell all he has and give the proceeds to the poor. But that is not what Jesus tells a Samaritan woman he meets at a well. He tells her to fetch her husband, and of course she cannot do it, for she has burned through five husbands and is currently living with a man who is not her husband: she must address the barrier of her broken relationships. The Gentile leader with a child whose life is threatened, the broken woman who washes Jesus's feet, the apostle who publicly disowns Jesus—in every case the Master's love is not only profound but pointed and shaped to address personal needs most accurately.

Equally wonderful is the way Jesus comes to those bowed down with the cares of life and says, "Come to me, all you who are weary and burdened, *and I will give you rest*. Take my yoke upon you and learn from me, for I am gentle and humble in heart, and you will find rest for your souls. For my yoke is easy and my burden is light" (Matt. 11:28–30, emphasis added). A theme of rest traces its own trajectory through the Bible. As God "rested" at the end of creation, as God commands in the Ten Commandments a Sabbath day for his people to rest, so the ultimate rest is secured in Jesus—a theme greatly expanded later in the New Testament (see Hebrews 3–4). This rest that God provides is a function of God's love for his people.

Then you find him on the cross. Did you see the film by Mel Gibson, *The Passion of the Christ*? A lot of the physical suffering was pretty accurately depicted. Whipped and beaten and broken, Jesus cries, "Father, forgive them, for they do not know what they are doing" (Luke 23:34). And that physical torment was not in any sense the whole of his suffering: as he bore the guilt and punishment of others, he experienced the deepest sense of abandonment by his heavenly Father (see Matt. 27:45–46).

For some of the New Testament writers, so moving is this love of God as shown in Christ Jesus that it is not uncommon for them to break out in delight at the theme. They may be describing something in precise theological expressions which make them think of the cross, and then they suddenly burst out with another joyful reiteration of their awareness of his love. For example, in one of Paul's letters, a letter to the Galatian Christians, he works through some deep material on what the cross achieved, what "justification" is (something we'll pick up two chapters from now), and then, as he mentions Jesus's death, he breaks out, "who loved me and gave himself for me" (Gal. 2:20). Elsewhere, when he is praying for another group of believers (this time in the city of Ephesus), the apostle Paul tells them *what* he prays for them, what he asks God for on their behalf. He mentions one or two things, and then he adds that he prays that they "may have power, together with all the Lord's people, to grasp how wide and long and high and deep is the love of Christ" (Eph. 3:18), using spatial metaphors to depict its limitless dimensions. Then he uses paradox: "to know this love that surpasses knowledge" (Eph. 3:19), that is, to know this love that is not knowable, that is past finding out, that is past knowledge—to know it, to experience it. The reason why Paul prays for this, Paul tells the Ephesians, is "that you may be filled to the measure of all the fullness of God" (Eph.

3:19)—that's an expression that means, roughly, "in order that you might be just as full as God will make you, perfectly mature; you cannot be a genuinely mature human being until you are richly aware that you are awash in the love of God expressed in Christ Jesus. And that's what I pray for you."

The measure of God's love for us is Jesus.

3. The Purpose of God's Love for Us Is That We Might Have Life

Look at the language of John 3:16–18:

> [16]For God so loved the world that he gave his one and only Son, that whoever believes in him *shall not perish but have eternal life*. [17]For God did not send his Son into the world *to condemn* the world, but *to save* the world through him. [18]Whoever believes in him is not condemned, but whoever does not believe stands condemned already because they have not believed in the name of God's one and only Son.
>
> John 3:16–18, emphasis added

Notice the pairs: (1) shall not perish versus shall have eternal life; (2) not to condemn the world versus to save the world. These are the opposites. The purpose of God's love for us is clear and directed. Occasionally some people have depicted the love of God in Christ Jesus as if it was somehow self-sacrificing without a purpose: Jesus dies on the cross to prove how much he loves us. But so what? More than a century ago, some wag in Britain countered this by saying, in effect, "Would it make any sense for someone to run down Brighton Pier and yell, 'World, world, world, I love you! I will show my love to you!' and then jump off the end of the pier and drown?" Would that prove love or that the fellow had lost it? Sad, maybe, but scarcely an example of love.

But Jesus doesn't go the cross because he is a victim of fate. He does not go to the cross as an abstract lesson. He does not go to the cross as a mere example (though he is an example). He has a purpose in going to the cross. It is to *save people from condemnation that is already hanging over them.* "Whoever believes in the Son has eternal life, but whoever rejects the Son will not see life, for God's wrath *remains on them*" (3:36, emphasis added); "whoever does not believe *stands condemned already*" (3:18, emphasis added). We are back to the Bible's storyline. Jesus does not come to neutral people and arbitrarily condemn a few here and save a few there. Rather, he comes to people who are already condemned. We stand this side of Genesis 3. We are already under God's judgment. We are already a lost and ungrateful brood. The purpose of his coming and his death on the cross is not to condemn but to save the world (see 3:17).

This passage does not describe at great length how Jesus accomplishes this. Other passages in John's Gospel make that pretty clear. One powerful example is John 6. In it, Jesus says that he is the Bread of Life and unless we eat him we will die. At a superficial level, the notion of eating Jesus might sound jolly close to cannibalism. Or those of us who are more religiously inclined might think, "Maybe it's the sacrament of holy communion or something like that." Originally, that was not what Jesus meant at all. We must not forget that in the ancient world just about everybody worked with their hands or on farms, so they were much closer to nature than we are today. If you ask a five-year-old or a seven-year-old today, "Where does food come from?" they will reply, "From Jewel-Osco" or whatever grocery store chain is in their region. But if you were to ask anybody in the first century where it comes from, they would reply, "From plants, fish, and animals." They have grown or caught this food themselves. So anybody in the first century knows that you live because the chicken died. You live because the carrots have been pulled up and killed. All of this organic material that we feed ourselves with—which we must have or we die—has given its life for us in substitution. Either we die or it dies.

Perhaps in the near future you will stop at a fast-food restaurant and pick up a hamburger. What will you eat? Dead cow. Dead lettuce. Dead tomato. Dead barley. Dead wheat. Everything you eat in that meal once lived and is now dead—except for a few minerals like salt, of which there may be too much. That is what you will eat. All of it has given its life for you. Either it dies or you die. Now, of course, the cow did not volunteer. Nor did the lettuce. The point is not the voluntary nature of such substitution but the reality of it. Either you die or something else living dies so that you may live. Jesus picks up on that language and says, "Unless you eat my flesh, you will die. I die so that you may live."

For the burden of the New Testament is that Jesus dies a substitutionary death. He does not deserve to die. But when God sent him to do his Father's will, to go to the cross and die, it was with a purpose: to die *our* death so that we do not have to die, so that we may have eternal life. That is what the text is saying. "God so loved the world that he gave his one and only Son. . . . For God did not send his Son into the world to condemn the world, but to save the world through him" (3:16–17) so that whoever believes in him may have eternal life. We do not ingest physically this Christ. We believe in him. We trust him and discover that his life becomes ours as our death becomes his. His life becomes ours! And much of the New Testament is given over to unpacking precisely that point.

4. The Means by Which We Come to Enjoy This Love and Life Is Faith

Look one more time at these verses:

[16]For God so loved the world that he gave his one and only Son, that whoever *believes* in him shall not perish but have eternal life. . . . [18]Whoever *believes* in

him is not condemned, but whoever does *not believe* stands condemned already [i.e., the verdict has already been passed] because they have *not believed* in the name of God's one and only Son.

John 3:16, 18, emphasis added

Two chapters from now I shall talk about faith at greater length. For now it is enough to recall we have come across this theme before: we saw it already in the last chapter. Just as the people were saved by simply looking at, by trusting in, by believing in the bronze snake that God had provided, so also we believe in Christ and find life (see 3:14–15). What Jesus wants us to do is not impress him, try to gain his attention, or try to pay for our own sins. What he wants us to do is trust him.

Conclusion

Let me end this way. If all of this is true, and I believe with every fiber of my being that it is, then the first response to it ought to be gratitude, contrition before God, thankfulness for what he has done, and frank faith. But there are loud voices in our world who argue that thankfulness before Jesus shows what an inferior, sappy, emotional, weak religion Christianity is. For example, Bishop Spong, a recently retired Episcopal bishop, writes,

> What does the cross mean? How is it to be understood? Clearly the old pattern of seeing the cross as the place where the price of the fall was paid is totally inappropriate. Aside from encouraging guilt, justifying the need for divine punishment and causing an incipient sadomasochism that has endured with a relentless tenacity through the centuries, the traditional understanding of the cross of Christ has become inoperative on every level. As I have noted previously, a rescuing deity results in gratitude, never in expanded humanity. Constant gratitude, which the story of the cross seems to encourage, creates only weakness, childishness and dependency.[1]

That is a very common stance today. One of the best brief responses to it I have seen is by John Piper, who says,

> "Yes," Bishop Spong, "a rescuing deity results in gratitude." That's true. We cannot stop the mercy of God from doing what it does. He has rescued us from our selfishness and its horrible endpoint, hell. Our hearts cannot stop feeling what they feel—gratitude.
>   You say this encourages "weakness." Not exactly. It encourages being strong in a way that makes God look good, and makes us feel glad. For example, Jesus said to the apostle Paul, "My grace is sufficient for you, for my power is made perfect in weakness." Paul responded, "Therefore I will boast all the more gladly of my *weaknesses*, so that the *power* of Christ may rest upon me. . . .

For when I am weak, then I am *strong*" (2 Corinthians 12:9). So his dependence made him stronger than he would have been otherwise. He is strong with the strength of Christ.

You say this "constant gratitude" produces "childishness." Not really. Children do not naturally say thank you. They come into the world believing that the world owes them everything they want. You have to drill "thank you" into the selfish heart of a child. Feeling grateful and saying it often is a mark of remarkable maturity. We have a name for people who don't feel thankful for what they receive. We call them ingrates. And everyone knows they are acting like selfish children. They are childish. No, Bishop Spong, God wants us to grow up into mature, thoughtful, wise, humble, thankful people. The opposite is childish.

In fact the opposite is downright cranky. C. S. Lewis, before he was a Christian, really disliked the message of the Bible that we should thank and praise God all the time. Then everything changed. What he discovered was not that praising and thanking made people childish, but that it made them large-hearted and healthy. He said, "The humblest, and at the same time most balanced and capacious, minds praised most while the cranks, misfits and malcontents praised least." That is my experience. When I am ungrateful, I am selfish and immature. When I am overflowing with gratitude I am healthy, other-oriented, servant-minded, Christ-exalting, and joyful.[2]

You see, we finally close with Christ. God is the kind of God who pursues *us*, and therefore we close with Christ. So many Christians across the centuries have testified to the way God pursued *them*. There is a wonderful poem by Francis Thompson that talks about God as if he were the hound of heaven, chasing him down. Some of its lines follow:

> I fled Him, down the nights and down the days;
>   I fled Him, down the arches of the years;
> I fled Him, down the labyrinthine ways
>   Of my own mind; and in the mist of tears
> I hid from Him, and under running laughter.
>   Up vistaed hopes I sped;
>   And shot, precipitated,
> Adown Titanic glooms of chasmèd fears,
> From those strong Feet that followed, followed after.
>   But with unhurrying chase,
>   And unperturbèd pace,
> Deliberate speed, majestic instancy,
>   They beat—and a Voice beat
>   More instant than the Feet—
> "All things betray thee, who betrayest Me."[3]

That is the God who loves. He is the hound of heaven. And he is the one who finally gives us meaning as we are restored to the living God. Our meaning does not come from being independent. That is what may destroy us. Our meaning does not come from being rich. That may destroy us; in any sense it is godless and will eventually damn us. Our meaning comes from basking in a right and ordered relationship to the living God, peculiarly and overwhelmingly loved by him. The alternative is death—not always as dramatic as what another poet, Edwin Arlington Robinson, describes, but certainly of the same order:

> Whenever Richard Cory went down town,
> We people on the pavement looked at him:
> He was a gentleman from sole to crown,
> Clean favored, and imperially slim.
>
> And he was always quietly arrayed,
> And he was always human when he talked;
> But still he fluttered pulses when he said,
> "Good-morning," and he glittered when he walked.
>
> And he was rich—yes, richer than a king,
> And admirably schooled in every grace:
> In fine, we thought that he was everything
> To make us wish that we were in his place.
>
> So on we worked, and waited for the light,
> And went without the meat, and cursed the bread;
> And Richard Cory, one calm summer night,
> Went home and put a bullet through his head.[4]

As Thompson said, "All things betray thee, who betrayest Me."

Or again, the testimony of Malcolm Muggeridge, who was a cranky, brilliant, eccentric journalist whose interests and comments ranged all over the map. He was creative, blasphemous, victorious, defeated, and had a spectacular career. He converted in his old age and wrote,

> I may, I suppose, regard myself, or pass for being, a relatively successful man. People occasionally stare at me in the streets—that's fame. I can fairly easily earn enough to qualify for admission to the higher slopes of the Inland Revenue [i.e., the British IRS]—that's success. Furnished with money and a little fame even the elderly, if they care to, may partake of trendy diversions—that's pleasure. It might happen once in a while that something I said or wrote was sufficiently heeded for me to persuade myself that it represented a serious impact on our time—that's fulfillment. Yet I say to you, and I beg you to believe me, multiply these tiny triumphs by a million, add them all together, and they are nothing— less than nothing, a positive impediment—measured against one draught of that living water Christ offers to the spiritually thirsty, irrespective of who or

what they are. What, I ask myself, does life hold, what is there in the works of time, in the past, now and to come, which could possibly be put in the balance against the refreshment of drinking that water?[5]

"For God so loved the world that he gave his one and only Son" (John 3:16).

10

The God Who Dies— and Lives Again

When you think of the biographies of important people, whether artists, football hunks, an Einstein, a political figure—it doesn't matter—never is there any suggestion that they were born in order to die. If the party is no longer living, then there is some mention of the person's death, no doubt, which may be heroic or ordinary, prolonged or quick, accidental or the result of old age—it may be all kinds of things. But never do we speak of someone being born in order to die. That is true for Muhammad. It is true for Gautama the Buddha. There may be stories of their deaths, but no one suggests that the purpose of their coming was to die.

This is why the four Gospels (the first four books of the New Testament: Matthew, Mark, Luke, and John) are so hard to classify. People have written scholarly volumes on what genre of literature they fall into. Is it a tragedy? Well, Jesus rises from the dead, which doesn't sound all that tragic. Is it, literally speaking, a comedy? But they are a different species. They are too serious for comedy: the centrality of the cross and what is achieved and the barbaric awfulness of it all amidst its splendor—they cannot be reduced to one-word expressions. Are the Gospels biographies? That is probably as close as you can get to an adequate label. A New Testament Gospel is somewhat akin to first-century Hellenistic biographies, I suppose. But there aren't any other first-century Hellenistic biographies where the plotline says that the reason the central figure came was to die. The New Testament Gospels feel very different from first-century Hellenistic counterparts.

Have you been exposed to some of the literature that gets promoted every Easter season? Around about Easter the press loves to drag out the latest scholar who has written something on the Gospel of Judas or the Gospel of Thomas or some other Gospel not included in the Bible. Various people line up to say, "These are as authoritative as the Gospels in the New Testament, and we should incorporate them again too. Originally, Christianity was much broader, and then it got narrow and orthodox and mean. But originally it was much, much broader. There were a lot of Gospels."

This revisionist history really cannot stand up to close scrutiny. The earliest of these other so-called Gospels is about mid-second century, and they drag on for another century and a half or two centuries. None of them is connected with the first generation of eyewitnesses the way the canonical Gospels are (that is, the Gospels in our Bible), not one of them. But there is more to it than that.

Consider the so-called Gospel of Thomas. It is a short book of 114 sayings supposedly credited to Jesus and includes two tiny historical snippets. That's it. In other words, it is completely unlike the Gospels in the New Testament, all of which drive toward the cross and resurrection of Jesus. The Gospel of Thomas leaves these climactic events out. In fact, in the first century people didn't speak of *four* Gospel books: Matthew, Mark, Luke, and John. They spoke, rather, of *one* gospel message: the gospel of Jesus Christ, the one gospel of Jesus Christ *according to* Matthew, according to Mark, according to Luke, and according to John. There is one gospel with various witnesses describing what this Good News about Jesus Christ consists of, telling this spectacular news about the Savior who invaded history to save his people from their sins. Only later did people start referring to them rather loosely as "the Gospel *of* Matthew" or "the Gospel *of* Mark," but even then it is really important to see that all four of these books (Matthew, Mark, Luke, and John) say something about Jesus's forerunner (John the Baptist, the one who announces Jesus), origins, and ministry (they talk extensively about what he did, what he said, how he preached, some of his miracles, his parables, his sayings, some of his sermons), and then at the end he is crucified and rises again. All along the story has been driving toward his death. This is essential to the plotline in each book.

An important part of this plotline is how Jesus starts talking about how he is going to die. In Matthew 16, when Peter confesses that Jesus really is the promised Messiah, the one who comes from David's line, the one whom they were expecting, Jesus goes on to say, in effect, "Yes, and you know, I must go to Jerusalem and suffer many things and be crucified and the third day rise again." Then one of the disciples replies with words to this effect: "No way. That cannot be. The promised Davidic figure, the promised Messiah, is so strong, and someone like you can do miracles. How are they going to stop *you*?" But Jesus keeps insisting again and again: he will be betrayed and killed, and this is the center of his heavenly Father's plan. Jesus came to die. That is why each of the Gospels finds Jesus insisting that he came for this purpose.

But Jesus adds some very strange clarifications: "I'm not going to die as a martyr. No one can take my life from me. I lay it down myself. I have the power to lay it down, and I have the power to take it again" (see John 10:17–18). He does not classify himself as a martyr but as a sacrifice. He is not simply the sad victim of a vicious conspiracy or a nasty historical mistake. He is a willing sacrifice.

That is why these books sound so strange to anyone who reads a lot of biographies. There is no one quite like him. Even when he is being arrested and dragged away, his disciples wonder if having courage now means to pull out a sword and slash at the attackers. Jesus's response is, "Don't you understand? I could in theory call twelve legions of angels. Do you really think an unruly mob is going to stand up to twelve legions of angels?" (see Matt. 26:50–54). But he didn't come to be rescued. He came to be butchered. He came to die.

Moreover, in ordinary biographies, once you do have people safely buried in the ground, they stay there. But Jesus comes to die *and rise again*. This pair of events, Jesus's death and resurrection, are so central to everything the Bible says about Jesus and all the purpose of his coming that the apostle Paul, writing a couple of decades after Jesus rose from the dead, announces to his readers in 1 Corinthians 15 that he is going to lay out the matters "of first importance" (15:3)—and he first says, "Christ died for our sins according to the Scriptures" (15:3), and then he spends much of the rest of the chapter talking about Jesus's resurrection. These are matters of first importance. They are the basis of everything in Christian belief, conduct, and understanding. We have to get this right, or we have no part of Christianity left.

There are many ways to go about studying Jesus's death and resurrection. We could go through all of the accounts of his death, for example, and all the allusions to his death. What I am going to do is direct your attention rather quickly to one of the actual accounts of his death, the one found in Matthew 27. Then I shall switch to a passage in John that talks about his resurrection. Much more could be said about these passages[1] (and of course there are many other passages), but I shall center this chapter on these two so that we have some focus to what we are saying.

The Ironies of the Cross (Matt. 27:27–51)

The account we have here of Jesus's death is carefully shaped by Matthew. Matthew is a skillful, God-inspired writer. Of the New Testament writers, the two who are most given to irony are Matthew and John. At one level Matthew is simply describing what happened, but he relates it in such a way that what he shows you are the ironies of the cross, the real meaning behind the raw events. By "irony" I mean words that convey in their context the exact opposite of what they formally say. That's irony. What you will discover is that in each of several paragraphs Matthew lays out what happened when Jesus died, describing it all with such a delicious dipping into irony that we begin to see what God is really doing in this death.

Instead of printing the entire narrative, we shall lay out the text section by section as we go along.

1. The Man Who Is Mocked as King Is King (Matt. 27:27–31)

[27]Then the governor's soldiers took Jesus into the Praetorium and gathered the whole company of soldiers around him. [28]They stripped him and put a scarlet robe on him, [29]and then twisted together a crown of thorns and set it on his head. They put a staff in his right hand as a scepter. Then they knelt in front of him and mocked him. "Hail, king of the Jews!" they said. [30]They spit on him, and took the staff and struck him on the head again and again. [31]After they had mocked him, they took off the robe and put his own clothes on him. Then they led him away to crucify him.

Matthew 27:27–31

Already Jesus has been savagely beaten as part of the interrogation process. That was standard procedure. Then after the sentence was passed, he was savagely beaten again. That too was standard procedure. Once you were condemned to be crucified, you were beaten again before you were taken out and crucified. He has already suffered all of that.

What takes place here is not standard procedure. This is barracks-room humor. They put some sort of robe on him as if he is an emperor, and they twist into a crown one of the spiked vines that they have in the Middle East. They ram it down onto his head. They put a stick in his hand as if it is a scepter and pretend that he is a great monarch. "Hail, king of the Jews!" they say, bowing down, slapping his face, laughing. Such fun. They take this stick that is supposed to be the symbol of his power and bash it against his head again and again. More laughter. Barracks-room humor.

But every time they say "Hail, king of the Jews!" they mean the opposite. In the context the words actually convey nothing but derision and scorn. They think that their humor is deeply ironic and very funny. But there is a deeper irony. Matthew knows, and God knows, and the readers know that Jesus *is* the king. The man who was mocked as king is the king. That is the first deep irony in this passage.

After all, how does the Gospel of Matthew begin? "This is the genealogy *of Jesus the Messiah the son of David*, the son of Abraham" (1:1, emphasis added). Jesus is in the Davidic line. He has the legal right to the throne. And all through the book there are allusions to Jesus being the king. He tells some parables in which—for those with eyes to see—the king in the parable is Jesus himself. In fact, as part of the procedure during Jesus's trial before Pilate, the Roman governor, Jesus is asked, "Are you the king of the Jews?" From Pilate's perspective, if Jesus says yes then he could be condemned: his words would be a confession of treason. Jesus would be setting himself up against the Herod family (which supplied the local petty monarchs in the area) or even setting himself up against Caesar in Rome. Jesus would be a usurping king. Jesus answers with a kind of affirmation: "It is as you say. You have said this." But he does not want simply to flatly say, "Yes, I am the promised king"—because what Jesus means by king is not exactly what Pilate means by king. Nevertheless, he is the king of the Jews.

In fact, when you read the whole New Testament, he is not only the king *of the Jews*, he is the king of you and me. How does Matthew end his Gospel? Jesus, risen from the dead, says, "All authority in heaven and on earth has been given to me" (Matt. 28:18). Quite frankly, he claims to be king of the universe. He is certainly the king of these soldiers who are laughing at his supposed power as king. Matthew wants us to see that the man who is mocked as king *is* king.

But what sort of a kingdom is it? What kind of kingdom is it where the king lays down his life not because he has been overpowered by a competitor but as an act of voluntary self-sacrifice? Most kings surely would want to go out and fight. Jesus refuses to do so. In fact, in one remarkable passage a few chapters earlier in Matthew, Jesus actually talks about the nature of his kingdom. I have alluded to it before. In Matthew 20, the mother of James and John and her two sons (two of Jesus's disciples) approach Jesus, and what they want is to sit one on the right and one on the left *in Jesus's kingdom*. They want political power. But Jesus goes on to say,

> [25]You know that the rulers of the Gentiles lord it over them, and their high officials exercise authority over them. [26]Not so with you. Instead, whoever wants to become great among you must be your servant, [27]and whoever wants to be first must be your slave—[28]just as the Son of Man did not come to be served, but to serve, and to give his life as a ransom for many.
>
> Matthew 20:25–28

Jesus is not recommending that his followers adopt the stance that makes them everybody's doormat, useful only for other people to wipe their feet on (that is not the point), nor that they should deny any sort of authority when they are put in a position of authority (that is not the point). The problem is that in this world, when we gain authority, we start lording it over people. We start thinking that it is our due. But Jesus is the sort of God—he is the God who is there—who loves because he is that kind of God. His aim is to serve. He does not come to be fawned over but to serve, and to serve finally by giving his life a ransom for many. That is why he comes. For the first three centuries of the church's history, ordinary Christians understood this very well, for they often depicted Jesus, with their own delicious irony, as the king who reigns from a cross.

That is the kind of kingdom over which he reigns, for he expects his followers to exercise authority in exactly that way.

There is the first irony: the man who is mocked as king is king.

2. The Man Who Is Utterly Powerless Is Transcendently Powerful (Matt. 27:32–40)

³²As they were going out, they met a man from Cyrene, named Simon, and they forced him to carry the cross. ³³They came to a place called Golgotha (which means "the place of the skull"). ³⁴There they offered Jesus wine to drink, mixed with gall; but after tasting it, he refused to drink it. ³⁵When they had crucified him, they divided up his clothes by casting lots. ³⁶And sitting down, they kept watch over him there. ³⁷Above his head they placed the written charge against him: THIS IS JESUS, THE KING OF THE JEWS.

³⁸Two rebels were crucified with him, one on his right and one on his left. ³⁹Those who passed by hurled insults at him, shaking their heads ⁴⁰and saying, "You who are going to destroy the temple and build it in three days, save yourself! Come down from the cross, if you are the Son of God!"

Matthew 27:32–40

Here is a horrible picture of the most abject weakness possible. When the sentence was passed, you were beaten again, and then you were forced to carry the crossbeam (the horizontal beam of the cross) on your shoulder out to the place of execution where the upright was already in the ground. There you were stripped and either nailed or tied to the crossbeam, which was then hoisted up and attached to the upright. You hung there not only in pain but in shame: when men and women were crucified, they were crucified naked.

In former times there had been occasions when the soldiers had left somebody hanging on a cross, and friends of the victim had actually managed to come along and take the person down. Victims had been known to survive. At this point in Roman history that wasn't possible: it was now imperial policy to leave a group of four soldiers at the site to guard the body until the victim was unambiguously dead. And you pulled with your arms and you pushed with your legs to open up your chest cavity so that you could breathe, and the muscle spasms started so that you collapsed. But then you couldn't breathe. So you pulled with your arms and you pushed with your legs so that you could breathe, and then the spasms started again and you collapsed. That could go on for hours, sometimes days, and the soldiers kept watch. If for any reason the soldiers wanted to finish you off a little faster (for example, because a special feast day was about to dawn), what they would do was smash your shin bones. Then you couldn't push with your legs anymore, and you would suffocate in a few minutes.

At this point Jesus is as powerless as you can imagine. There is no way out. There is no hope. And he is so weak from his repeated beatings, he isn't even strong enough to hoist the crossbeam on his shoulders and take it out to the place of execution. By trade a carpenter, Jesus is now so weak he cannot lift a piece of wood, so they have to conscript somebody else to do it for them, a man identified as Simon from Cyrene.

Then the mockery begins: "You who are going to destroy the temple and build it in three days, save yourself! Come down from the cross, if you are the Son of God!" (Matt. 27:40). Now where does this insult come from? It seems strange in our ears. But it too showed up in the trial—not the trial before Pilate but the trial before the high priest in the previous chapter (Matthew 26). Some had tried to make this part of the charge against Jesus. The reason it could, in theory, have been very dangerous, was this: the Roman Empire was a highly diverse place, religiously speaking, so one of the things that the Romans did to keep the peace among competing religions was make it a capital crime to desecrate a temple, any temple. If you desecrate a temple, any temple, then under Roman law you die. So if someone heard Jesus saying, "Destroy this temple, and in three days I'll raise it again," perhaps the first part of his utterance could be worked into conspiracy for a capital crime, that is, destroying a temple. Because the witnesses couldn't get their stories straight, this charge actually went nowhere. Jesus was finally charged with treason, with setting himself up as king over against Caesar. Apparently, however, some who had heard this charge at the trial find it amusing. They look at Jesus in his most abject weakness, and they say, in effect, "So, big mouth—you're so strong, aren't you? You who are going to destroy the temple and build it in three days—look at you now, strong man!"

If you have ever helped build a house with Habitat for Humanity, you know that with a decent foundation laid, a lot of planning, a good engineer, a certain amount of pre-fab, and forty strong-backed volunteers, you can put up a small house in a day. But you could not put up one of the temples in the ancient world in a day. In fact, you could not put up one of the cathedrals in Europe in a lifetime. Not one of the original architects of the great cathedrals in Europe ever saw the finished product. It took more than one lifetime to build one. In Jesus's day, just the current beautification project of the temple in Jerusalem had already been going on for forty-six years. Moreover, by Jewish law you were not allowed to hammer a stone within hearing distance of the temple. All those stones had to be measured, cut, brought in, and set in place without hydraulics. No wonder the temple took a long time to build. Yet Jesus did say, "Destroy this temple, and in three days I'll build it again" (see John 2:19). When the mockers hurl Jesus's words back in his face, they think they are using irony to be funny. When they say, "You who are going to destroy the temple and build it in three days," they mean precisely the opposite: he can do nothing of the kind. He is in fact hopelessly weak, dying, and damned on a cross.

But Matthew knows, and God knows, and the readers know, that by this death and the resurrection around the corner Jesus is destroying the temple and rising again. When early in his ministry Jesus used these words, "Destroy this temple, and I will raise it again in three days" (John 2:19), his disciples did not have a clue what he was talking about. They probably muttered under their breath, "Jesus is saying something deep again, very mysterious." But then John comments, "After he was raised from the dead, his disciples recalled what he had said. Then they believed the scripture and the words that Jesus had spoken" (John 2:22).

The point is that the temple in the Old Testament was the great meeting place between God and human beings, as we have seen. It was the place of sacrifice. Now Jesus, referring to his own body, says, "Destroy this temple, and I will raise it again in three days." He means that by the destruction of his own life and its resurrection, *he* becomes the great meeting place between God and human beings. By rising again after his death, *he* becomes the great temple with all the power that is required to bring someone back from the dead. The great meeting place between God and human beings is no longer a building in Jerusalem with its sacrificial system. It is Jesus himself.

Thus, while the mockers think their mockery is cast in humorous irony, we cannot help but see an even deeper irony, for the man who is utterly powerless is in fact powerful. He is the temple of the living God.

3. The Man Who Can't Save Himself Saves Others (Matt. 27:41–42)

The mockery continues: "In the same way the chief priests, the teachers of the law and the elders mocked him. 'He saved others,' they said, 'but he can't save himself! He's the king of Israel! Let him come down now from the cross, and we will believe in him'" (Matt. 27:41–42).

What do we mean by the verb "to save"? What does it mean on the streets of Minneapolis or Chicago or London? It depends who is using it. If you are a banker, saving is something that we are supposed to do (if the market does not wipe it all out) to protect our investments and prepare for retirement. If you are gifted in sports, saving is what the goalie does to stop a goal, whether in soccer or ice hockey. If you are a geek, saving is what you are supposed to do so that you do not lose too much data if your hard drive crashes. So we use the verb "to save" in a variety of different contexts, don't we? What does Matthew mean?

We had a glimpse of the answer three chapters back. When Joseph is told that Mary is pregnant, he is told that he must give the baby "the name Jesus [Yahweh saves], because he will *save* his people from their sins" (Matt. 1:21, emphasis added). "Saving" in Matthew's Gospel means saving people from their sin: from its guilt, consequences, eternal effects, and power in this life. That is why Jesus came. Even when Jesus "saves" people by healing them, this is a function of his determination to save his people from their sin, including the temporal effects in this life (see Matt. 8:14–17).

But now the mockers are chanting, "He saved others"—that is, he helped them, he cured them, he was such a good savior. "But he can't save himself!" In other words, "Look at him. He is completely shackled; he is completely tied down. There is no way he can save himself, which shows that he is not much of a savior at all." So when they say, "He saved others," again they mean with cheap irony, "He is no savior to be respected at all."

But Matthew knows, and God knows, and the readers know, that it is by *staying* on that cross that he saves others. Strictly speaking, he cannot save himself and save others. If he saves himself, he will not be able to save others. When they say, "He can't save himself," they mean that he is so attached to the cross, so nailed to the cross, that physically he cannot get down. But Matthew knows that he *could* get down. He could still call his twelve legions of angels. But he cannot save himself if he is to save others because the very purpose of his hanging on that cross is to bear my sin in his own body on the tree. If he does save himself, I am damned. It is only by *not* saving himself that he saves me.

So once again, there is a deeper irony hidden behind the mocking irony of the mockers. Unlike what the critics thought, their words are true. He saved others; he can't save himself.

I suspect that part of the reason that we have initial trouble absorbing this is that we live at a time in Western culture where a lot of conduct is constrained by force of law or just by force. In other words, we do not have much place left for a kind of internal moral imperative.

Did you see the film *Titanic* when it came out? As the great ship is going down, people are scrambling for the lifeboats, of which there are too few. There are a lot of well-to-do men on the boat, and they start scrambling and shoving the women and children aside so that they can reserve their own places. The sailors pull out handguns and fire in the air and say, "Women and children—the boats are for women and children." Historically, of course, that is rubbish. There were numerous wealthy men on that boat. John Jacob Astor was there, the Bill Gates of 1912, the richest man. He got his wife to the boat, and when others said to him, "You get in too, sir," he said, "No, this is for women and children," and he stepped back and drowned. Benjamin Guggenheim was there. He was pulled apart from his wife and yelled to someone between, "Tell my wife that Guggenheim knows his duty." Guggenheim stepped back and then drowned. She was saved. Despite the fact that in third class many people were locked down, there was not a single report of wealthy men on deck scrambling to save themselves by jeopardizing women and children.

Isn't that stunning? When Fareed Zakaria commented on this in a *New York Times* article,[2] he brought to mind the obvious question: Why did the producer and director distort history and say what isn't true? Why didn't they tell the truth about what happened at this point? Zakaria's answer to this question: because if they had told the truth today, nobody would have believed them. For at the time there was still enough of a culture of chivalry, often fed by Christian self-denial for the sake of others, that an internal moral imperative drove many men, out of resources from within themselves, to do something self-sacrificial for others.

That is what drove Jesus supremely: he came to do his Father's will, and his Father's will is that he should sacrifice himself for all those who in grace would believe. To a lesser degree, that is the way Christian motivation must operate in us once we become Christians, followers of Jesus. *We* are changed by the new birth; *we* are strengthened by the Holy Spirit living and working within us. There is an internal moral imperative, a transformation of heart—doubtless not more than a pale reflection of Jesus, but in the same line, wanting to sacrifice for the sake of others.

4. The Man Who Cries Out in Despair Trusts God (Matt. 27:43–51)

The people are still mocking:

[43]"He trusts in God. Let God rescue him now if he wants him, for he said, 'I am the Son of God.'" [44]In the same way the rebels who were crucified with him also heaped insults on him.

[45]From noon until three in the afternoon darkness came over all the land. [46]About three in the afternoon Jesus cried out in a loud voice, *"Eli, Eli, lema sabachthani?"* (which means "My God, my God, why have you forsaken me?").

[47]When some of those standing there heard this, they said, "He's calling Elijah."

[48]Immediately one of them ran and got a sponge. He filled it with wine vinegar, put it on a staff, and offered it to Jesus to drink. [49]The rest said, "Now leave him alone. Let's see if Elijah comes to save him."

[50]And when Jesus had cried out again in a loud voice, he gave up his spirit.

Matthew 27:43–50

So is Jesus actually giving up at this point, caught up in the web of miserable circumstances, drowning in despair? Is that the message we are to learn? "Push me far enough, and I too will collapse"? Oh, his cry is much deeper than that. Because of Jesus's death, because of his willingness to stay there, in the very next verse beyond this paragraph, "the curtain of the temple was torn in two from top to bottom" (Matt. 27:51)—the veil of the temple that set off the very presence of God from the rest of the people. Then the Most Holy Place, where only the high priest could enter once a year, is exposed. The veil is torn apart as if to indicate that you and I—ordinary human beings without priestly pretensions—can actually get into the presence of God because Jesus's sacrifice really has paid all the debt that the blood of bulls and goats could never ever pay for through the sacrifices we saw a few chapters back. Now Jesus dies, and in his cry "My God, my God, why have you forsaken me?" he is crying in the bleakest, darkest, most pitiable despair, not because he does not know that he is doing his Father's will but precisely because he *does* know that he is doing his Father's will. He *is* trusting God, and that Father's will is to bear my sin in his own body on the tree, absorbing the curse, discharging the debt, paying the guilt, and tearing the veil so that I can get into the Most Holy Place, into the very presence of the living God.

Can God Die?

I titled this chapter, in part, "The God Who Dies." In some ways that title is a bit slippery, even potentially misleading. By and large the New Testament does not talk of God dying. It speaks of Jesus being the God-man, and it speaks of Jesus dying. Never is there a hint that the Father dies. Of course not: he is not a human being that he could die. Only the Son can die, only the "Word made flesh." Jesus can die because he is a human being, a man. But if he is also confessed to be God and worshiped as God (see for example John 20:28), is there not a sense in which we may speak of God dying?

By and large the Bible avoids such choice of words. Once in a while, however, we find passages that come so close to this. When the apostle Paul gives a speech to some church elders from Ephesus, he says, "Keep watch over yourselves and all the flock of which the Holy Spirit has made you overseers. Be shepherds of the church of *God*, which *he bought with his own blood*" (Acts 20:28, emphasis added). Isn't that remarkable? "God . . . with his own blood"? Now, of course, if pressed, Paul could parse that a bit. He could say, "Of course, the person I have in mind is not God the Father but the Son of God, Jesus, who is himself God, and because he is God and because he does give his life and shed his blood, therefore, it is appropriate to say that God sheds his blood." If you want to unpack it, that is what Paul means.

Nevertheless, do not let the shock of the language stop you. This is *God's* action in Christ Jesus, the man who is also God. This is not the death of one human individual and no more. It is a human individual who is also the living God who hangs on that cross, not because he is forced to do so by circumstance but because he is fulfilling in himself all of the strands of the Old Testament's sacrificial system, the temple system—all the strands from the fall and the promise of the seed of the woman coming to crush the serpent's head by his own death. Elsewhere Paul can write, "*God* demonstrates his *own* love for us in this: While we were still sinners, *Christ* died for us" (Rom. 5:8, emphasis added). As the old hymn says,

> Bearing sin and scoffing rude,
> In my place condemned he stood.
> Sealed my pardon with his blood!
> Hallelujah, what a Savior!
>
>   Philip P. Bliss

It is appropriate to speak of the God who dies.

At the end of World War I, that bloodiest and most stupid of wars, several English poets (Wilfred Owen, Rupert Brook, one or two others) wrote some very moving poetry about the sheer savagery of the war. One of the minor poets was Edward Shillito, whose piece "Jesus of the Scars" deserves wide circulation. The poem ends by saying,

> The other gods were strong, but Thou wast weak;
> They rode, but Thou didst stumble to a throne;
> But to our wounds only God's wounds can speak,
> And not a god has wounds, but Thou alone.[3]

So when we face the ravages of uncertainty, when there is suffering and agony in our lives or in the world, and we wonder what God is doing and we have no answers and we reread the book of Job (that piece of wisdom literature we saw in chapter 6) and we hear God saying through four chapters of rhetorical questions, "Be still, Job; there are many things you do not understand at all," we can now actually add something more that we *do* understand:

> But to our wounds only God's wounds can speak,
> And not a god has wounds, but Thou alone.

You can trust a God who not only is sovereign but bleeds for you. Sometimes when there are no other answers for your guilt or your fears or your uncertainties or your anguish, there is one immovable place on which to stand. It is the ground right in front of the cross.

The Resurrection

As important as the cross is, it is not the end of the story, for all of the New Testament writers focus equally on the resurrection of the Lord Jesus. The resurrection accounts are rich and diverse. There is no way they can be reduced to mass hallucination. Jesus appeared to many people many times over a period of forty days or so. He appeared to ones and twos; he appeared to as many as five hundred at a time; he appeared to the apostles more than once; he appeared in locked rooms; he appeared on the seashore and ate some fish that he was cooking for them. The witnesses multiply. He shows up when they are not expecting him, and he shows up when they are. He cannot be categorized or dismissed or domesticated. The resurrection appearances are simply too frequent, too diverse, and supported by too many witnesses. What do you do with them?

If you think that the early Christians made this up or were somehow hood-winked or fell victims to mass psychology of some sort, it is hard to explain why they were willing to die for their faith. If the resurrection is a fairy story a bit like "Hansel and Gretel," my question is, "How many have offered to die for Hansel and Gretel?" But the early Christians were willing to die for their conviction that Jesus had risen from the dead. They had seen him, touched him, handled him, eaten with him, *after he had risen from the dead*—and they were transformed by him. In fact, he promised them resurrection bodies of their own one day. They believed that he was Lord.

Why Doubt the Resurrection of Jesus? (John 20:24–28)

One of the most moving scenes describes what takes place on the second Sunday, the Sunday after the Sunday when Jesus rose from the dead. The first Sunday, resurrection Sunday, Jesus appeared to some women, to Peter and John, to a couple walking to the little town of Emmaus, and to ten of the apostles. Now on the second Sunday, we read these words:

> [24]Now Thomas (also known as Didymus), one of the Twelve, was not with the disciples when Jesus came. [25]So the other disciples told him, "We have seen the Lord!" But he said to them, "Unless I see the nail marks in his hands and put my finger where the nails were, and put my hand into his side, I will not believe."
>
> John 20:24–25

This is the kind of doubt that springs from hurt. He did not want to be duped. He had believed that Jesus was the Messiah, and then Jesus had died. That made no sense. He was lonely and scared. He was still a pious, Jewish monotheist, but he had been snookered (he thought) once and now he wasn't going to talk himself into believing that Jesus was back after all. He was going to have to see for himself. He was not going to have an easy faith, just believing somebody else's account. He wasn't going to do that. In other words, he wanted to distinguish between faith and gullibility, so he therefore laid out the most extreme test he could imagine. He wanted to be sure that the body that went into the tomb was the same as the one that supposedly came out or had some sort of genuine, organic connection with it. So he specifies, "Unless

I see the nail marks in his hands and put my finger where the nails were, and put my hand into his side, I will not believe" (20:25).

I chair The Gospel Coalition. Our executive director is a chap called Ben Peays. Ben is an identical twin, and when I say identical twin, I mean *identical* twin. They look alike generally, but also have the same little smirks and smiles and so on—they are spitting images of each other. I'm sure that if you know them well enough you can tell them apart; I can only barely do so, unless they are side by side. So last year when we had our council meeting, Ben was around, of course, but we did not tell anybody on the council that his brother was showing up too. So at one point in the council meeting I said, "Guys, I should tell you that our executive director has been working so hard with so much work to do we decided to clone him and get two of him." And I pointed at the other one.

Maybe Jesus has a twin. Maybe he can pretend to come out of the tomb. Maybe he can be the new Jesus. But then where are the wounds—not only the wounds from the nails but the shaft that went up under his rib cage into the pericardium and pierced the flesh such that blood and water flowed out? Where are the wounds? "Unless I put my hands in his wounds, I will not believe." That was the test.

> [26]A week later his disciples were in the house again, and Thomas was with them. Though the doors were locked, Jesus came and stood among them and said, "Peace be with you!" [27]Then he said to Thomas, "Put your finger here; see my hands. Reach out your hand and put it into my side. Stop doubting and believe."
> [28]Thomas said to him, "My Lord and my God!"
>
> John 20:26–28

On first reading Thomas's response, one wonders why he says so much. Why doesn't he simply say, "You *are* alive!" or "Oops, I was wrong" or something more modest? Why does he infer so much ("My Lord and my God!") from the fact that Jesus is now alive? After all, some chapters earlier Lazarus had been raised from the dead, and nobody said to Lazarus after he was raised from the dead, "My Lord and my God!" So why is Thomas saying this to Jesus?

What you have to do is put yourself into the very account. Put yourself—so far as it is possible—in Thomas's place. You have a whole week between the first reports of Jesus's resurrection and the second appearance. The fellow apostles are coming along and saying, "We actually saw him. Peter saw him on his own. Peter and John saw the empty tomb. The two on the road to Emmaus saw him. Together we saw him—ten of us all at once. And then there are the reports of the women. We have all seen him." So now all week long Thomas is saying, in effect:

Can't be. I just can't believe it. I know the tomb is empty, but who knows, a grave robber might have come. Maybe we got the wrong tomb; it was dark when they put him in. But supposing he is alive, what would that mean? Oh no, it can't be. It doesn't make any sense. But he did do some strange things in his life. I mean, after all, he said the very night that he was going to the cross, "Have I been with you such a long time, and have you not known me? He who has seen me has seen the Father" [see John 14:9]. And there was that strange utterance from Jesus sometime back where he said, "Before Abraham was born, I am" [John 8:58]. That's more than just bad timing. Abraham has been dead for two millennia. Why didn't he say, "Before Abraham was born, I *was*"? This would have been claiming some sort of preexistence, maybe—hard enough to believe. But still, that's just preexistence. But "Before Abraham was born, I *am*"? That's taking the name of God!

What do you do with passages like that? All during the years of Jesus's ministry, when Jesus said things that were hard to understand, doubtless his disciples scratched their heads, smiled devotedly, and thought, "More mystery. Maybe we'll understand it someday." They could remember that Jesus had insisted that it was the Father's determination that all should honor the Son even as they honor the Father (see John 5:23). You do not say that about a mere human being.

Maybe Thomas during that week before the second Sunday had also thought through some Old Testament texts a bit more, in the light of the claims that Jesus had risen from the dead. And then, of course, historically speaking, the other New Testament Gospels report other instances in which he had opportunity to observe Jesus. I shall mention one.

Only the Offended Party Can Forgive

There's a spectacular account in two other Gospels (not in John) where Jesus is preaching in a packed house—no chairs, people are just packed in. By this time Jesus has quite a reputation as a preacher and teacher but also as a healer. Four men bring along a paralyzed friend. He cannot walk, so he is brought on some sort of pallet. The four bearers try to get into the house where Jesus is preaching and simply cannot get in. People are saying, "Hush, hush, the master is preaching. Wait your turn. He's busy. Don't bother him." But the four men with their litter will not be stopped. So they go up the outside stairs (many houses had outside stairs in those days because people would cool down in the evening on the flat roofs with the breezes wafting over the city of Jerusalem). Reaching the flat roof, they listen carefully for where Jesus is speaking. They find the right area and start taking off the tiles. Then they lower their friend down on ropes in front of Jesus. If the crowd will not make room for him through the doorway, they will make room for him because a bed is coming down on their heads. Then this bed and its paralyzed man is in front of Jesus, and Jesus says, "Son, your sins are forgiven" (Mark 2:5).

Theologians who are present are indignant. "Who can forgive sins but God alone?" (Mark 2:7). That's a good observation, isn't it?

Supposing, God forbid, that on your next trip to work you are brutally attacked by a gang of thugs. You are viciously beaten up, left half dead, maybe gang-raped. Emergency services take you to a hospital, and I go and visit you two days from now. You are bandaged up with your legs on pulleys. You can barely talk. And I say to you, "You know, you can be glad, for I found the thugs, and I have forgiven them." What would you say to me? Wouldn't you be outraged? "Who do you think you are? You're not the one who was gang-raped! You're not the one lying in the hospital! How can *you* possibly forgive them? The only person who can forgive is the offended party. Only the offended party can forgive."

At the end of World War II, a Jew by the name of Simon Wiesenthal was still clinging to life in Auschwitz, even after all of his extended family had been wiped out. At this juncture he was only weeks away from the end of the terror and horror of Auschwitz: the Russians were moving in from the East. Wiesenthal was in a work party when suddenly he was pulled out by the German guards and shoved into a room. There was a young German Nazi soldier there—maybe nineteen years old. He had suffered grievous wounds and was clearly going to die. Before he died he wanted to talk to a Jew. In God's peculiar providence, the Jew who was pulled out of the line and shoved into that room was Simon Wiesenthal. The young Nazi explained why he wanted to see him. Gasping for breath, not long to live, he acknowledged that the Nazis had treated the Jews horribly and that he himself had been engaged in horrible things. Now he wanted the Jews' forgiveness.

Wiesenthal was quietly reasoning it out in his mind. He later wrote up his reflections in a little book called *The Sunflower*. Most of the pages of that short book describe what flashed through Wiesenthal's mind. The reasoning is this: Who can forgive but those who have been offended? The most offended parties of the Holocaust are dead. In Auschwitz they have already been burned in the ovens. How can a survivor like Wiesenthal pronounce forgiveness on behalf of those who died? How can he speak for the dead? If the most brutalized victims of the Nazis are dead, then there is no one qualified to pronounce forgiveness, *so there is no forgiveness for the Nazis*. Without saying a single word, Wiesenthal listened to the young man, then turned and walked out of the room.

After the war was over and he had written his little book, Wiesenthal sent it to ethicists all around the world—Christian and Jewish, various backgrounds—and asked them to answer the question, "Did I do what was right?" He kicked off a furious exchange among ethicists all over the world.

Wiesenthal almost got it right. He was surely right to insist that only the offended party can forgive. That is right. But according to the Bible, the most offended party is always God. That is what David understood when he dared to write, "Against you, you only, have I sinned and done what is evil in your sight" (Ps. 51:4).[4]

Now this young paralytic is lowered before Jesus—a young man who has not offended Jesus in the flesh, not man-to-man, person-to-person—and Jesus looks at him and says, "Your sins are forgiven" (Mark 2:5). The theologians ask, "Who can forgive sins but God alone?" (Mark 2:7).

Just so. And Thomas remembered that too. Combined with all the other memories of what Jesus had said and done, combined with all his reflections on the Old Testament Scriptures, he came to the only reasonable conclusion: Jesus is not only a resurrected man—miracle enough!—but somehow, incredibly, wonderfully, he is God, with all of God's right to forgive sins. And he bowed before the resurrected Jesus and said, "My Lord and my God!" (John 20:28).

That is what each of us must do: recognize that what Jesus has accomplished on the cross was suffering for the sake of his own people who put their faith in him, who recognize that what he bore was their sin. As the God-man, only he can forgive. We must have his forgiveness to be reconciled to God. We must have it. Then we bow before him and cry with joy and thankfulness, with mystery, adoration, and awe, "My Lord and my God."

Concluding Prayer

We rejoice, heavenly Father, in the truth that Jesus rose from the dead. Yet we begin to see that this is not simply a truth in the public arena of history to be absorbed quickly and then set to one side. For if indeed your dear Son, the God-man, rose from the dead, then everything is changed. His victory over death is confirmed. The sacrifice he provided has been vindicated. Already he is the head of a new humanity that will one day share in his resurrection-likeness. And his people, heavenly Father, rejoice to bow before him and cry, "My Lord and my God." Grant that each one who reads these pages may cry, "Forgive my sin as you forgave the sin of that paralyzed man, my Lord and my God." In Jesus's name, Amen.

11

The God Who Declares the Guilty Just

At a certain level the title of this chapter almost seems perverse. The following, I think, is how we would prefer that things work:

Members of the jury, I am not asking for mercy or pardon. I want justice. I am demanding full acquittal. Yes, I committed the murder of which I am accused. But I am not guilty. Members of the jury, you must consider all my good deeds—not merely as mitigating circumstances but as reason for exonerating me. The goodness of my other deeds outweighs the crime I committed. My good deeds *require* a "not guilty" verdict. If justice is to be done, you must find me innocent.

So writes Todd Wilken.[1] We grin because the argument is so ridiculous. Yet suddenly we see that an approach to God that depends finally on our balancing of good deeds and bad deeds must be no less ridiculous. For this is the lamest of all forms of *self-justification*—yet this is the case we want to make before God. This argument is not a plea for leniency; rather, it is a bold assertion of innocence. It assumes that guilt is cancelled by good deeds. God *must* acquit us and declare us "not guilty" because we have done enough compensating good things. This is *self*-justification. And it is no more believable before the bar of God's justice than it would be in a contemporary court.

So how should we think that God looks at things, this God who is himself spectacularly holy and who does not see our good deeds as things that are weighed in a balance against bad deeds but sees even this futile effort at self-justification as one more example of our mortal defiance against him? What is the Bible's solution? God does not pretend that good deeds make up for bad deeds. Rather, he has found a way to declare the guilty *just*—and retain his integrity while doing it. Instead of *self-justification*, he finds a way to *justify* us; he finds a way to grant us *justification* that is not *self*-justification but justification from the God who is our Maker and our Judge. That is what this chapter is about.

We shall shortly focus on Romans 3:21–26. Martin Luther, a Reformer who lived five hundred years ago, called this paragraph the center of the book of Romans and indeed of the whole Bible. But before we actually look at these verses, we should remind ourselves where they fall within Paul's letter to the Romans.

Romans 3:21–26 in Light of Romans 1:18–3:20

Paul's letter to the Christians in Rome falls within the New Testament. The New Testament opens with the four Gospels (Matthew, Mark, Luke, and John) followed by the book of Acts (which recounts "the acts of the apostles" from Christ's resurrection on through the first three decades or so of the church) and then a sheaf of letters written by the apostle Paul. The first of Paul's letters in the New Testament is written to the Romans. But before we get to Romans 3:21–26, which is our focus of interest, we must recognize that Paul's entire argument in Romans 1:18–3:20 shows us we are guilty. What these two and a half chapters do is unpack in theological terms the thrust of what the Bible says about human beings from Genesis 3 on.

This long section begins with the words, "The wrath of God is being revealed from heaven against all the godlessness and wickedness of human beings who suppress the truth by their wickedness, since what may be known about God is plain to them, because God has made it plain to them" (Rom. 1:18–19). The following two and a half chapters show that whether you come from the line of Abraham through the covenant with Moses and have received a lot of revelation from God, or, alternatively, you have come from outside that line from some sort of Gentile heritage, nevertheless, both lines—Jews and Gentiles alike—without exception end up guilty before God. Knowing what God wants does not enable you to meet those standards. Alternatively, if you come from a heritage where you have been exposed to very little of what God has said, and you adopt some lesser standard, you do not even come up to that standard. On every front we are a guilty people.

This is so out of line with contemporary self-perception that when you read some of what Paul says without developing a feel for the whole of the Bible's storyline, it can easily be dismissed as over the top. He finishes the section in 3:9–18 with a raft of quotations from the Old Testament:

9What shall we conclude then? Do we [i.e., Jews] have any advantage? Not at all! We have already made the charge that Jews and Gentiles alike are all under the power of sin. 10As it is written [and now you get these quotations, all snippets from the Old Testament Scriptures]:

> "There is no one righteous, not even one;
>   11there is no one who understands;
>   there is no one who seeks God.
> 12All have turned away,
>   they have together become worthless;
> there is no one who does good,
>   not even one."
> 13"Their throats are open graves;
>   their tongues practice deceit."
> "The poison of vipers is on their lips."
>   14"Their mouths are full of cursing and bitterness."
> 15"Their feet are swift to shed blood;
>   16ruin and misery mark their ways,
> 17and the way of peace they do not know."
>   18"There is no fear of God before their eyes."
>
> Romans 3:9–18

Now if you come from a thoroughly secular background and you opened this book in your hand at this page and read the lines quoted above, you might well think, "Has the author taken leave of his senses? Oh, I know that there are some bad people out there—Stalin, maybe, and Pol Pot, I suppose, and Hitler, of course—but what about 'Doctors without Borders'? Aren't there a lot of people doing good things out there?"

At a certain level, Paul would agree with that conclusion. Historically, Christians have often seen in such good things the fruit of common grace, that is, grace that God gives commonly to all kinds of people. But Paul's probing cuts deeper into the human heart. The question is not whether many good things are done (e.g., pieces of art, a wonderful symphony, self-sacrificing doctors on the frontier of a horrible disease, and much, much more). We have already seen that the Bible presents human beings to be horrible contradictions: we have so much potential reflecting something of the goodness of creation and the glory of God, and on the other hand we are corrupt, abusive, twisted, and above all self-focused. The heart of evil, according to the entire storyline of the Bible, is the broken relationship with God that sets up idols that de-god him. This results in destroying the beauty and goodness of the created order. The heart of all evil is not Auschwitz, as unimaginably evil as it is. The heart of all evil is first of all human beings, you and me, wanting to go our own way and disowning the God who has made us.

When you probe these texts line by line and discern that this is what God has in mind when he talks about evil, all the lines make sense. "There is no one righteous, not even one" (3:10). It makes sense if you remember the quotation from Todd Wilken with which we began the chapter: the issue is not a matter of balancing good deeds and bad deeds. None of us can claim to be righteous, "not even one"—and most of us recognize the truth of this assertion, if we are honest enough.

"All have turned away, they have together become worthless" (3:12)—not worthless in the sense that there is no intrinsic value in human beings, in God's image-bearers, but worthless in the sense that we have all violated our Creator God. This is easier to understand when we remember what Jesus told us is the "most important" commandment: "'Love the Lord your God with all your heart and with all your soul and with all your mind and with all your strength.' The second is this: 'Love your neighbor as yourself'" (Mark 12:29–31). I confess with shame that I do not love God with all my heart and soul and mind and strength. If Jesus says that this is the most important commandment, then I am guilty of breaking it. Aren't you? In fact, loving God with all your heart and soul and mind and strength might be thought in our culture to be a bit fanatical. But God says, in effect, "Listen, don't you understand? This the way I created the universe in the first place. If you don't see it, that is already a mark of how fallen this order is." Similarly with the second command, the command to love our neighbors as ourselves: it seems so over the top, ridiculously utopian. But God says that such inferences show how badly we have forsaken what he sees as normal, healthy, good, godly, right, clean. No wonder, then, these quotations say,

> [12]"All have turned away,
>   they have together become worthless. . . ."
> [13]"Their throats are open graves;
>   their tongues practice deceit."
> [14]"The poison of vipers is on their lips."
> "Their mouths are full of cursing and bitterness."
>
>   Romans 3:12–14

Oh, I know many of us come from civilized backgrounds where there is not all that much cursing and bitterness unless we bang our thumbs with a hammer or get fired from work when we think it is unjust. Despite all of our civilized behavior, however, when we face enough pressure we find it desperately easy, in the back of our minds (even if we are disciplined enough not to let it actually escape from our mouths), to nurse bitterness and curse our perceived opponents. This is scarcely a mark of loving our neighbors as ourselves; it is not a way of praising God; it is not a reflection of the *shalom*—the utter well-being that only God can establish—God intends us to enjoy.

The truth of the matter is that, as the last line of these biblical quotations puts it, "There is no fear of God before their eyes" (3:18). So we are still enmeshed in the central problem disclosed in the drama of the entire Bible. How do we human beings get restored to God? If, as we saw at the beginning of this chapter, *self-justification* will not work, how about simple denial? Here is part of the testimony of a philosopher named Budziszewski. He writes,

> Everything goes wrong without God. This is true even of the good things he has given us, such as our minds. One of the good things I've been given is a stronger than average mind. . . . The problem is that a strong mind that refuses the call to serve God has its own way of going wrong. When some people flee from God they rob and kill. When others flee from God they do a lot of drugs and have a lot of sex. When I fled from God I didn't do any of those things; my way of fleeing was to get stupid. Though it always comes as a surprise to intellectuals, there are some forms of stupidity that one must be highly intelligent and educated to achieve. . . .
>
> Paul said that the knowledge of God's law is "written on our hearts, our consciences also bearing witness" [that's a quotation of Romans 2:15]. . . . That means that so long as we have minds, we can't not know them. Well, I was unusually determined not to know them; therefore I had to destroy my mind. . . .
>
> Visualize a man opening up the access panels of his mind and pulling out all the components that have God's image stamped on them. The problem is that they all have God's image stamped on them, so the man can never stop. No matter how many he pulls out, there are still more to pull. I was that man. Because I pulled out more and more, there was less and less that I could think about. [That is what he means by saying that he became stupid. Christians have so much to think about. People who write God off and all of his truth have much less to think about. They become stupid.][2]

He goes on to say that before he was converted, he thought he was becoming more focused, he thought that he was brighter than the fools around him—until he saw that he was himself the fool.

Now this is the background Paul has established and now simply presupposes as he writes the spectacular paragraph that Martin Luther calls the center of the entire Bible: Romans 3:21–26. We shall add a few verses more.

> [21]But now apart from the law the righteousness of God has been made known, to which the Law and the Prophets testify. [22]This righteousness is given through faith in Jesus Christ to all who believe. There is no difference between Jew and Gentile, [23]for all have sinned and fall short of the glory of God, [24]and all are justified freely by his grace through the redemption that came by Christ Jesus. [25]God presented Christ as a sacrifice of atonement [propitiation], through the shedding of his blood—to be received by faith. He did this to demonstrate his

justice, because in his forbearance he had left the sins committed beforehand unpunished—[26]he did it to demonstrate his justice at the present time, so as to be just and the one who justifies those who have faith in Jesus.

[27]Where, then, is boasting? It is excluded. Because of what law? The law that requires works? No, because of the "law" that requires faith. [28]For we maintain that a person is justified by faith apart from observing the law. [29]Is God the God of Jews only? Is he not the God of Gentiles too? Yes, of Gentiles too, [30]since there is only one God, who will justify the circumcised by faith and the uncircumcised through that same faith. [31]Do we, then, nullify the law by this faith? Not at all! Rather, we uphold the law.

Romans 3:21–31

Frankly, these paragraphs are so condensed that even if you have been a Christian for quite a while, when you hear them read you may start hearing strings of God-words going by you without being able quite to follow the flow. The only way to understand the thought is to go slowly enough through these lines that you unpack the logic and discover how the entire passage is put together. The passage will certainly repay careful reading: I know no passage in all of the Bible clearer on what the cross achieves than this one. This is what Jesus did on the cross.

So we shall follow the argument, first of all, in verses 21–26, and then, secondly, in verses 27–31.[3]

Romans 3:21–26

1. The Revelation of God's Righteousness in Its Relationship to the Old Testament (Rom. 3:21)

Now remember, Paul just spent two and a half chapters showing how much guilt, ingratitude, idolatry, and sin there is—and this in the face of God being a righteous God. So how will we be righteous in his eyes? How will we live under him?

"But now" (3:21) means at this point in the Bible's storyline, at this point in redemptive history: now that Jesus has come.

"Apart from the law" refers to the law given by Moses, the law-covenant under which the Hebrews, the Israelites, lived for a millennium and a half.

"But now apart from the law the righteousness of God has been made known." That is to say, the righteousness of God that transcends the ages, the very character of God, his perfect righteousness, has now been disclosed or made known not in the framework of that old law-covenant with its sacrificial system and its priesthood and so forth. God's righteousness has *now* been made known *apart from* that. To use language that Paul uses elsewhere, what he is saying is, "We have now arrived at the *new* covenant; now a *new* frame of reference, a *new* covenant has arrived." He has not yet explained how it is grounded or how it works.

But that does not mean that this new situation is entirely off from the old law-covenant, for Paul adds an interesting clause at the end of verse 21: "But now apart from the law the righteousness of God has been made known, *to which the Law and the Prophets testify*" (emphasis added). That is, if you read the Old Testament carefully and listen well, you will see that the law-covenant that Moses gave actually anticipated what is coming now. For example, the blood of bull and goat borne by the high priest into the Most Holy Place in the tabernacle on Yom Kippur, the Day of Atonement, pointed toward the ultimate sacrifice that pays for sin, the sacrifice of Christ.

Even those laws that we call moral laws (e.g., "You shall not murder," "You shall not commit adultery")—these point forward too. For example, imagine the final state of things, a new heaven and a new earth, perfect righteousness, resurrection existence, with absolutely no sin or death or decay anywhere. Do you think there are going to be little signs posted here and there saying, "You shall not murder" or "You shall not commit adultery"? Probably it is pretty hard to commit murder and adultery in resurrection bodies in the perfection of paradise anyway! But quite apart from such considerations, do you really think that those sorts of laws will be needed? If you say yes, then you have not yet imagined perfection. If you say no, then you might ask yourself, "Does this mean that God's law has changed?" Oh no, that misses the point entirely, because ultimately the laws that say "You shall not murder" and "You shall not commit adultery" anticipate a time when murder and adultery, hatred and selfish sexual lust, will all be gone. In that sense, the laws point to the perfect righteousness when people love one another, when murder and adultery are not so much prohibited as unthinkable.

So the law-covenant, which set out many commands and prohibitions, along with its sacrificial system and its structures for the nation—in many ways these things pointed forward to what is now being introduced by Christ. If the righteousness of God is now made known "apart from the law," that very law bore witness to this new state of affairs and anticipated this day.

2. The Availability of God's Righteousness to All without Racial Distinction but on Condition of Faith (Rom. 3:22–23)

"This righteousness [which has now been made known in a fresh way] is given through faith in Jesus Christ to *all* who believe. There is no difference between Jew and Gentile, for *all* have sinned and fall short of the glory of God" (Rom. 3:21–23). Observe the two italicized instances of the word "all": it is this pair of "all's" that connects this paragraph with the previous two and a half chapters. The previous two and a half chapters have argued at great length and in immaculate detail that *all* people need this righteousness. We are *all* guilty before God. But now there is a righteousness from God that meets our needs. It can be *our* righteousness. And it is "given through faith in Jesus Christ to *all* who believe," Jews and Gentiles, "for *all* have sinned."

The old covenant was for the Israelites. Of course, even in the Old Testament, God presents himself as sovereign over all the nations of the world. Even in the Old Testament it is written, "Righteousness exalts a nation, but sin condemns any people"—and God holds all to account. That is why, for example, the God of Israel in the Old Testament can be depicted as holding, say, Babylon or Assyria to account. Today he holds America and China to account. He is still the sovereign Lord who holds all to account. Nevertheless in Old Testament times the focus of the law-covenant tied God to the Israelites, the descendants of Abraham, Isaac, and Jacob.

But now, we are told, this righteousness from God that is in some ways detached from that old covenant, is given through faith in Jesus Christ. It is not given on the old covenant grounds where you were supposed to be born into the nation or adopted into the nation in some sense. No, it is "given through faith in Jesus Christ to *all* who believe. There is no difference between Jew and Gentile, for *all* have sinned and fall short of the glory of God." In other words, the grace is extended as far as the need, and the need is everywhere: Jew and Gentile alike.

One of the wonderful things about the last book of the Bible is that it pictures around the throne of God on the last day men and women from every language and ethnicity and nation. Millions of them! On that last day around the throne, there will be lots of Chinese, Hutus, Tutsis, Serbs, Russians, Bolivians, Arabs, Europeans—different colors, different senses of humor, different languages, different ethnicities. God draws out his people from all of those nations. Today, Christians who travel discover that wherever they go, they will find Christians in amazing places. I've been in Papua New Guinea with brothers and sisters in Christ who a generation-and-a-half ago would have been cannibals. I have visited Hong Kong: what a spectacular city with such a mix of styles: Gucci and Saks Fifth Avenue, and two blocks over an open meat market. Such a colorful array of people—and a fair number of Christians in that lot, too. And on and on all around the world: Africans, Asians, Europeans, Americans. Around the throne on that last day people will be found from all over the globe and from every ethnicity, *because* under the terms of this new covenant God has made available the righteousness that we so desperately need to *all* who believe because *all* have sinned and fall short of the glory of God.

Now Paul has still not explained how God has done this. But that is the thrust of the point he establishes.

3. The Source of God's Righteousness in the Gracious Provision of Christ Jesus as the Propitiation for Our Sins (Rom. 3:24–25)

"There is no difference between Jew and Gentile, for all have sinned and fall short of the glory of God, and all are justified freely by his grace through the redemption that came by Christ Jesus. God presented Christ as a sacrifice of atonement [propitiation], through the shedding of his blood—to be received by faith" (Rom. 3:22–25).

Now we are getting into some theological words that have to be unpacked.

REDEMPTION

What does *redemption* mean? For us, *redemption* is a word belonging to God-talk. We do not use this word very much in ordinary speech anymore. A generation or two ago we still used *redemption* in some business dealings. If you went to a pawn shop and hawked your grandfather's watch to obtain a little money, and then you managed to earn some money a few weeks later, you would go back and *redeem* the watch. You bought it back and thus freed it from where it was. Likewise people would speak in economic terms of redeeming their mortgage, finally paying it off.

In the ancient world, redemption terminology was used even more commonly. It was not restrictively God-talk vocabulary. For example, in the ancient world you could become a slave because there were no Western-style bankruptcy laws (like Chapter 11 or 13 here in America). Supposing you borrow some money, you start a business, the economy flounders, and your business goes belly-up. What do you do? In the ancient world what you have to do is sell yourself and/or your family into slavery. That is what you do; there is no Chapter 11.

But suppose you have a rich cousin twenty miles away, close to a day's journey, who hears that that you have had to sell yourself into slavery. Suppose he cares for you and decides that he is going to do something about it. What he might well do is come along and buy you back. Now, there was a complicated process for doing that through pagan temples, a process we need not go into— but what he would be doing would be redeeming you. He is buying you back and thus freeing you from your slavery.

So now what Paul is saying, in effect, is this: "We too have received a redemption, a liberation from our slavery to sin. We have been bought back, and as a result we have been freed from what would otherwise enslave us." In fact, what Paul asserts is that all of us "are justified freely by his grace through the redemption that came by Christ Jesus" (3:24). This is astounding: we are all *justified*—declared just before God, declared righteous before God—how so, when we are not just, when we are not righteous? We have just traversed two and a half chapters to say that we are not righteous. Yet now we are told that this righteousness from God has declared us righteous. We are justified freely by his grace through this redemption, this buying us back, our freedom now secured by Christ Jesus, through the redemption that came by Christ Jesus. How does this work? What does it mean?

To understand, we must come to grips with another word Paul uses.

PROPITIATION

"God presented Christ as a *sacrifice of atonement*, through the shedding of his blood—to be received by faith" (3:25, emphasis added). Or as the ESV rightly has it, God presented Christ "as a *propitiation* by his blood, to be received by faith" (emphasis added). Now what does that mean? We need to pause for a moment and work through this word "propitiation" or "sacrifice of atonement."

Propitiation is that sacrificial act by which God becomes propitious, which doesn't tell you very much, does it? "Propitious" simply means favorable: to say that propitiation is an act by which God becomes propitious is to say it is an act by which God becomes favorable to us. He is set over against us in wrath, but now by this sacrificial act he becomes favorable to us. That is propitiation.

Others prefer to use the expression "expiation." Expiation is the act by which sin is cancelled, wiped out, taken off the board. So the object of expiation is sin. The object of propitiation is God. God becomes favorable.

In the pagan world of the first century, when pagans offered sacrifices to their gods, very often it was with the desire to make them propitious, to make them favorable. So if you want to make a sea voyage, you make a propitiating sacrifice to Neptune, the god of the sea, in the hope that he will not be bad-tempered or angry with you, and then you will have a safe sea voyage. It was a sacrifice to Neptune to make him propitious. It was a propitiating sacrifice.

But this text says something rather astonishing. In that old pagan way of looking at things, the human worshiper offers a propitiating sacrifice to the gods. But this text says that *God* presented Christ as a propitiating sacrifice. So does that mean that God, presenting Christ as a propitiating sacrifice, propitiates God? How can God offer a sacrifice that propitiates himself?

Partly because of the strangeness of this thought, many have rejected this interpretation entirely. They think it is silly. How can God propitiate himself? Besides, some of them just do not like the notion of blood sacrifice or God being wrathful. In the 1930s an influential professor in the United Kingdom, a man by the name of C. H. Dodd, argued strongly that "propitiation" makes no sense as a translation. Surely God cannot propitiate himself; therefore, this must be *expiation*, in which by the sacrifice of his Son, sin is cancelled. Further, Dodd argued, God so loved the world that he gave his Son (see John 3:16). If he was already so favorable to the world that he gave his Son, how could we properly imagine that the Son is then propitiating God, making God favorable? God is already favorable. So surely what is happening must be expiation (cancelling sin), not propitiation (averting God's wrath).

Those who responded to Professor Dodd pointed out that in the Old Testament when propitiation is mentioned, it is regularly in the same context where the wrath of God is mentioned. In fact, the word rendered *propitiation* is used two-thirds of the time in the Greek translation of the Old Testament to refer to the top of the ark of the covenant, where on the Day of Atonement the blood of the bull and goat was shed—precisely to turn away God's wrath. God ordained that this sacrifice be offered for this purpose. And in the passage here in Romans, we have just had two and a half chapters that begin, "*The wrath of God* is being revealed from heaven against all the godlessness and wickedness" that we human beings have deployed in suppressing the truth (1:18, emphasis added). So the wrath of God is the backdrop to the usage here in Romans 3:25.

God's response to our sin is deep, personal, unavoidable. That wrath must be set aside, or we cannot be "justified," declared just in his eyes. But how can God propitiate himself? The answer, of course, is that the entire storyline of the Bible has taught us that God stands over against us in wrath because of his holiness, but he stands over against us in love because he is that kind of God. Both are important.

On the one hand, if God does not stand over against us in wrath when we have sinned, then he is immoral: "Oh, I don't care, they can blaspheme and kill and rape and steal and lie. No sweat. I don't care. No skin off my nose." But God is righteous; he *does* stand over against us in wrath, especially because we have marginalized him. We have de-god-ed him.

God knows that it is for our *good* that he be at the center of absolutely everything. It is not that he wants to have a certain preference among peers: he is not our peer! When you and I want to be especially praised by our peers, by our fellow human beings, we want to be stronger or wiser or richer or more beautiful than they are; we want to be thought of as in some sense superior. But God *is* superior. He is not just like us. He is *God*. Equally important, God in his love knows that we *must* see him at the center of everything or we are lost and undone. To see him this way is for our good. It is out of love that God insists that he be God, that idols must be banished. And he is correspondingly angry when by our actions, thoughts, and deeds we declare, "It will not be so."

God does stand over against us in wrath because of his holiness, but, on the other hand, he stands over against us in love because that is the kind of God he is. This text says that God presented Christ to be the propitiation for our sins. Now in fact you cannot have propitiation (i.e., the turning aside of the wrath of God) without expiation (i.e., the cancelling of sin). The two hang together in the Bible. Even in the sacrifice on the Day of Atonement that was so, which is why some people have preferred the more embracing expression "sacrifice of atonement": "God presented Christ as a sacrifice of atonement" (3:25) for our sins, cancelling our sin and turning aside the wrath of God in one act. What you must not lose sight of in the context of Romans is that the righteous wrath of God must be set aside without tarnishing God's justice.

We need to think about this just a little more. It is not as if the Father stands over against us in wrath, really angry, and dear Jesus comes along and stands over against us in love. That would be a barbaric notion: the Triune God would not be pulling together in harmony to free us human beings, his image-bearers, from the tyranny of our sin. The whole Triune God (Father, Son, and Spirit) stands over against us in wrath, and equally he stands over against us in love.

I think that one of the reasons we find it hard in the West to visualize this is because of our judicial system. In virtually every Western country, the judiciary is independent, and the judge is someone who must not be a victim of the criminal who is under review. Suppose, for example, some person charged with mugging is brought before a judge, and it turns out that the judge is the one who was mugged. In our system the judge must therefore recuse himself or herself because the judge is not to stand in judgment of any person where the judge himself or herself is the victim of the crime. That is because the judge administrates a bigger judicial system. That is all a judge does. The judge is supposed to be administering, in an equitable way, the larger system. The criminal has not in any sense sinned against the judge. The criminal sins against the state, the law, the constitution, the people. If you are in a monarchy as in Great Britain, then you sin against the crown. But you do not sin against the judge. The judge is supposed to be an independent arbiter who is using the structure of the judicial system to apply the law fairly and evenhandedly to the person who is under review.

But that is not the way it is in God's court. God, as we have seen again and again, is always the most offended party. He is the one we have mugged, and he is our Judge: he never recuses himself. Yet his justice is not for that reason unfair. He is perfectly fair. He is himself the very embodiment of justice. He is perfectly righteous. He knows everything. Nothing can be hidden from him, not even our thoughts. His justice is perfect. But he is also the most offended party. Always. Thus, in wrath he demands that justice be done. Then in the person of his own dear Son, he pays the penalty.

In our system of courts, that is just so stupid it is unbelievable. Perhaps you have heard illustrations where you picture someone who is brought before a judge and the judge finds the person guilty and orders a fine of five thousand dollars or, alternatively, confines the criminal to five years in jail. Then the judge descends from his bench, takes out his checkbook, and writes the check for five thousand dollars, or, alternatively, takes off his robe and goes to jail for five years in place of the guilty criminal. That is called substitution. I suppose the illustration does get across the notion of substitution, but in our system it would nevertheless be incredibly corrupt. No judge in our system could do that. The judge is supposed to be an independent arbiter whose passion is the fair administration of the law, the majesty of the law. He does not have the right to take the prisoner's place. That would be a corruption of justice.

But in the courts of heaven, God sets up the system. He is not only perfectly just, but he is also the offended party. And in the person of his own dear Son he absorbs the penalty on behalf of the people who put their faith in him. This last point is searingly important.

4. The Demonstration of God's Righteousness through the Cross of Jesus Christ (Rom. 3:25–26)

"He did this [i.e., God set forth Jesus to be the propitiation for our sins] to demonstrate his justice, because in his forbearance he had left the sins committed beforehand unpunished—he did it to demonstrate his justice at the present time, so as to be just and the one who justifies those who have faith in Jesus" (Rom. 3:25–26).

God "did this to demonstrate his justice," not simply to love, forgive, or redeem us—but to demonstrate his justice. If God had forgiven our sin without sin in any sense being paid for, where would the justice be? If justice is not served, how could God say, "I forgive you," without fostering *in*justice? The sin must be paid for.

"In his forbearance [God] had left the sins committed beforehand unpunished" (3:25). This refers to all the sins of God's own covenant people in the past. They had often received temporal punishments of some sort or another. For example, under God's justice the corrupt people of Israel did go into exile. They faced pressures and earthly punishments of various kinds. But now Paul points out that they never faced the full weight of God's condemnation. That was coming on Christ himself. They had been spared this condemnation. In some deep way, God had left their sins still unpunished. God now demonstrates his justice in sending Christ to the cross "because in his forbearance he had left the sins committed beforehand unpunished." Jesus bears their sins as he bears my sins. Jesus does this "to demonstrate his justice at the present time, so as to *be just* and the one who justifies those who have faith in Jesus" (3:26, emphasis added). In other words, not only by this means does God declare guilty people like you and me just (i.e., he justifies us because someone has paid for our sin), but he demonstrates his own justice while he is doing it.

Do you want to know where God's justice is most powerfully demonstrated? On the cross. Do you want to know where God's love is most powerfully demonstrated? On the cross. There Jesus, the God-man, bore hell itself, and God did this both to be just and to be the one who declares just those who have faith in him. There is thus a sense in which God views me, Don Carson, through the lens of Jesus. That is to say, my sin is now viewed as his, and he has paid for it. And his justice, his righteousness, is now viewed as mine. God looks at me and declares me just, not because I am (I am guilty!) but because he has set forth his Son to be the propitiation for our sins.

Romans 3:27–31

Repeatedly in Romans 3:21–26, Paul tells us that the way we receive this righteousness, this justification, from God is *faith*. In the last few verses of the chapter, Romans 3:27–31, Paul underscores three emphases on faith. Briefly:

1. Faith Excludes Boasting (Rom. 3:27; 4:1–2)

"Where, then, is boasting? It is excluded. Because of what law? The law that requires works? No, because of the 'law' that requires faith" (Rom. 3:27).

That is to say, I cannot come before you and say, "I am a superior person. That is why I am accepted by God." At the end of the day I am declared to be just before God not because I try harder but because I have received God's gift by faith. The very nature of faith excludes boasting. No one in the new heaven and the new earth will brag about the way personal merit attracted God's approval.

2. Faith Is Necessary to Preserve Grace (Rom. 3:28; 4:3–8)

"For we maintain that a person is justified by faith apart from observing the law" (Rom. 3:28).

If somehow I can get pardon from God (i.e., God can look on me with favor) because I earn it, then grace is no more grace. We have already seen that when we are dealing with a God with whom we cannot barter, the only way that we are going to be forgiven is by his sovereign grace worked out in the cross. That grace is demonstrated in the cross, and we receive it by faith. Faith preserves God's sovereign grace. If somehow we earned God's favor, then God's favor would not be dispensed on the ground of God's grace.

Not only does faith exclude boasting, not only is it necessary to preserve grace, but . . .

3. Faith Is Necessary If Jews and Gentiles Alike Are to Be Saved (Rom. 3:29–30; 4:9–17)

"Is God the God of Jews only? Is he not the God of Gentiles too? Yes, of Gentiles too, since there is only one God, who will justify the circumcised [i.e., Jews] by faith and the uncircumcised [i.e., Gentiles] through that same faith" (Rom. 3:29–30).

One of the necessary implications of monotheism, belief in one God, is that in some sense he is the God of all, acknowledged or otherwise. He is the God of Jews and Gentiles alike. The way that you and I receive this bold declaration that we are just before God is by faith. For on the basis of the cross, and only on that basis, God justifies believing Jews (the circumcised) and believing Gentiles (the uncircumcised).

4. Christian Faith, Far from Overturning the Old Testament, Fulfills and Upholds It (Rom. 3:31; 4:18–25)

"Do we, then, nullify the law by this faith? Not at all! Rather, we uphold the law" (Rom. 3:31). Paul thus closes the circle: he brings us back to verse 21, where he has already established that this wonderful display of God's righteousness, though it now appears apart from the law-covenant, was anticipated and announced by that same law-covenant. By saying something similar here, he is emphatically insisting that the whole Bible hangs together. God's purposes have been unified all along—layered, complex, interwoven, but wonderfully unified, so that now, in the cross and resurrection of Jesus, the law-covenant is fulfilled and its long-term purpose in the plan of God spectacularly fulfilled. Guilty men and women are declared just and reconciled to God, not because they are just, not because they try to balance up good deeds and bad deeds, but because by faith they trust Christ's sacrifice on their behalf—a sacrifice that simultaneously pays for their sin and establishes God's justice.

A Final Word on Faith

We cannot have failed to observe that "faith" or "believing" are crucial terms in this chapter of Romans. Yet we can easily misconstrue these words, because today in the Western world the word "faith" commonly has one of two meanings, neither of which Paul uses:

1. In some contemporary contexts "faith" is the equivalent of "religion." We say there are many faiths, many religions. You have your faith, and I have my faith; you have your religion, and I have my religion. In this usage, "faith" is simply a synonym of "religion."

2. But when it is not used in that way, in our culture "faith" means something like personal, subjective, religious choice. That is, it is not tied in any sense to truth or to fact. It is a personal, subjective, religious choice. So if you say to some people today, "You must have faith in Jesus," it sounds like an invitation to a blind leap: some opt for Jesus, others opt for Allah and Muhammad, and others opt for Buddhism. But although the word "faith" is used in a variety of ways in the Bible, not once is it ever used that way. Not once.

In the Bible it is crucially important to establish faith's object, that is, *what* or *whom* you believe. For example, in another of Paul's letters, a letter in which he is writing to the Christians in Corinth, Paul insists that Christians believe that Jesus rose from the dead (see 1 Cor. 15). Suppose, he argues, that Jesus did not rise from the dead; suppose that claim is historical nonsense. Then what happens to your faith if Jesus did not rise from the dead?

One, the first witnesses are all deceived or liars; you cannot trust any of the five hundred of them from different sites, different times, different circumstances. They are all liars. Two, it means that you are still lost because the Bible teaches that it was Christ's dying and rising again that brought our redemption. That's how we are reconciled to God. Three, your faith is useless. In other words, if you believe that Jesus rose from the dead when in fact Jesus did not rise from the dead, your faith is worthless because *faith's validation depends in part on the truthfulness of faith's object.* That is why the Bible never encourages you to believe something that is not true or something that it is not prepared to declare to be true. That is why in the Bible faith is strengthened by articulating and defending the truth. The Bible never says, "Just believe, believe, believe, believe, believe—it doesn't matter if it's true, just believe. So long as you are sincere in your belief, that is good." And four, Paul goes one step farther and says that if you believe something that is not true (like the resurrection of Jesus, if it never happened), you are in fact of all people most to be pitied. Your life is a joke. You are believing something that is nonsense.

So as long as you are convinced that Christ did not rise from the dead, I am the last person who is going to urge you to sort of tighten up your stomach muscles and pretend to believe it. That is not faith. It might be the onset of a stomach ulcer, but it is not faith.

Even here, however, it is important that we avoid deluding ourselves. If someone were to object, "I prefer not to have *any* faith. I shall live my life solely on the basis of verifiable evidence," the obvious answer is that faith is unavoidable. If you hold that *any* claim to superior knowledge about God *cannot* be true, that itself is an object of faith, an object of religious belief—that is, a belief that shapes your frame of reference about everything you hold to be important. If you insist that no one can decide which faith is true, you are yourself making a claim grounded on a certain kind of faith, a perception of reality you have come to trust. So why should we believe you? All of us, without exception, make truth-claims of some kind or other. Doubtless it is difficult to evaluate them. But we have no alternative except to try.

Thus when Paul here in Romans 3 commends faith, what he is wanting from us is a God-given ability to perceive what God has done by hanging Jesus on the cross, reconciling us to himself, setting aside his own just wrath, demonstrating his love, and declaring us just even though we are not, because the righteousness of Christ Jesus is now counted as ours and our sin is now counted as his. And he has anchored this in God's gracious self-disclosure across enormous tracts of time, across the Bible's entire storyline, climaxing in the shattering reality that the God who made us, the God who is our Judge, bled and died for us and rose again.

Certainly that is the kind of Jesus you can trust. It is the kind of God in whom you can place your faith.

Concluding Prayer

Dilemma wretched: how shall holiness
Of brilliant life unshaded, tolerate
Rebellion's fetid slime, and not abate
In its own glory, compromised at best?
Dilemma wretched: how can truth attest
That God is love, and not be shamed by hate
And wills enslaved and bitter death—the freight
Of curse deserved, the human rebels' mess?
The Cross! The Cross! The sacred meeting-place
Where, knowing neither compromise nor loss,
God's love and holiness in shattering grace
The great dilemma slays! The Cross! The Cross!
This holy, loving God whose dear Son dies
By this is just—and one who justifies.[4]

Open our eyes, heavenly Father, that we may see the truth of what you have done in Jesus, and in seeing the truth, believe. For Jesus' sake, Amen.

The God Who Gathers and Transforms His People

In one of his more recent books, *God Is Not Great: How Religion Poisons Everything*, the articulate and very interesting atheist and critic of Christianity Christopher Hitchens argues that the entire record of religion—all religion—is toward war, hatred, and strife, whether it is the Protestant-Catholic strife of Belfast in recent decades, or Beirut between peoples of Christian and Muslim heritage, or Belgrade or Baghdad or Bombay. All around the world religion poisons everything. It has to be said that there is some truth to the charge. It is not for nothing that centuries back the Thirty Years' War was at least in substantial measure a war of religion.

The reason that there is some truth to the charge Hitchens levels is that one of the things that religion does—all religion—is to treat some issues as matters of staggering importance. Today the current round of dominant terrorists are Muslims, and undoubtedly they would like to see Islamic culture and faith enjoy a bigger share of the world's financial and cultural pie. But what makes their beliefs crushingly important in their own eyes is their conviction that they represent the mind of God himself.

Mind you, it has also been shown by Alister McGrath in his book on atheism[1] that if you do not have religion to transcendentalize things, you end up transcendentalizing something else. In other words, the act of making something out to be of transcendental importance is not exclusively a function of religion. It may be a function of human desire to control. In the twentieth century, the powerful movements of Nazism and Stalinism were not religiously driven. Some in the Nazi party laid claim to their reconstruction of

Christianity, but the purpose was to domesticate Christianity and harness its energies. In reality, what drove the two movements—Nazism and Stalinism—were distinct visions of reality: on the one hand, the transcendentalizing of ethnicity, a sense of intrinsic Aryan superiority, a hate-filled blaming of Jews and of the Treaty of Versailles; on the other hand, a transcendentalizing of the state grounded in Marxist social and economic theory. So it is not as if religion poisons everything while everything else is good. The century characterized by the greatest bloodshed, the twentieth century, generated most of its violence in movements that were distinctly anti-religious. The world did not lose one-third of the population of Cambodia because of Christianity but because of communism.

Nevertheless, Christianity has had its fanatics. Still, the notion of fanaticism needs to be analyzed. Probably most people think that Christians can be placed on a spectrum between nominalism (Christians in name only) and fanaticism (Christians who are extremely intense about their beliefs and morals). On this scale, we might be most drawn to the middle of the scale, to the nice moderates. The problem is that the scale itself is mischievous. It assumes that Christianity itself is primarily about effort and moral improvement, so that the high-intensity end of the scale is peopled with self-righteous, over-confident, superior, condescending folk who are, at best, terribly off-putting.

Yet that is not what Christianity is about. Where one sees that Christianity is being lived out in a fashion reasonably faithful to the Bible's emphasis on salvation by grace, on what God has done for us in Christ and not on what we have achieved, it ought to change everything. Tim Keller writes,

> Belief that you are accepted by God by sheer grace is profoundly humbling. The people who are fanatics, then, are not so because they are too committed to the gospel, but because they are not committed enough.
>
> Think of people you consider fanatical. They're overbearing, self-righteous, opinionated, insensitive, and harsh. Why? It's not because they are too Christian but because they are not Christian enough. They are fanatically zealous and courageous, but they are not fanatically humble, sensitive, loving, empathetic, forgiving, or understanding—as Christ was. . . . What strikes us as overly fanatical is actually a failure to be fully committed to Christ and his gospel.[2]

If you really do drink deeply from what we have been seeing in the Bible and see that ultimately our hope is in God's grace, it changes everything. This is why biblical Christianity has always had within its heritage the capacity to challenge and reform itself: it returns to the grace of God. That is why, however ghastly and defenseless the Crusades were, it is the Christian heritage in the West that has apologized for them countless times. After all, Islam took over the Middle East first with *equal* bloodthirstiness, and there is no trace in the heritage of Islam of any apology for any of it.

Thus the slavery that was enacted and developed in the West, in which Christians participated, was also eventually destroyed by Christians who were trying to become more biblical and who challenged the entire wretched enterprise. Thomas Sowell analyzes what took place under Wilberforce and other Christian leaders in Great Britain until first the slave trade across the Atlantic and then eventually slavery itself was abolished in the British Empire. He notes that what drove the abolition movement initially were evangelical Christians determined to put a stop to an evil, and eventually enough public opinion was mobilized over successive generations of government officials that the antislavery movement was pushed further and further to its logical conclusion.[3]

Despite revisionist arguments advanced to prove that abolitionists had discovered it was more economical to abolish slavery than to maintain it, the realities were very different. For example, when slavery was finally abolished, the British government undertook to pay all the great sugarcane farmers of Jamaica and elsewhere under the British crown the price of the slaves to free them. The promise was for *half* the national GDP, and they undertook it not because it was going to save them money but because of Christian influence regarding what is right and wrong. That does not justify in the slightest all the wickedness that was done beforehand, but it does remind us that although the Bible can be used in all kinds of shameful ways, it can ground followers of Jesus so deeply in the sheer grace of God that entire ethical systems are transformed. When you come across what the gospel is genuinely about, it is humbling. It does not make people arrogant. It transforms them.

In the previous chapter we saw how the cross of Jesus is the ground of our reconciliation. God propitiates himself. He sets aside his own wrath because he is the God of love. He satisfies his sense of justice in the person of his own dear Son and in grace reconciles ungrateful rebels to himself. The result is that they come to him humbly, not imagining for a moment that they are doing him a favor. Quite the reverse: they take hold of this reconciliation, this justification from God, by faith. We saw that this salvation is granted by grace alone and received by faith alone. This is true for Jews and Gentiles alike.

In other letters written by Paul, however, the apostle develops his argument in slightly different directions. What I shall do in the remainder of this chapter is a bit different from what I have usually done. Instead of focusing primarily on one short passage or chapter from the Bible, I shall cite a handful of passages at length and offer some brief comments along the way so that you can hear Paul's argument with slightly different emphases, emphases that insist that the Good News about Christ and his cross, what the Bible calls "the gospel," calls out people, gathers them together, and transforms them. Any so-called Christianity that does not incorporate this reality into its vision is not worthy of the name it carries.

Ephesians 2:1–22

Paul is writing to believers in the city of Ephesus, and he describes their conversion:

> [1]As for you, you were dead in your transgressions and sins, [2]in which you used to live when you followed the ways of this world and of the ruler of the kingdom of the air [that's a way that Paul alludes to Satan, our old friend from Genesis 3], the spirit who is now at work in those who are disobedient. [3]All of us also lived among them at one time, gratifying the cravings of our sinful nature and following its desires and thoughts. Like the rest, we were by nature deserving of wrath [which is, of course, exactly what we discovered in the first two and a half chapters of Romans]. [4]But because of his great love for us [despite the fact that we deserve the wrath!], God, who is rich in mercy, [5]made us alive with Christ even when we were dead in transgressions—it is by grace you have been saved. [6]And God raised us up with Christ [that is, Christ's life is now ours] and seated us with him in the heavenly realms in Christ Jesus [God now views us as acceptable in his very presence as Christ himself is; we are united to him; that's the way God sees us, belonging to Christ and therefore enjoying free access to God], [7]in order that in the coming ages he might show the incomparable riches of his grace, expressed in his kindness to us in Christ Jesus. [8]For it is by grace you have been saved, through faith [that sounds like Romans 3]—and this is not from yourselves, it is the gift of God—[9]not by works, so that no one can boast [that again sounds like Romans 3]. [10]For we are God's handiwork, created in Christ Jesus to do good works, which God prepared in advance for us to do.
>
> Ephesians 2:1–10

In other words, Paul's concerns are not restricted to seeing men and women legally acquitted before God and nothing more. Certainly the guilt must be dealt with. The ground of God's wrath must be set aside. God himself must be propitiated. The sin must be expiated. But that still leaves me functionally a sinner. True, we need to be reconciled to this God; but we ourselves must be changed.

We witnessed this theme when we surveyed what the new birth is about (in chapter 8), but now we are discovering something similar, but with different terminology, in the writings of the apostle Paul. "For we are God's handiwork, *created in Christ Jesus to do good works*, which God prepared in advance for us to do" (Eph. 2:10, emphasis added). There *must* be transformation, for this is God's very purpose in salvation, in his "handiwork." This change, this new creation, this handiwork of God within us empowers us so that we will do good works—not because the good works have secured our place in God but precisely because they are the inevitable outcome of it.

In fact, if you recall, Romans 3 talks about Jews and Gentiles, both under wrath, both being saved by grace through faith. Paul now talks about Jews and Gentiles again. Observe what he says as he goes on in this chapter of Ephesians:

> [11]Therefore, remember that formerly you who are Gentiles by birth and called "uncircumcised" by those who call themselves "the circumcision" (which is done in the body by human hands) [that is, the Jews]— [12]remember that at that time you were separate from Christ, excluded from citizenship in Israel and foreigners to the covenants of the promise [that is, the covenant with Abraham and the covenant of law with Moses; you Gentiles are not part of that heritage], without hope and without God in the world. [13]But now [with the coming of Christ] in Christ Jesus you who once were far away have been brought near by the blood of Christ [that is, his death on our behalf].
>
> [14]For he himself is our peace, who has made the two [that is, Jews and Gentiles] one and has destroyed the barrier, the dividing wall of hostility, [15]by setting aside in his flesh the law with its commands and regulations [that is, we are no longer under that law-covenant that was only for the Israelites and therefore distinguished them from others]. His purpose was to create in himself one new humanity out of the two, thus making peace [a new locus of the people of God made up of Jews and Gentiles, people drawn from every tongue and tribe and people and nation, a new humanity], [16]and in one body to reconcile both of them to God through the cross [that is, not only reconciling them to each other and thus making peace, but reconciling them to God and thus making peace so that his wrath does not rest on us; all of this the cross achieves], by which he put to death their hostility. [17]He came and preached peace to you who were far away [that is, Gentiles] and peace to those who were near [that is, Jews]. [18]For through him we both have access to the Father by *one Spirit*.

Ephesians 2:11–18, emphasis added

"One Spirit." I briefly introduced the theme of God's Spirit, the Holy Spirit, earlier in this book. A little review will prepare us for learning a little more about him. Sometimes the Bible speaks of God sending his Spirit, but also of the Spirit talking. The Spirit is regularly presented not merely as an abstract power but as somehow like the eternal Word, like the eternal Son, the very self-disclosure, self-manifestation of God himself. Indeed, on the night that he is betrayed and then taken off to trial and crucifixion, Jesus talks at length of the Spirit whom he will send. He calls him the Holy Spirit; he also calls him another word that is harder to translate: *paraklētos* in the original. We sometimes transliterate it *Paraclete*. It means someone who comes alongside and helps in a variety of ways. For example, in John's Gospel the Paraclete, the Holy Spirit, helps by bringing conviction of sin to people who are otherwise self-righteous. He comes also to be the very presence and manifestation of God now that the Son is going to the cross and rising again and returning to his heavenly abode. It is the Spirit who is poured out upon us as the presence of God himself among us. He is said to be the one who takes up residence in people's lives, transforming them, giving them power.

Indeed, in Paul's letters, the Holy Spirit is sometimes called—this is stunning—the down payment or the deposit of the promised inheritance (see 2 Cor. 1:22; 5:5; Eph. 1:14). This promised, ultimate inheritance that we are to receive is a new heaven and a new earth, the home of righteousness, along with transformed resurrection bodies, a perfect world. The down payment or deposit of that inheritance, according to Paul, is the Holy Spirit himself. It will take God's immeasurable power to bring about the ultimate transformation on the last day, but already his formidable power, the same power that raised Jesus from the dead (see Eph. 1:18–21), is at work in us by his Holy Spirit to transform us, to begin the work of changing our hearts and minds.

So Paul talks about this new humanity that forms because of what Christ has done on the cross—a new humanity made up of Jews and Gentiles alike, with the Triune God at work to form it. For *Christ* came and preached peace to Jews and Gentiles alike (see 2:17), such that through *him* both groups have access to the *Father* by the *one Spirit*—Father, Son, and Spirit at work in this one new humanity. Paul adds:

> [19]Consequently, you are no longer foreigners and strangers, but fellow citizens with God's people and also members of his household, [20]built on the foundation of the apostles and prophets, with Christ Jesus himself as the chief cornerstone. [21]In him the whole building is joined together and rises to become a holy temple in the Lord. [22]And in him you too are being built together to become a dwelling in which God lives by his Spirit.
>
> Ephesians 2:19–22

Here is a vision of Christianity that goes way beyond the individual: it extends to the *church*. The church is God's "household." In another metaphor, the church is a building that is put together to serve as "a holy temple in the Lord," a building in which Jesus Christ himself is "the chief cornerstone." In the Old Testament the tabernacle, succeeded by the temple, was the place where God met sinful human beings; we have already seen that in John's Gospel, Jesus himself is the temple, the place where God meets sinful human beings. But the same language is now applied to the church: this is where the Good News of what Jesus has done is announced, where sinful human beings meet with God. As God displayed his presence in the Old Testament temple, so he does in the church, for God lives in this dwelling "by his Spirit."

One of the marks of the old covenant believers was circumcision. So important was this sign that Paul can refer to Jews collectively as "the circumcision." In this new covenant community that he describes, however, made up of Jews, Gentiles, and every other ethnicity, circumcision is no longer a decisive mark. Indeed, elsewhere the New Testament writers teach us that the public sign of becoming a Christian and joining together with other believers in the encouraging discipline of the local church is baptism. In the first century it was simply unthinkable that someone would become a Christian and not simultaneously join a local church and be baptized. For this community has been set free by Christ's death and resurrection, and empowered by the Holy Spirit himself. This community, the church, is the matrix in which individual believers grow, flourish, are encouraged and admonished, and frequently become leaders themselves.

Something is disastrously awry when the word "church" refers to nothing more than a building, or when a local "church" is made up of many people who do not know God, do not trust Christ, know nothing of having their sins forgiven, and have experienced nothing of the power of the Spirit to transform their lives. That is simply not what the New Testament says the church really is. Imagine the impact on the world if local churches lived out the high privileges Paul here describes.

And Paul can get more practical yet, as we shall see.

Ephesians 4:17–5:10

[17]So I tell you this, and insist on it in the Lord, that you must no longer live as the Gentiles do, in the futility of their thinking [that is, the Gentiles in their pre-Christian days]. [18]They are darkened in their understanding and separated from the life of God because of the ignorance that is in them due to the hardening of their hearts [that sounds like Romans 1: suppressing the truth in unrighteousness]. [19]Having lost all sensitivity, they have given themselves over to sensuality so as to indulge in every kind of impurity, and they are full of greed.

[20]That, however, is not the way of life you learned [21]when you heard about Christ and were taught in him in accordance with the truth that is in Jesus. [22]You were taught, with regard to your former way of life, to put off your old self, which is being corrupted by its deceitful desires; [23]to be made new in the attitude of your minds; [24]and to put on the new self, *created* to be like God in true righteousness and holiness.

Ephesians 4:17–24, emphasis added

"Created"? The power of God in creation in Genesis 1–2 is now being displayed again in a *new creation* that is every bit as real as the first creation—not yet consummated in the transformation of the ultimate creation but already working out in the lives of believers. Here is a picture of lives *transformed* by the gospel.

[25]Therefore each of you must put off falsehood and speak truthfully to your neighbor, for we are all members of one body. [26]"In your anger do not sin": Do not let the sun go down while you are still angry, [27]and do not give the devil a foothold. [28]Those who have been stealing must steal no longer, but must work, doing something useful with their own hands, that they may have something to share with those in need.

[29]Do not let any unwholesome talk come out of your mouths, but only what is helpful for building others up according to their needs, that it may benefit

those who listen. [30]And do not grieve the Holy Spirit of God [which presupposes that the Holy Spirit is a person; you don't grieve a power], with whom you were *sealed for the day of redemption.*

Ephesians 4:25–30, emphasis added

"Sealed for the day of redemption" means marked out as God's because he is already within you, he has already come as the down payment of the promised inheritance. You are set aside for him—so if you live as if none of this has happened, you grieve God as he has disclosed himself by his Spirit within you.

[31]Get rid of all bitterness, rage and anger, brawling and slander, along with every form of malice. [32]Be kind and compassionate to one another, forgiving each other, *just as in Christ God forgave you.*

Ephesians 4:31–32, emphasis added

So we are again back at the cross.

Biblical Christianity does not come along with a lot of pre-packaged rules, as if that were the essence of Christianity. We who are Christian pastors and preachers sometimes get this wrong ourselves. Perhaps we think we discern signs of decay in our culture, and if we are not careful our very first instinct will be to say, "Don't do that. Do this instead," and give the impression that we can fix things by imposing a fresh set of rules. You will show how righteous, good, and disciplined you are if you adopt all of these rules in your life. And after all, this text certainly talks about things we should do and should not do: for example, speaking the truth and getting rid of bitterness and malice. Of course there are some moral structures there.

And yet the fundamental Christian motivation is not adherence to more rules. Rather, we are told, "Forgive each other *as God in Christ has forgiven you.*" God's Spirit transforms us by bringing us back to the cross so that all of our morality is first and foremost a function of gratitude to God for what Christ has already done. If you begin to see just how much you were forgiven by what Christ did on the cross, how on earth can you possibly nurture bitterness toward others? If you see what is still in store for the future, that you have already received in part by the down payment of the Spirit who strengthens your moral resolve and gives you vistas of a new heaven and a new earth, how can you possibly be locked into the agonizing, painful, limited concerns of a world that will pass away? You are destined for eternity with God Almighty. That changes everything. When there is a moral slide in the church or in the broader world, what we must have more of is an accurate, thick, rich understanding of the gospel, for it transforms us. The Holy Spirit whom Jesus sent empowers us to live in a way that is different from the way we lived before. Everyone who has this life in himself does not live the way he or she used to live. Like the mysterious wind whose effects we can see but whose mechanisms are frequently obscure, we might not understand the mechanisms of the Spirit, but we see the results. So it is with those who are born of God.

So we read:

> [1]Follow God's example, therefore, as dearly loved children [2]and walk in the way of love, just as Christ loved us and gave himself up for us as a fragrant offering and sacrifice to God.
>
> Ephesians 5:1–2

Do you see this intermingling again of God's love and Christ's love? "Follow *God's* example [who loved us so much he gave his Son] . . . just as *Christ* loved us and gave himself up for us" (5:1–2, emphasis added). You cannot have one without the other. They are together. And because we have received so much from God in Christ Jesus, and we are the objects of such love, how can we not also love? Christ loved us and gave himself up for us as a fragrant sacrifice and offering to God.

> But among you there must not be even a hint of sexual immorality, or of any kind of impurity, or of greed, because these are improper for the Lord's people.
>
> Ephesians 5:3

That is, it is not simply improper because it is against the law, though doubtless that is true. It is improper because you have been bought with a price. You are the Lord's people. To play with sexual immorality is to dishonor the Lord, the Lord who loved you even to the death of the cross.

> Nor should there be obscenity, foolish talk or coarse joking, which are out of place, but rather thanksgiving.
>
> Ephesians 5:4

Thanksgiving is the underpinning of all Christian morality, not least Christian speech.

> For of this you can be sure: No immoral, impure or greedy person—such a person is an idolater—has any inheritance in the kingdom of Christ and of God.
>
> Ephesians 5:5

Isn't this statement remarkably penetrating? Greed is idolatry because what you most want becomes your god. What you most urgently pursue becomes your god. Idolatry does not require some little figurine made of stone or clay or pottery or some giant figure of a god somewhere carved out of a mountainside. Idolatry is anything and everything that displaces God, that makes me try to find my identity and place in the universe by appealing to something or someone other than God. Thus greed itself establishes who our real gods finally are. But for Christians? They have been reconciled to God by the death of Christ and have been exposed to something of God's spectacular glory and grandeur—not least in the cross.

> [5]No immoral, impure or greedy person—such a person is an idolater—has any inheritance in the kingdom of Christ and of God. [6]Let no one deceive you with empty words, for because of such things God's wrath comes on those who are disobedient. [7]Therefore do not be partners with them.
>
> [8]For you were once darkness, but now you are light in the Lord. Live as children of light [9](for the fruit of the light consists in all goodness, righteousness and truth) [10]and find out what pleases the Lord.
>
> Ephesians 5:5–10

Here again the change of heart and life that is part and parcel of being a Christian cannot be overlooked. The change of heart has come about such that we *want* to please the Lord, and we are eager to find out what pleases him. Biblical transformational Christianity gathers men and women together in the church, these people who have been called out—Jew or Gentile, it doesn't matter—and under the lordship of Christ they look back to the cross and look forward to what is still ahead. By the power of the Spirit and because of the change in their lives, they *want* to find out what pleases the Lord.

God help us! We who are Christians are still painfully inconsistent in these matters. We still await the final transformation that lies ahead of us. But we look back and see that we are not what we were. The point was well made by John Newton. His name might mean something to you if you saw the film on William Wilberforce, *Amazing Grace*. John Newton was the old slave trader who had become a preacher of the gospel. Looking back on his life, he estimated that he had transported twenty thousand slaves across the Atlantic. He said that in his nightmares he could still hear them scream. At some point he was genuinely converted. He became a Christian, and his life changed. Eventually he became a pastor. In his senior years, he declared,

> I am not what I ought to be—ah, how imperfect and deficient! I am not what I wish to be—I abhor what is evil, and I would cleave to what is good! I am not what I hope to be—soon, soon shall I put off mortality, and with mortality all sin and imperfection. Yet, though I am not what I ought to be, nor what I wish to be, nor what I hope to be, I can truly say, I am not what I once was; a slave to sin and Satan; and I can heartily join with the apostle, and acknowledge, "By the grace of God I am what I am."[4]

"For you were once darkness, but now you are light in the Lord. Live as children of light (for the fruit of the light consists in all goodness, righteousness and truth) and find out what pleases the Lord" (Eph. 5:8–10).

Let us look at one more passage with a similar contrast.

Galatians 5:13–26

Much of the argument in Galatians parallels some of what Romans explains: what justification is, what the cross achieves. As soon as you emphasize such things, however, you must also talk about how people need changing. It is not enough for us to stand acquitted before God and be reconciled to him. We must also be transformed. So in Galatians we read:

[13]You, my brothers and sisters, were called [that is, called when you became Christians] to be free. But do not use your freedom to indulge the sinful nature; rather, serve one another humbly in love. [14]For the entire law is fulfilled in keeping this one command [it points in this direction]: "Love your neighbor as yourself." [15]If you keep on biting and devouring each other, watch out or you will be destroyed by each other.

[16]So I say, walk by the Spirit [the Spirit who has been poured out upon us because of what Christ has achieved], and you will not gratify the desires of the sinful nature. [17]For the sinful nature desires what is contrary to the Spirit, and the Spirit what is contrary to the sinful nature. They are in conflict with each other, so that you are not to do whatever you want. [18]But if you are led by the Spirit, you are not under the law.

Galatians 5:13–18

So now Paul distinguishes for us the acts of the sinful nature and the fruit of the Spirit. The former are listed first:

[19]The acts of the sinful nature are obvious: sexual immorality, impurity and debauchery; [20]idolatry and witchcraft; hatred, discord, jealousy, fits of rage, selfish ambition, dissensions, factions [21]and envy; drunkenness, orgies, and the like [which pretty much covers it!]. I warn you, as I did before, that those who live like this will not inherit the kingdom of God.

Galatians 5:19–21

But now over against the acts of the sinful nature stands the fruit of the Spirit. After all, God is the God who not only gathers his people into one community but also transforms them. In one old Christian hymn we sing, "He breaks the power of canceled sin and sets the prisoner free." That is, he cancels sin through what Christ has done on the cross, but he also pours out his Spirit and enables believers to live differently: he "breaks the power of canceled sin." So we read,

[22]But the fruit of the Spirit is love, joy, peace, patience, kindness, goodness, faithfulness, [23]gentleness and self-control. Against such things there is no law. [24]Those who belong to Christ Jesus have crucified the sinful nature with its passions and desires. [25]Since we live by the Spirit, let us keep in step with the Spirit. [26]Let us not become conceited, provoking and envying each other.

Galatians 5:22–26

In other words, Christ by his Spirit so begins the work of transformation in the hearts and lives of his followers that two things follow: (1) we are given incentive to "keep in step with the Spirit," to pursue conduct and attitudes in line with the Spirit of God; conversely, (2) where no transformation at all is evident, there is scant reason for thinking the person is a Christian.

Take Up Your Cross

Another way we can get at this broader theme of God's gathering and trans-formation of his people is by considering how he tells his followers to take up their cross. Many New Testament passages adopt expressions like this. One of the most striking comes from the teaching of Jesus himself. After announcing very clearly that he himself must be crucified, he says to his disciples that if they want to be his disciples they "must deny themselves *and take up their cross* and follow me" (Matt. 16:24, emphasis added). Today when people hear expressions like "We all have our cross to bear!" the image is no longer powerful. "Ohhhh," someone complains, "this horrible toothache! But we all have our cross to bear!" So bearing the cross becomes nothing more than some minor irritation—or a nasty in-law, perhaps. But in the first century no one ever made jokes about crucifixion. In the first century crucifixion was viewed with such horror that in handbooks of conduct parents were told not to talk about crucifixion to their children. If a crucifixion site lies on their route, they should lead their children around that site by taking some other route. You could no more joke about crucifixion in the ancient world than you could joke about Auschwitz today. It was simply unthinkable.

Yet here Jesus has the cheek to say to his disciples, in effect, "Unless you take up your cross, you cannot be my disciple." Taking up the cross in those circumstances did not mean taking up your particular little bit of suffering. It meant that you pick up the cross-member, the horizontal piece, and carry it out to the place of crucifixion where you will suffer and die. It meant death to self-interest.

Most of us are not going to be crucified in a literal sense, but we follow a Master who was crucified literally. It is as if Jesus now says, "If I have been crucified, don't you understand? If you are to be my disciple, you must be crucified too"—not, for most of us, in the same physical way he suffered, but in death to self-interest. We are to take up our cross *and follow him*, coming under his lordship as he himself obeyed his own heavenly Father perfectly.

That is why Paul in another of his letters can say, "For it has been granted to you [Christians] on behalf of Christ not only to believe on him, but also to suffer for him" (Phil. 1:29). The assertion is stunning. It has been *granted* to you (that is, as a gracious gift, a grant) not only to believe (faith is a gift) but also to suffer for Jesus (equally a gift!). You take up your cross, and in Christ's way of looking at it that is a privilege. In the perspective of the earliest Christians, it was such a privilege that when the apostles were first beaten up it is reported of them, "The apostles left the Sanhedrin, rejoicing because they had been counted worthy of suffering disgrace for the Name" (Acts 5:41).

Amy Carmichael, missionary to India where she rescued hundreds of orphans amidst much suffering, wrote this poem:

> Hast thou no scar?
> No hidden scar on foot, or side, or hand?
> I hear thee sung as mighty in the land;
> I hear them hail thy bright, ascendant star.
> Hast thou no scar?
>
> Hast thou no wound?
> Yet I was wounded by the archers; spent,
> Leaned Me against a tree to die; and rent
> By ravening beasts that compassed Me, I swooned.
> Hast thou no wound?
>
> No wound? No scar?
> Yet, as the Master shall the servant be,
> And piercèd are the feet that follow Me.
> But thine are whole; can he have followed far
> Who hast no wound or scar?[5]

The insight in this poem springs from a life that abounded in compassion and was ready for self-sacrifice, a life that carefully avoided nurtured self-pity. This is merely the mark of a normal, transformed, Christian life.

Not long ago I read the following paragraph in a journal:

In April 1942, Jacob DeShazer was a bombardier in the Doolittle raid over Japan [that's the raid that basically turned Tokyo into a furnace]. With four other crewmen, he bailed out. Two of them were executed. The others spent the rest of the war—three years and four months—in prison camps. They were beaten, tortured, and starved. At some point, DeShazer asked for a Bible.

They brought him one, allowing him to keep it for three weeks. "I eagerly began to read its pages," he later wrote. "I discovered that God had given me new spiritual eyes and that when I looked at the enemy officers and guards who had starved and beaten my companions and me so cruelly, I found my bitter hatred for them changed to loving pity." He survived, and dedicated his life to missionary work in Japan. One of his converts was Mitsuo Fuchida—the lead pilot in the Pearl Harbor attack. Fuchida became an evangelist. Jacob DeShazer died in Salem, Ore., age 95. R.I.P.[6]

This is a God who gathers and transforms his people.

I must include one more quote. It was written by a self-confessed atheist, Matthew Parris. Parris was born in Nyasaland, now Malawi. He returned after 45 years, and came to a conclusion which, by his own admission, confounded his own atheism:

> It confounds my ideological beliefs, stubbornly refuses to fit my world view, and has embarrassed my growing belief that there is no God. . . . I've become convinced of the enormous contribution that Christian evangelism makes in Africa: sharply distinct from the work of secular NGOs, government projects and international aid efforts. These alone will not do. Education and training alone will not do. In Africa Christianity changes people's hearts. It brings a spiritual transformation. The rebirth is real. The change is good. . . .
>
> We had friends who were missionaries, and as a child I stayed often with them; I also stayed, alone with my little brother, in a traditional rural African village. In the city we had working for us Africans who had converted and were strong believers. The Christians were always different. Far from having cowed or confined its converts, their faith appeared to have liberated and relaxed them. There was a liveliness, a curiosity, an engagement with the world—a directness in their dealings with others—that seemed to be missing in traditional African life. They stood tall.
>
> At 24, travelling by land across the continent reinforced this impression. . . . Whenever we entered a territory worked by missionaries, we had to acknowledge that something changed in the faces of the people we passed and spoke to: something in their eyes, the way they approached you direct, man-to-man, without looking down or away. They had not become more deferential towards strangers—in some ways less so—but more open.
>
> This time in Malawi it was the same. I met no missionaries. . . . But instead I noticed that a handful of the most impressive African members of the Pump Aid team (largely from Zimbabwe) were, privately, strong Christians. . . . It would suit me to believe that their honesty, diligence and optimism in their work was unconnected with personal faith. Their work was secular, but surely affected by what they were. What they were was, in turn, influenced by a conception of man's place in the Universe that Christianity had taught.[7]

Listen: The God who is there, the God who has named himself supremely in Jesus, gathers and transforms his people. Without this transformation so-called Christianity is no Christianity at all. For this God gathers and transforms his people.

13

The God Who Is Very Angry

As solemn as the subject of this chapter is, for anybody who has followed the Bible's storyline this far it should not be too surprising. Any residual ideas of God as a slightly sleepy grandfather figure and nothing more simply will not stand up to the way that the Bible portrays God's righteousness, his sense of the most profound offense when his creatures wish to distance themselves from him. When you stop to think through what the Bible says about judgment, there is quite a lot there from Genesis 3 on: the judgment of the flood, the sacrificial system with all those dead animals, the cycles of decay under the judges in Israel when the nation sank down again and again and faced various kinds of judgment, the judgment that fell on the kings of Israel when they were increasingly perverse and corrupt, and on and on all the way through. Then there is Jesus himself with blistering language in Matthew 23 condemning some of the sins in his day, and Jesus again saying more about hell than any other person in the Bible. So none of this should surprise us if we have followed the Bible's storyline at all.

In our culture it is hard to think about this topic because anger is often connected in the public mind with intolerance, narrow-mindedness, and bigotry. The category of righteous anger is not for us near the top of our scale of virtues.

In this chapter we will focus on one particular passage from the last book of the Bible and then reflect a little on the place of God's anger in the Bible as a whole.

Revelation 14:6–20

One of the most frightening passages in the Bible is found in Revelation 14. We have come to the last book of the Bible. There are many passages to which we could turn to explore the theme of God's wrath, but we shall focus on Revelation 14:6–20.

This section is divided into two: the heralds (three angels) and the harvest (two metaphors about harvest), and both sections talk about judgment in frankly horrendous terms. The literary genre of this last book of the Bible is often called apocalyptic literature. It is full of symbolism and figures that one does not find in other kinds of writing. We cannot here unpack how all the symbolism in this book "works," but the main thrusts of this chapter are easy enough to understand.

> [6]Then I saw another angel flying in midair, and he had the eternal gospel to proclaim to those who live on the earth—to every nation, tribe, language and people. [7]He said in a loud voice, "Fear God and give him glory, because the hour of his judgment has come. Worship him who made the heavens, the earth, the sea and the springs of water."
>
> [8]A second angel followed and said, "'Fallen! Fallen is Babylon the Great,' which made all the nations drink the maddening wine of her adulteries."
>
> [9]A third angel followed them and said in a loud voice: "If anyone worships the beast and its image and receives its mark on their forehead or on their hand, [10]they, too, will drink of the wine of God's fury, which has been poured full strength into the cup of his wrath. They will be tormented with burning sulfur in the presence of the holy angels and of the Lamb. [11]And the smoke of their torment will rise for ever and ever. There will be no rest day or night for those who worship the beast and its image, or for anyone who receives the mark of its name." [12]This calls for patient endurance on the part of the people of God who keep his commands and remain faithful to Jesus.
>
> [13]Then I heard a voice from heaven say, "Write: Blessed are the dead who die in the Lord from now on."
>
> "Yes," says the Spirit, "they will rest from their labor, for their deeds will follow them."
>
> [14]I looked, and there before me was a white cloud, and seated on the cloud was one like a son of man with a crown of gold on his head and a sharp sickle in his hand. [15]Then another angel came out of the temple and called in a loud voice to him who was sitting on the cloud, "Take your sickle and reap, because the time to reap has come, for the harvest of the earth is ripe." [16]So he who was seated on the cloud swung his sickle over the earth, and the earth was harvested.
>
> [17]Another angel came out of the temple in heaven, and he too had a sharp sickle. [18]Still another angel, who had charge of the fire, came from the altar and called in a loud voice to him who had the sharp sickle, "Take your sharp sickle and gather the clusters of grapes from the earth's vine, because its grapes are ripe." [19]The angel swung his sickle on the earth, gathered its grapes and threw

them into the great winepress of God's wrath. [20]They were trampled in the winepress outside the city, and blood flowed out of the press, rising as high as the horses' bridles for a distance of 1,600 stadia.

Revelation 14:6–20

As I have already indicated, the passage neatly divides into two parts.

The Heralds (Rev. 14:6–13)

Angels are often found in apocalyptic literature. In this case, the proclamations they bring are interrelated and progressive.

In verse 6 the first angel summons all humankind to fear God and worship him. "I saw another angel flying in midair"—that is, mid-heaven, to be seen and heard by all. Now he issues a proclamation "to those who live on the earth." His proclamation is not for the angelic hordes of heaven but for people living on the earth. "He had the eternal gospel to proclaim to those who live on the earth." That is what he was there for: to proclaim "the eternal gospel." To whom? The author stipulates "to those who live on the earth"—and in case the sweep of that designation escapes us, he adds, "to every nation, tribe, language and people." But what is this "eternal gospel" he is proclaiming? There are two views:

(1) One group says that the "eternal gospel" in verse 6 is given its content in verse 7. So the eternal gospel is what this angel says in verse 7: "Fear God and give him glory, because the hour of his judgment has come. Worship him who made the heavens, the earth, the sea and the springs of water." In this case it sounds like the eternal gospel is some kind of generic idea like "you might not have heard of Jesus and might not have known the truth, but sort of worship the God who has manifested himself in nature and you will be all right." As popular as this interpretation is, it does not make much sense, for two reasons:

(a) By the time this book was written, about AD 90, the word "gospel" already enjoys fixed meaning. That "gospel" is the great news of what God has done in Jesus Christ's death and resurrection on behalf of his desperately needy image-bearers.

(b) Earlier on in this book, in two spectacular chapters, Revelation 4–5, the author John has a vision that shows us what the gospel really is, what it looks like. It is spectacular. I wish I had time to expound those two chapters to you. Revelation 4 is to Revelation 5 what a setting is to a drama. In highly apocalyptic imagery, God is presented in the setting as transcendent, so spectacularly glorious that even the highest order of angels cover their faces before him and cry, "Holy, holy, holy is the Lord God Almighty!" (4:8). There we are told that he is the God of creation, and the entire created order lives and moves and has its being entirely because of him. That is Revelation 4.

Then in Revelation 5, a drama begins. In the right hand of this God, we are told, is a scroll sealed with seven seals, and this scroll turns out to be the book that contains all of God's purposes for judgment and blessing for the entire universe. As the drama is set up in this vision, an angel proclaims to the whole universe, "Who is worthy to break the seals and open the scroll?" (Rev. 5:2). But that means one must be worthy to approach this God and take the scroll from the right hand of God himself, and serve as God's agent to break the seals. In the symbolism of the day the breaking of the seals meant bringing to pass everything that was written down in the scroll. What angel could approach this God and be God's agent for bringing to pass all of God's purposes? No one is found who is worthy: no angelic being, no human being, no one in the abodes of the dead, no one. After all, he is the God who is described in such transcendent terms in the previous chapter. If even the highest order of angels dare not look on him, who is going to come along and say, "Here, I'll do that; no problem"?

So John, in his vision, weeps. He weeps not because he is a busybody who is frustrated because he is not allowed to see into the future. He weeps because in the symbolism of the vision, unless somebody does come along with the qualifications to approach this God, take the scroll, and break the seals, God's purposes for judgment and blessing will not come to pass. That is, history becomes meaningless. There is no final accounting. There is no righteousness. The sufferings of the church are useless. So John weeps.

Then one of the interpreting figures taps him on the shoulder and says, in effect, "Stop your crying, John. Look! The lion of the tribe of Judah has triumphed so as to open the scroll!" "So I looked," John says, "and I saw a lamb." A lion has been introduced, but what he sees is a lamb. We are not to think of two animals parked side by side. This is apocalyptic literature, and one of the characteristics of apocalyptic literature is that mixed metaphors are very common: the lion *is* the lamb. The lion of the tribe of Judah means "the one who comes from the royal tribe." The tribe of Judah is the tribe of David, the tribe from whom the king comes, the tribe of the Messiah, the promised one. The lion comes from the tribe of Judah. He is a royal figure. He has "triumphed," suggesting that he has prevailed after a struggle. Yet the lion is a lamb—a slaughtered lamb, a sacrificial lamb. How is it that this lion-lamb can approach the transcendent God so boldly? The answer is that he himself does not approach God from the outside, as it were, but he himself emerges from the center of the throne (see Rev. 5:6). He is one with God himself. We have returned by another route to the complexity of the one God. As he manifests himself as the lion-lamb, all around the throne countless millions break out in a new song as they address this Christ-figure, this lion-lamb, and sing,

> You are worthy to take the scroll
> and to open its seals,

because you were slain,
> and *with your blood* you purchased for God
> members of every tribe and language and people and nation.

Revelation 5:9, emphasis added

In other words, the gospel is the same gospel as you find in Paul. It is what God has ordained through his Son, this lion-lamb, to pay the price of sin, to take on the effects of the curse, to release his people, to gather and transform men and women from every tongue and tribe and people and nation. This is the good news.

(2) So in Revelation 14:6–7, the connection between these two verses has got to be seen the other way. It is not that verse 7 gives us the *content* of the gospel. The content of the gospel is defined by Jesus on the cross and has already been laid out for us in Revelation 4–5. The connection between Revelation 14:6 and 14:7 is a little different. It runs like this: "Granted that the gospel is here, granted that it is being proclaimed to everyone, granted that this is the sole means by which God's purposes for salvation and judgment come to pass, then fear God and give him glory because the hour of his judgment has come. Worship him who made the heavens, the earth, the sea, and the springs of water."

In other words, verse 7 does not give us the *content* of the "gospel" mentioned in verse 6, but the *motive to respond* to the gospel, since the end is so close. People everywhere are called to respond in worship to their Creator, since "the hour of his judgment has come."

The second angel announces the impending downfall of paganism. This angel follows and says, "'Fallen! Fallen is Babylon the Great,' which made all the nations drink the maddening wine of her adulteries" (14:8). The historic city of Babylon, of course, was the capital of the Babylonian Empire and was located in the Tigris and Euphrates river system. At one point it was the capital of the regional superpower that destroyed the southern part of the land of Israel, that is, the tribes of Judah and Benjamin. It destroyed the temple in 587 BC. By the time the book of Revelation was written, however, it was nothing but ruins and a small fishing village. Nevertheless, in the Bible Babylon becomes a kind of symbol for paganism that runs amuck and is finally destroyed. The book of Daniel reports that at one juncture the Babylonian emperor boasted, "Is not this the great Babylon I have built as the royal residence, by my mighty power and for the glory of my majesty?" (Dan. 4:30). Small wonder that "Babylon" became synonymous with the spirit of godlessness that in every age lives in those who worship themselves, their successes, and their possessions—anything but the Creator. Society set free from God is its own worst enemy. So although by New Testament times the ancient city of Babylon had long since been destroyed, the name of Babylon was still useful to refer to the city of Rome, which at that time was the capital city of the regional superpower and center of fresh rounds of pagan arrogance.

That is what is being picked up by the cry of the second angel: "Fallen! Fallen is Babylon the Great": that is, this is an announcement of the impending destruction of every culture, not least Rome itself, that arrogantly sets itself up against God. Pagan Rome "made all the nations drink the maddening wine of her adulteries." In biblical language these "adulteries" are not primarily sexual; rather, adultery becomes a figure of speech rejecting God. As in ordinary adultery a spouse betrays a spouse, so in spiritual adultery people betray the God who is there and chase after idols. The massive pagan voice of Rome has made the nations drunk with the maddening wine of her adulteries.

The third angel vividly portrays the torments awaiting those who worship the beast (see 14:9–11). The reference to the beast is from the previous two chapters. Revelation 12:9 pictures the devil himself, referred to as "that ancient serpent," which again calls to mind Genesis 3. That old serpent then calls forth two "beasts" as his functionaries. The first beast is particularly strong and powerful, while the second beast is deceptive and sometimes called a false prophet. And in John's vision the devil, the first beast, and the second beast function together as a kind of aped trinity, pretending to be God, trying to act like Father, Son, and Spirit, but only evil, only destructive, never able to be God. The beast, then, wants everybody to be stamped by his image and come under his sway and control. That is part of the language of the previous chapter.

So this third angel says in a loud voice:

> [9]If anyone worships the beast [that is, Satan's own emissary] and its image and receives its mark on their forehead or on their hand, [10]they, too, will drink of the wine of God's fury, which has been poured full strength into the cup of his wrath. They will be tormented with burning sulfur in the presence of the holy angels and of the Lamb. [11]And the smoke of their torment will rise for ever and ever. There will be no rest day or night for those who worship the beast and its image, or for anyone who receives the mark of its name.
>
> Revelation 14:9–11

God's wrath poured out in full strength? What does that mean? The image is drawn from wine-drinking practices in the ancient world. When you produce wine, it comes out about 30 proof, that is, about 15 percent alcohol. It can go up or down a bit, but it is not a distilled product where you can control the amount of alcohol. It is a fermented process, so it depends on the sugar content, the temperature, the kind of berry, and so on, but commonly wine is about 30 proof. In the ancient world, however, it was very common to "cut" the wine with water, somewhere between one part in ten (one part of wine to ten parts of water) and one part in three. Most table wines that people drank in the ancient world were cut. This image is a way of saying that in the past, God's wrath has been diluted. It is as if the text were saying, "This is now the wine of God's wrath poured out full strength. Any manifestation of God's wrath that you have seen so far—the exile, for example, plagues in the Old Testament, disease, war—any of these things that you have seen as horrible manifestations of God's wrath, they were the diluted form. Now God's wrath is poured out full strength."

Various images are used to get the point across: "burning sulfur in the presence of the holy angels and of the Lamb" (14:10) does not mean that the angels and the Lamb are sitting there laughing and saying, "I told you so." It means that there is enough awareness in these people of the angels and the Lamb to whom they no longer can have access, that that is part of their torment. There is no way out. "And the smoke of their torment will rise for ever and ever" (14:11).

The Harvest (Rev. 14:14–20)

Here the arrival of God's judgment is depicted in two agricultural portraits.

1. THE GRAIN HARVEST (REV. 14:14–16)

The point of these three verses is very simple: a set time is coming when the harvest will take place, and there is no escaping it. The "one like a son of man" is Christ himself with "a sharp sickle in his hand," and the angel that comes out of the temple (i.e., from his heavenly Father) says, "'Take your sickle and reap, because the time to reap has come, for the harvest of the earth is ripe.' So he who was seated on the cloud swung his sickle over the earth, and the earth was harvested" (Rev. 14:15–16).

In other words, life does not go on and on endlessly. This is not Hinduism where there are cycles of existence. History in the Bible is teleological—that is, it is heading somewhere, to a *telos*, a goal, an end. It begins somewhere, and it ends somewhere; it heads toward the end God has appointed. When the time comes and the Lord himself swings his sickle, time as we know it will be no more, and judgment will be final.

2. THE TREADING OF THE WINEPRESS (REV. 14:17–20)

This final vision emphasizes the violent thoroughness of God's wrath when it is finally poured out. In the ancient world, vine keepers would take the grapes they gathered and put them into a great stone vat. At the bottom of the vat were little holes, and when the grapes were squashed the juice would run out through those holes and along stone channels into collecting pots. So you would put the grapes into this vat and the servant girls would kick off their sandals, pick up their skirts, jump in, and stamp down the grapes. That would make the juice flow. Then the juice would be collected, and from it would come the fermentation and the wine that marked the vineyard's prosperity.

But now this imagery is used to portray people being thrown into the great winepress of God's wrath, people who are being trampled underfoot so thoroughly and in such numbers that their blood flows out from the channels to a height of a horse's bridle for a distance of almost two hundred miles.

Now I know this is imagery. The sulfur is imagery too. And elsewhere darkness and chains, no doubt, are imagery. But they are not imagery of nothing. In each case they are meant to tell us something important about the awfulness of the final judgment on those who have spurned the "eternal gospel." Here the point of the imagery is the violent thoroughness of God's wrath when it is finally poured out.

Biblical-Theological Reflections on God's Wrath

What shall we make of this? A lot of Christians today want to say, "Surely it is better to think of hell as a place where there will be some temporary punishments until eventually people simply lose all consciousness: annihilation." Others think that it is manipulative and cruel to think of hell at all: "Just talk about the love of God." There are several things that really must be said. This is not an easy topic, but they have to be said.

1. The Person in the Bible Who Talks Most of Hell Is Jesus

Jesus is the one who introduces most of the horrendous and colorful images. He can openly say to those of his followers who are at risk of being crucified and beaten and sawn apart and all the rest: "Do not be afraid of those who kill the body but cannot kill the soul. Rather, be afraid of the One who can destroy both soul and body in hell" (Matt. 10:28). He talks about dungeons and chains, outer darkness. People sometimes say, "I'd like to go to hell. All my friends will be there." There are no friends in hell. Jesus speaks of weeping and wailing and gnashing of teeth. So it is not surprising that he weeps over the city when people in it do not repent and believe.

So if people think that warning people of hell is manipulative, they must charge Jesus with manipulation. Yet the charge of manipulation is sensible only if the threat of hell is not real. One would never speak of manipulating people to leave a burning building by warning them of the terrible consequences of staying inside and entreating them to leave. Granted that hell is real, terrifying, and eminently to be avoided, it would be unkind and uncharitable of me *not* to warn you, in exactly the same way that it would have been unkind and uncharitable of Jesus *not* to warn the people of his day.

The only thing that many Americans know of the New England Puritan Jonathan Edwards is that he preached a sermon titled "Sinners in the Hands of an Angry God." Many high school students have read it as part of their American literature or American history courses. The main point of the sermon is, in Edwards's words, "There is nothing that keeps wicked men, at any moment, out of hell, but the mere pleasure of God."[1] Not a little of Edwards's language is graphic. Countless generations of students have read the sermon and dismissed it as barbaric or worse.[2] Yet it is not as if preaching about hell constituted the exclusive core of Edwards's ministry: he preached and wrote on a broad array of themes, and his book expounding 1 Corinthians 13, known as the love chapter, is a rich pleasure to read even today. In this Edwards follows Jesus, who also preached on a broad array of themes yet devoted some space to warning against the terrible danger of going to hell. Even in the degree of graphic detail, Edwards does not differ greatly from Jesus. If Edwards is barbaric, so also is Jesus; if Jesus is to be thanked for telling the truth and bringing needed warning, so also must Edwards be thanked.

2. There Are Some Small Hints That This Place of Suffering Goes On

Did you notice the line in Revelation 14:11? "The smoke of their torment will rise for ever and ever." This does not sound like a place where suffering comes to an end. Or again, a few chapters on:

> [9]But fire came down from heaven and devoured them. [10]And the devil, who deceived them, was thrown into the lake of burning sulfur, where the beast and the false prophet had been thrown. They will be tormented day and night for ever and ever.
>
> Revelation 20:9–10

It is an illusory comfort to suppose that those who end up here will eventually be annihilated.

3. Those in Hell Can No Longer Repent

Hell is not going to be filled with people who say, "All right, all right, you win. I'm so sorry. I repent. I really would like another chance. I would like to trust Jesus. I would like to go to heaven."

I cannot prove this, but I think that there are enough biblical hints to hold that it is true. The last chapter of the Bible says, "Let those who do wrong continue to do wrong; let those who are vile continue to be vile; let those who do right continue to do right; and let those who are holy continue to be holy" (Rev. 22:11). That is, you move into the new heaven and the new earth—or you move into hell itself—and you remain in principle what you are already. If as a Christian you are already seen as righteous in Christ, if you have already been increasingly conformed to the likeness of Christ, you move into a new heaven and a new earth, and righteousness becomes yours without footnotes or exceptions or tendencies to fall away or the influences of the old nature. "Let those who do right continue to do right." Righteousness is consummated. Or you move into hell, and you do not suddenly turn over a new leaf and become spotless: "Let those who do wrong continue to do wrong; let those who are vile continue to be vile." Evil is consummated.

Hell is full of people who do not want to be there but who still do not want to bend the knee. For all eternity they still hate God. They still despise the cross. They still nurture sin; they still hate others in this endless cycle of self-chosen sin, iniquity, thanklessness, idolatry, and their consequences. The prospect is horrendous. This ongoing sin is so much a part of their stamp and makeup that if they were suddenly transported to heaven, they would hate it. In exactly the same way as we saw in John 3 in the passage on God's love, when the light comes, people love darkness rather than light because their deeds are evil. That is the horrible awfulness of it: ongoing punishment and still—God help us—no repentance. Not ever. That's why the Bible tells us to "flee from the coming wrath" (Matt. 3:7).

Biblically faithful Christianity does not present itself as a nice religious structure that makes happier parents and well-ordered children and good taxpaying citizens. It may produce better parents and taxpaying citizens, but the issues at stake in biblical Christianity have to do with eternity: heaven and hell, matters of the utmost significance, your relationship to your Maker, what God has provided in Christ, what the cross is about, the resurrection. At the end of the day, what hell measures is how much Christ paid for those who escape hell. The measure of his torment (in ways I do not pretend to begin to understand) as the God-man is the measure of torment that we deserve and he bore. And if you see that and believe it, you will find it difficult to contemplate the cross for very long without tears.

4. Any Christian Who Teaches on These Things without Tears Is Betraying Jesus

Christian faith and thought are not helped by angry preachers whose tone almost suggests that they take a kind of vicious glee from the tragic end of others. For a start, we Christians will be the first to acknowledge, as Paul understands in Ephesians 2, that we are *all* by nature children of wrath—starting with us who have become Christians. If we have come to experience the forgiveness of sins and reconciliation with the living God, it is only because of the grace of the gospel. We are never more than poor beggars telling others where there is bread; we are never more than condemned prisoners who have found pardon and who want others to enjoy the same.

Concluding Prayer

Open our eyes, Lord God, so that we can see the eternal significance of the glorious gospel of Christ. Help us to see that the terrors found in this world, the threats and torments displayed often enough across the history of the world, are nothing compared to the wrath of the Lamb. We face a choice: either we will live our lives frightened of people and what they think, people who at most can do a little damage to us in this world, or we will live our lives in submissive fear of him who can destroy body and soul in hell—and justly so. O Lord God, help us to turn to our only escape, to him who bore our sin with its guilt and penalty in his own body on the tree that we might be made the righteousness of God in him. Help us to sing with that old converted slave trader, John Newton,

> *I saw One hanging on a tree*
> *In agony and blood;*
> *He fixed His loving eyes on me,*
> *As near His cross I stood.*

> *My conscience felt and owned the guilt*
> *And plunged me in despair;*
> *I saw my sins His blood had spilt*
> *And helped to nail Him there.*

> *A second look He gave, which said,*
> *"I freely all forgive:*
> *This blood is for thy ransom paid,*
> *I die that thou may'st live."*

> *Thus, while His death my sin displays*
> *In all its blackest hue,*
> *Such is the mystery of grace,*
> *It seals my pardon, too.*

> *O can it be, upon a tree,*
> *The Savior died for me?*
> *My soul is thrilled, my heart is filled,*
> *To think He died for me!*

Lord God, be merciful to me, a sinner. For Jesus' sake, Amen.

14

The God Who Triumphs

We come now to Revelation 21–22: the last two chapters of the last book of the Bible. We shall begin, however, rather tangentially. In the Sermon on the Mount, which is recorded in Matthew 5–7, Jesus says,

> [19]Do not store up for yourselves treasures on earth, where moth and rust destroy, and where thieves break in and steal [or where the stock market can erode it all]. [20]But store up for yourselves treasures in heaven, where moth and rust do not destroy, and where thieves do not break in and steal [and where the stock market has no effect whatsoever]. [21]For where your treasure is, there your heart will be also.
>
> Matthew 6:19–21

That last sentence is astonishingly important. Note carefully what Jesus says. He does not say, "Guard your heart"; he says, rather, "Choose your treasure." There are other passages where we are told to guard our hearts: "Above all else, guard your heart, for everything you do flows from it" (Prov. 4:23). But in this passage in the Sermon on the Mount, that is not what Jesus says. What he presupposes is something like this: "Your heart will follow your treasure, so choose your treasure aright."

In other words, if what you value the most has to do with treasures down here—things that may in themselves be good, things to appreciate and for which to give thanks—if that is the entire horizon of your treasure, that is where your heart will go. "Heart" does not refer merely to one's emotions or to one's romantic impulses. Often in the Bible "heart" has to do with the essence of what any human being is: who you are, what you think, what you cherish. And if what you value out there has to do with everything in this life *and that's all*, then that is where your heart will go. That is where your creative imagination goes; that is where your energy goes; that is what you think about; that is what you hope for, what you dream about. Of course, if you are a Christian, then at some sort of level you will also believe, say, that there is a new heaven and a new earth to be gained, but such belief will not mean a blessed thing about how you live unless the new heaven and the new earth are something you yearn for, something you treasure. If all your treasures belong to this life, then belief that a new heaven and a new earth are coming will not shape you in any powerful way.

If, on the other hand, though you can thoroughly appreciate all the good things that God gives us in this life (and there are so many of them), what you treasure the most has to do with the new heaven and the new earth, then that is where your imagination will go; that is where your energy will go; that is where your heart goes. Christians in parts of the world where there is a lot of persecution, violence, or suffering have no difficulty understanding that at all. You meet Christians in the southern Sudan or Iran, and they instinctively understand the point.

By contrast, if we live in parts of the world that are lavish in the goods of this world, our hearts will easily pursue what is here and rarely get excited about what is to come. That means that one of the things we ought to do if we are to take the injunction of the Lord Jesus seriously is take time pretty often to reflect on passages from the Bible that tell us what the new heaven and the new earth are like. We need to fire up our imagination so we see what it is that the Lord Jesus is commanding us to treasure, to think about, to value, to run after.

Few passages in all of the Bible are more calculated to do that than Revelation 21–22. These chapters are deeply symbol laden, and there is too little time for me to go through every verse step-by-step to unpack all the symbols. Nevertheless, even with a superficial flyby, one begins to see what Jesus is on about.

> [1]Then I saw "a new heaven and a new earth," for the first heaven and the first earth had passed away, and there was no longer any sea. [2]I saw the Holy City, the new Jerusalem, coming down out of heaven from God, prepared as a bride beautifully dressed for her husband. [3]And I heard a loud voice from the throne saying, "Look! God's dwelling place is now among the people, and he will dwell with them. They will be his people, and God himself will be with them and be their God. [4]He will wipe every tear from their eyes. There will be no more death' or mourning or crying or pain, for the old order of things has passed away."
>
> [5]He who was seated on the throne said, "I am making everything new!" Then he said, "Write this down, for these words are trustworthy and true."
>
> [6]He said to me: "It is done. I am the Alpha and the Omega, the Beginning and the End. To the thirsty I will give water without cost from the spring of

the water of life. [7]Those who are victorious will inherit all this, and I will be their God and they will be my children. [8]But the cowardly, the unbelieving, the vile, the murderers, the sexually immoral, those who practice magic arts, the idolaters and all liars—they will be consigned to the fiery lake of burning sulfur. This is the second death."

[9]One of the seven angels who had the seven bowls full of the seven last plagues came and said to me, "Come, I will show you the bride, the wife of the Lamb." [10]And he carried me away in the Spirit to a mountain great and high, and showed me the Holy City, Jerusalem, coming down out of heaven from God. [11]It shone with the glory of God, and its brilliance was like that of a very precious jewel, like a jasper, clear as crystal. [12]It had a great, high wall with twelve gates, and with twelve angels at the gates. On the gates were written the names of the twelve tribes of Israel. [13]There were three gates on the east, three on the north, three on the south and three on the west. [14]The wall of the city had twelve foundations, and on them were the names of the twelve apostles of the Lamb. . . .

[22]I did not see a temple in the city, because the Lord God Almighty and the Lamb are its temple. [23]The city does not need the sun or the moon to shine on it, for the glory of God gives it light, and the Lamb is its lamp. [24]The nations will walk by its light, and the kings of the earth will bring their splendor into it. [25]On no day will its gates ever be shut, for there will be no night there. [26]The glory and honor of the nations will be brought into it. [27]Nothing impure will ever enter it, nor will anyone who does what is shameful or deceitful, but only those whose names are written in the Lamb's book of life.

[1]Then the angel showed me the river of the water of life, as clear as crystal, flowing from the throne of God and of the Lamb [2]down the middle of the great street of the city. On each side of the river stood the tree of life, bearing twelve crops of fruit, yielding its fruit every month. And the leaves of the tree are for the healing of the nations. [3]No longer will there be any curse. The throne of God and of the Lamb will be in the city, and his servants will serve him. [4]They will see his face, and his name will be on their foreheads. [5]There will be no more night. They will not need the light of a lamp or the light of the sun, for the Lord God will give them light. And they will reign for ever and ever.

Revelation 21:1–14; 21:22–22:5

In one of the first-year courses I teach to seminary students, I sometimes assign them an essay in which they are to work through Revelation 21–22 and pick up every single allusion to anything in the Old Testament. There are scads of them. What these two chapters do is pull together a great deal from the Old Testament—much of what we have seen in the thirteen previous chapters of this book. We can pick up only a small part of them, but they are wonderful.

What does the author John see in this his final vision? He sees what is new (Rev. 21:1–8), what is especially symbol laden (21:9–21), what is missing (21:22–27), and then what is central (22:1–5).

What Is New (Revelation 21:1–8)

What John sees initially is nothing less than "a new heaven and a new earth" (21:1). Of course, that calls to mind the opening words of Genesis 1: "God created the heavens and the earth." So the opening of the Bible connects with the very closing of the Bible. But now this new heaven and new earth (as we will see in the following verses) is untainted by any of the residue of the sin of Genesis 3. It is a *new* heaven and earth. That is what John sees: a transformation of existence. John adds, "and there was no longer any sea" (21:1). For those of us who love the sea, that seems a bit harsh, doesn't it? But what you must understand is that for the ancient Israelites the sea was associated with chaos. The Israelites were not a seagoing people.

I was born in Canada, but my parents were both born in the United Kingdom. British people are born with saltwater in their veins, doubtless owing to the fact that they are an island nation. That geographical reality has made them a seafaring people, with the result that their literature and their poetry are full of sea images. Even as a boy growing up in Canada, I memorized poems like this:

> I must go down to the seas again, to the lonely sea and the sky,
> And all I ask is a tall ship and a star to steer her by,
> And the wheel's kick and the wind's song and the white sail's shaking,
> And a grey mist on the sea's face and the grey dawn breaking. . . .
>
> John Masefield[1]

But the ancient Israelites were not like that. They were a landlocked people, and the one time under Solomon when they tried to build a navy, the ships had to be manned by people from seagoing pagan ports up the coast. So as a result Israelite poetry is full of negative uses of the sea; the sea may be associated with chaos and danger and the like. So in Isaiah, "the wicked are like the tossing sea, which cannot rest, whose waves cast up mire and mud" (Isa. 57:20). This is not talking about the properties of water in the new reality, whatever they will be. It is saying that in this new heaven and new earth, there is no more chaos, no more destruction, no more muck and mire.

This expression, "a new heaven and a new earth," goes all the way back to Isaiah (see Isa. 65:17) and crops up from time to time in the Bible. It appears, for example, in one of Peter's writings (see 2 Peter 3:13). Sometimes the same essential vision is described in other terms. The apostle Paul writes about this present world order groaning like a woman in pregnancy, waiting for the final transformation of God's people when the whole universe will be transformed as well (see Rom. 8:19–22).

That is how John's vision begins in Revelation 21:1. Almost immediately, it changes. "I saw the Holy City, the new Jerusalem, coming down out of heaven from God" (Rev. 21:2). We are not to think of a new creation into which the new Jerusalem comes, thus melding the two images. Rather, John is simply changing the metaphor; apocalyptic literature happily piles disparate metaphors on top of one another. The point is that the ultimate state can be thought of as a new heaven and a new earth, or it can be thought of as a new city, the new Jerusalem. The change enables readers to glimpse different facets of the same reality.

The vision of a "new Jerusalem" calls to mind the old Jerusalem, which was the city of the great king, the city of the temple, the city where God manifested himself to his people. But now what John sees in his vision is a new Jerusalem without taint or corruption. This new Jerusalem was never defeated by the Babylonians or by anyone else. It is a profoundly social vision. So many of us in the West think of spirituality in highly individualistic terms, but this is the people of God in a social context: a city.

I know that in some of our Western literature the city is perceived to be the cesspool of iniquity, but in the Bible the city can be seen both as a sink or a reservoir of evil and as a glorious place of beauty where God lives with his people. As a result of this tension between two quite different associations with the word "city," some people, only half jokingly, call the book of Revelation "a tale of two cities" because this book contrasts two symbol-laden cities: Babylon, proverbial for pagan idolatry, and the new Jerusalem.

Then John changes the symbolism again: he sees the new Jerusalem "coming down out of heaven from God, *prepared as a bride beautifully dressed for her husband*" (Rev. 21:2, emphasis added). The city is now a bride. If any young man reading these pages is about to get married, I strongly urge you not to tell your wife on the first night, "Oh, you're such a lovely city" or "You remind me of a big city." I suspect she will not be amused. True to its nature, however, apocalyptic literature piles up the images without making them hang together. John leaps from one to the other.

Again and again in the Old Testament, God presents himself as a kind of bridegroom of his people Israel. The image is extended in the New Testament, with Christ now the bridegroom and the church his bride, the two of them engaged until the great consummating marriage supper. This is a powerful way of saying, in effect, "The joy, the intimacy, the pleasure, the knitting together of soul and mind and heart and body, which we best know in our small corner in a well-ordered marriage, is only an indication of the kind of intimacy and joy we will experience when the church is united with Christ forever." Because Jesus is also said to be, in another metaphor, a sacrificial lamb, the final wedding banquet can be called "the wedding supper of the Lamb" (Rev. 19:9), and even here in chapter 21 the city is later again referred to as a "bride," "the wife of the Lamb" (Rev. 21:9).

"And I heard a loud voice from the throne saying, 'Look! God's dwelling place is now among the people, and he will dwell with them'" (Rev. 21:3).

That notion of God making his dwelling with his people appears again and again in the Old Testament. In Leviticus 26, when the tabernacle is being put together in the desert for the ancient Israelites, long before there was an established temple, God says, "I will put my dwelling place among you, and I will not abhor you. I will walk among you and be your God, and you will be my people" (Lev. 26:11–12). So here, God's "dwelling place" is associated with the tabernacle, and then later with the temple. That the Israelites will be God's people is bound up with the tabernacle ritual. Many centuries later, however, when he promises that there will be a new covenant, God says, "I will put my law in their minds and write it on their hearts. *I will be their God, and they will be my people*" (Jer. 31:33, emphasis added). You have similar language, but if under the old covenant it was bound up with God's self-disclosure in the tabernacle, under the terms of the new covenant it is bound up with God's self-disclosure in the minds and hearts of his people. It is the same language, but the entire notion gets ratcheted up. Now in the *last* stage, the same language ("I will be their God, and they will be my people") is ratcheted up to such a place that the intimacy is so great, and God is so much present with them, that it is unthinkable that any residue of sin, decay, judgment, loss, or death can prevail anymore. The ratcheting up of expectations is so intense that perfection itself is envisioned. So we read,

> [3]Look! God's dwelling place is now among the people, and he will dwell with them. They will be his people, and God himself will be with them and be their God. [4]"He will wipe every tear from their eyes. There will be no more death" or mourning or crying or pain, for the old order of things has passed away.
>
> Revelation 21:3–4

Here eternal blessedness is couched in negation—that is, no tears, no pain, no mourning, no death, nothing bad. And that is only the negative side of the glory to come. The positive side is depicted in the imagery that still follows: to be with him in glory and splendor, to see the limitless perfections that all of eternity will still not exhaust because he is our God and we his people dwell with him and he with us forever. Incalculable pleasure!

Almost as if our faith needs to be reassured, John adds:

> [5]He who was seated on the throne [that is, God himself] said, "I am making everything new!" Then he said, "Write this down, for these words are trustworthy and true."
>
> [6]He said to me: "It is done. I am the Alpha and the Omega [the first and last letters of the Greek alphabet], the Beginning and the End [from creation to the consummation to the new creation; from creation in its perfection with its horrible dip of sin and destruction and decay to the work that I have done in the sending of my own Son and the pouring out of the Spirit now to the consummation; I am the Alpha and Omega, and the turning point is Jesus;

now we arrive at the consummation]. To the thirsty I will give water without cost [there is grace all over again] from the spring of the water of life. ⁷Those who are victorious [in this book, this refers to those who persevere to the end in confidence in Jesus; it does not refer to the kind of Christian who sails through life with nothing ever sticking to them; to be victorious in Revelation means that you persevere in faithfulness by God's grace to the very end] will inherit all this, and I will be their God and they will be my children. ⁸But the cowardly, the unbelieving, the vile, the murderers, the sexually immoral, those who practice magic arts, the idolaters and all liars—they will be consigned to the fiery lake of burning sulfur. This is the second death."

Revelation 21:5–8

So what is new? The new heaven, the new earth, the new Jerusalem, the consummated union between Christ and his people. Spectacular!

What Is Especially Symbol Laden (Rev. 21:9–21)

Much of what has already been said has been deeply symbol laden, but in these verses the symbols pile on top of each other so quickly that a reader may feel swamped by the imagery. It would take many pages just to work through all the symbols. Instead, I shall unpack two or three of them.

We are told that the city that John sees shines "with the glory of God" (21:11). That is, the people, this city coming out of heaven, shines "with the glory of God." Let us be quite frank: even the very best churches here today (churches that are full of the gospel, where there is discipline and accountability, where Christians really do love each other) are a flawed bunch. The church still has its share of sin. It is made up of sinners like you and me, sinners who have been declared just, yes, but sinners still, not yet perfected, not even close to what we will be. But one day the city itself will glow with the presence of God. No taint anywhere. The language is drawn from Old Testament prophets who anticipated the Jerusalem that would be built after the exile, looking forward to the ultimate Jerusalem. This is addressed to Zion, to Jerusalem:

> ¹Arise, shine, for your light has come
>   and the glory of the LORD rises upon you.
> ²See, darkness covers the earth
>   and thick darkness is over the peoples,
> but the LORD rises upon you
>   and his glory appears over you.

Isaiah 60:1–2

Now God's glory is manifested in the church, in the new Jerusalem. Notice the strange dimensions of this city:

[15]The angel who talked with me had a measuring rod of gold to measure the city, its gates and its walls. [16]The city was laid out like a square, as long as it was wide. He measured the city with the rod and found it to be 12,000 stadia in length, and as wide and high as it is long. [17]He measured its wall and it was 144 cubits thick, by human measurement, which the angel was using.

                                                                Revelation 21:15–17

The significance of the 12,000 and the 144: apocalyptic literature loves symbolism, and it is calling to mind the twelve tribes of Israel and the twelve apostles: 12 multiplied by 12 equals 144. It is a way of saying that all of the old covenant people and all of the new covenant people together constitute this unified people (like the "one new humanity" in Christ in Eph. 2:15).

But a city built like a cube? Even the most spectacular of our high-rise cities does not look cube-like. Once again, this must be symbol laden. So you stop and ask yourself, "Okay, where is there a cube in the Old Testament?" There is only one: it is the Most Holy Place of the tabernacle or the temple. You will recall that the tabernacle was built three times as long as it was wide, and two-thirds of it took up the first part, the Holy Place, and the last third—perfectly cube-like—was the Most Holy Place. This is where the ark of the covenant was found, including the top, on which the blood of bull and goat was sprinkled in the presence of God on the Day of Atonement. It was the place where God manifested himself in his glory when the blood was poured out. Now we are told that the entire New Jerusalem, the whole city, is built like a cube. This is a way of saying that all of us are forever in the very presence of God. We no longer need a mediating priest. We no longer need any blood sacrifices. It is equivalent to what we discovered when Christ was crucified: the veil of the temple was torn, the way into the Most Holy Place, the presence of God, was opened. And now the whole new Jerusalem is built like a cube.

What Is Missing (Rev. 21:22–27)

John tells us what he did *not* see in the city, what was missing:

1. Temple

"I did not see a temple in the city, because the Lord God Almighty and the Lamb are its temple" (Rev. 21:22). There is no temple in the city because the whole city is built like a cube: we are already in the Most Holy Place. One cannot imagine a temple *in* the Most Holy Place! Or to change the language just a wee bit, God himself, the one who sits on the throne, and the Lamb are the temple, the focal point, the heart of the universe, the heart of the temple—and that is where his people are. We no longer need mediating temples that have served us across the centuries to prepare us for the coming of Christ, for Christ has come.

2. Sun and Moon

"The city does not need the sun or the moon to shine on it, for the glory of God gives it light, and the Lamb is its lamp" (Rev. 21:23). This is not a way of unpacking for us the astronomical structures of the new heaven and the new earth any more than the absence of a sea discloses the hydrological arrangements. As usual, the language is symbol laden. In the ancient world, in a culture where there is no electric light, the night hours brought great darkness, especially if there was no moon. It was customary to shut down the city gates in order to enhance security. You made yourself safe because the nighttime was bound up with danger and wickedness. In such a culture, the sun and the moon not only give structured time by providing the normal cycles of life, but they signal relative safety. But now we are told, "The city does not need the sun or the moon to shine on it, for the glory of God gives it light, and the Lamb is its lamp. The nations will walk by its light, and the kings of the earth will bring their splendor into it. On no day will its gates ever be shut, for there will be no night there" (21:23–25).

No danger, no curse, no sin, no rebellion.

3. Impurity

More sweepingly, there will be no impurity. "Nothing impure will ever enter it, nor will anyone who does what is shameful or deceitful, but only those whose names are written in the Lamb's book of life" (21:27).

Have you ever tried to imagine what it would be like not only to be immaculately, perfectly pure but also to live in a culture that was immaculately, perfectly pure? It is so hard to imagine. What would it be like never ever to have lied about anybody or anything? What would it be like always, always to have loved God with heart and soul and mind and strength and your neighbor as yourself? What would it be like to live in a society where that was true of absolutely everyone around you? Don't you see? This is normal in God's mind. It is the way it was at the beginning. It is the way it will be at the end. But now with resurrection existence and no possibility of falling again, no impurity will ever be allowed to enter there. None. No one-upmanship. No greed. No holocausts. No hate. No betrayal. No jealousy. Above all, no idolatry. All who enter will be completely and utterly and totally and joyfully God-centered, *because that is the way it should be*. Finding all of our supreme joy and contentment in the God who is there, this God who discloses himself forever and perfectly, inexhaustibly, before his own blood-bought people, means that all of the culture of the new heaven and the new earth will be suffused with *shalom*, with the well-being, the flourishing, the social peace whose measureless source is the one who sits on the throne, and the Lamb.

What Is Central (Rev. 22:1–5)

This is the culmination of the vision: we see what is central. Two things are emphasized:

1. The Water of Life Flowing from the Throne of God and of the Lamb (Rev. 22:1–3)

The language is once again drawn, in part, from Genesis:

> ¹Then the angel showed me the river of the water of life, as clear as crystal, flowing from the throne of God and of the Lamb ²down the middle of the great street of the city. On each side of the river stood the tree of life, bearing twelve crops of fruit, yielding its fruit every month. And the leaves of the tree are for the healing of the nations. ³No longer will there be any curse. The throne of God and of the Lamb will be in the city, and his servants will serve him.
>
> Revelation 22:1–3

"The throne of God and of the Lamb" harks all the way back to the great vision of Revelation 4–5 mentioned in the previous chapter: this Lamb, Christ Jesus himself, is the one who emerges from the throne and who brings all of God's purposes to pass because he is the lion-king. The throne is a shared throne, as it were: it is the throne of God and of the Lamb, and all that we need for eternal life comes from his reign. The water of life comes from his throne, utterly dependent upon him with a pure supply. The twelve months bring forth twelve fruits, the "twelve" reminding us once again of the twelve tribes and of the twelve apostles: all the people of God.

There is such a transformation that there is healing of the nations.

2. The Vision of God (Revelation 22:4–5)

Indeed, the most spectacular part of the whole vision is found in verses 4–5. It is sometimes called the beatific vision, the blessed vision—the vision of God.

> ⁴They will see his face, and his name will be on their foreheads. ⁵There will be no more night. They will not need the light of a lamp or the light of the sun, for the Lord God will give them light. And they will reign for ever and ever.
>
> Revelation 22:4–5

"They will see his face." Do you remember Exodus 32–34, where Moses asked to see more of God's glory, to see God's face? God replied, "You cannot see my face, for no one may see me and live" (Exod. 33:20). The closest we can get to seeing God before the consummation is Jesus himself, the God-man. But now we have been so transformed that our sinfulness, as it were, has been burned away, the last stages of the old nature and its sinful desires all gone. Now in God's grace we have the privilege of gazing at God in all of his transcendent holiness. We sometimes sing these things even when we scarcely understand them:

> Face to face with Christ, my Savior,
> Face to face—what will it be,
> When with rapture I behold him,
> Jesus Christ who died for me?
>
> Only faintly now I see him,
> With a darkling veil between,
> But a blessed day is coming
> When his glory shall be seen.[2]

The wonder of the new heaven and the new earth is not in the first instance that you may link up with your mother who has gone on ahead. Undoubtedly there will be a reunion of the people of God. But the Bible says very little about such reunions compared with how much it says about the sheer God-centered, spectacular, unimaginable glory that will be ours forever as we contemplate God in his perfections. All the other biblical descriptions of the final state, everything that is said in other parts of the Bible about the work we will do and about our increased joy and responsibility and about the peacefulness of everything ("The wolf will live with the lamb, the leopard will lie down with the goat, the calf and the lion and the yearling together; and a little child will lead them," says Isa. 11:6), as wonderful as these prospects may be, they all pale in comparison of this vision of the sheer Godhood of God, which consumes us and empowers us and leaves us perpetually transformed.

Part of my job takes me to many different parts of the world. I fly far too much. But once in a while I am heading to some place closer to home, and I drive. And when I drive, I bring lots of music, and my musical tastes are painfully eclectic. Not too long ago I was listening to Roger Whittaker, a folk singer whose trademark is to sing the folk songs of many different parts of the world. On this recording he sang a folk song from Canada, which immediately perked up my ears. He sang a song of Cape Breton. The song describes the location in extravagant lyrical terms. In the last stanza Whittaker sings that if he could end his time perfectly,

> God's gift of heaven would be made up of three:
> My love, Cape Breton, and me.[3]

And I thought to myself, "My dear Roger, you just defined hell." Roger and his "love" would breed like rabbits, sinners still. Pretty soon you'd have Cain and Abel all over again, and another downward spiral. "God's gift of heaven would be made up of three"? He is still thinking in entirely self-focused terms: *his* love, *his* preference for Cape Breton, and *himself.* Absolutely nothing about God—which means that idolatry reigns.

In the Bible, what the song calls "God's gift of heaven" is first and foremost consumed with the centrality of God such that for the first time without any exceptions or caveats or failures, we will know by experience what it means to obey what Jesus calls the most important commandment: to love God with heart and soul and mind and strength. And we will be so transformed in this beatific vision that we will know by experience what it means to love our neighbors as ourselves.

So Christians in every generation and every location come together and pray using words drawn from the end of this chapter, "Yes, amen—come, Lord Jesus."

Concluding Prayer

How constrained is our vision, how inadequate our words, how paltry our love for you, Lord God, in the wake of all that you have done, in the wake of all that you have disclosed of yourself in your Son through your Word. Fill our hearts with joy that we may not only be ashamed of sin and loathe it, but also that we may be drawn to your own dear Son, to holiness, to transparent love for one another—all secured by Christ and his work on the cross on our behalf. Draw us on to the new heaven and the new earth precisely because that will also make us better stewards of your grace here. Grant that even now we may understand in our own experience how the Holy Spirit is the deposit of the promised inheritance, the anticipation of what will one day be. Grant us the power to grasp, together with all of God's people, the limitless dimensions of your love for us. Shape our lives by gratitude and adoration. Give us courage and stamina and with it holy joy and a love for all that is holy. Open our eyes to see Jesus, the cost that he bore, the grace that he pours out upon us, until we are ravished by his beauty, consumed by a heart full of adoration. For Jesus' sake, Amen.

Notes

Chapter 1: The God Who Made Everything

1. Ron Rosenbaum, "Is the Big Bang Just a Big Hoax? David Berlinski Challenges Everyone," *New York Observer*, June 7, 1998. This article providing a brief summary of Berlinski and his work can be found online at http://www.observer.com/node/40610.

2. Sometimes in the Old Testament, i.e., in the first two-thirds of the Bible, the word "Lord" is found in small capital letters, like this: LORD. Where that happens, as in the sentence just quoted, there is a particular Hebrew word behind it, a name for God often transliterated in English as "Yahweh." The name means something like "I am" or "I am what I am."

Chapter 2: The God Who Does Not Wipe Out Rebels

1. Sir Arthur Conan Doyle, "The Adventure of the Speckled Band," in *The Complete Works of Sherlock Holmes* (New York: Doubleday, 1930), 268.

2. F. Derek Kidner, *Genesis: An Introduction and Commentary*, Tyndale Old Testament Commentaries (Leicester: Inter-Varsity, 1981), 68.

3. Augustine, *The City of God*, vol. 2, Everyman's Library ed. (London: J. M. Dent, 1945), 9–10.

4. Blaise Pascal, *Pensées*, ed. A. J. Krailsheimer (London: Penguin, 1995), 34.

5. Daniel L. Migliore, *Faith Seeking Understanding: An Introduction to Christian Theology*, 2nd ed. (Grand Rapids: Eerdmans, 2004), 139.

Chapter 4: The God Who Legislates

1. A millennium and a half later, the apostle Paul would make exactly the same points about the function of law in the sweep of the Bible's storyline (see Galatians 3).

2. Remember this pair of words: they will show up again in chapter 7.

Chapter 6: The God Who Is Unfathomably Wise

1. This is usually attributed to Daniel O'Connell in the eighteenth century, following Plato.

Chapter 7: The God Who Becomes a Human Being

1. One New Testament document infers exactly that point: Hebrews 8:13.

Chapter 8: The God Who Grants New Birth

1. Ronald J. Sider, *The Scandal of the Evangelical Conscience: Why Are Christians Living Just Like the Rest of the World?* (Grand Rapids: Baker, 2005).

Chapter 9: The God Who Loves

1. John Shelby Spong, *Jesus for the Non-Religious: Recovering the Divine at the Heart of the Human* (San Francisco: HarperSanFrancisco, 2007), 277.

2. John Piper, "Ganging Up on Gratitude," Desiring God, November 21, 2007, http://www .desiringgod.org/ResourceLibrary/TasteAndSee/ByDate/2007/2504_Ganging-Up_on_ Gratitude/.

3. Francis Thompson, "The Hound of Heaven," online at http://bartelby.net/236/239.html.

4. Edwin Arlington Robinson, "Richard Cory," in *Collected Poems* (New York: MacMillan, 1921). Available online at www.bartleby.com/233.

5. Malcolm Muggeridge, *Seeing Through the Eye: Malcolm Muggeridge on Faith*, ed. Cecil Kuhne (San Francisco: Ignatius Press, 2005), 97.

Chapter 10: The God Who Dies—and Lives Again

1. I include more sustained exposition of these two passages in my book *Scandalous: The Cross and Resurrection of Jesus* (Wheaton: Crossway, 2010).

2. Fareed Zakaria, "To Hell in a Handbasket," review of *A Thread of Years* by John Lacaks, *New York Times*, April 19, 1998, http://www.fareedzakaria.com/articles/nyt/041998.html.

3. Edward Shillito, "Jesus of the Scars," in *Jesus of the Scars and Other Poems* (London: Hodder & Stoughton, 1919).

4. This was discussed in chapter 6.

Chapter 11: The God Who Declares the Guilty Just

1. Todd Wilken, "God Is Just: The Art of Self-Justification," *Modern Reformation* 16/5 (Sept./Oct. 2007): 31.

2. J. Budziszewski, "Escape from Nihilism," *re:generation Quarterly* 4/1 (1998): 13–14.

3. For a slightly fuller exposition of Romans 3:21–26, see my book *Scandalous: The Cross and Resurrection of Jesus*.

4. D. A. Carson, *Holy Sonnets of the Twentieth Century* (Grand Rapids: Baker, 1994), 101.

Chapter 12: The God Who Gathers and Transforms His People

1. Alister McGrath, *The Twilight of Atheism: The Rise and Fall of Disbelief in the Modern World* (New York: Doubleday, 2004).

2. Timothy Keller, *The Reason for God: Belief in an Age of Skepticism* (New York: Dutton, 2008), 57.

3. See Thomas Sowell, *Race and Culture: A World View* (New York: Basic Books, 1994), 210–14.

4. Perhaps because this was taken down from one of his sermons, this quotation has come down to us in several forms. Compare, for instance, Joseph Foulkes Winks, ed., *The Christian Pioneer* 10 (1856): 84; and Josiah Bull, *The Life of John Newton* (Edinburgh: Banner of Truth, 2007 [1868]), 289.

5. Amy Carmichael, "No Scars?" from *Mountain Breezes: The Collected Poems of Amy Carmichael*, ©1999 by the Dohnavur Fellowship. Used by permission of CLC Publications. May not be further reproduced. All rights reserved.

6. *National Review* 60, no. 7 (April 21, 2008): 12.

7. Matthew Parris, "As an Atheist, I Truly Believe Africa Needs God," *Times Online*, December 27, 2008, http://www.timesonline.co.uk/tol/comment/columnists/matthew_parris/article5400568.ece.

Chapter 13: The God Who Is Very Angry

1. The sermon has been reprinted many times in many places. An accessible version is the booklet by Jonathan Edwards, *Sinners in the Hands of an Angry God* (Phillipsburg, NJ: P&R Publishing, 1992), 12.

2. See for example the useful treatment by Douglas A. Sweeney, *Jonathan Edwards and the Ministry of the Word* (Downers Grove, IL: InterVarsity, 2009), 132–36.

Chapter 14: The God Who Triumphs

1. John Masefield, "Sea-Fever," *Salt Water Ballads*, 1902.

2. Carrie E. Breck, "Face to Face with Christ, My Savior," 1898.

3. Roger Whittaker, "My Love, Cape Breton, and Me," *Roger Whittaker's Greatest Hits*, audiocassette, RCA AYK1-4743, 1972.

Scripture Index

D. A. Carson teaches New Testament at Trinity Evangelical Divinity School and serves as president of the Gospel Coalition. He is the author of numerous books.

COMPANION LEADER'S GUIDE AND DVD AVAILABLE

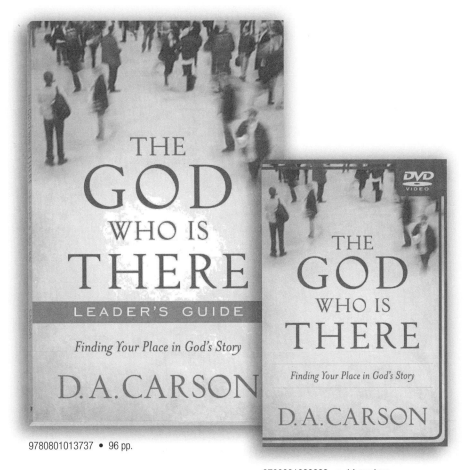

9780801013737 • 96 pp.

9780801030666 • 14 sessions

In this basic introduction to faith, D. A. Carson takes seekers, new Christians, and small groups through the big story of Scripture. He helps readers to know what they believe and why they believe it. The companion leader's guide and DVD help evangelistic study groups, small groups, and Sunday school classes make the best use of this book in group settings.